THE LONELY SOLDIER

THE LONELY SOLDIER

The Private War of Women Serving in Iraq

HELEN BENEDICT

BEACON PRESS, BOSTON

Beacon Press
25 Beacon Street
Boston, Massachusetts 02108-2892
www.beacon.org

Beacon Press books
are published under the auspices of
the Unitarian Universalist Association of Congregations.

12   11   10   09   8   7   6   5   4   3   2   1

This book is printed on acid-free paper that meets the uncoated paper
ANSI/NISO specifications for permanence as revised in 1992.

Text design by Yvonne Tsang at Wilsted & Taylor Publishing Services

Library of Congress Cataloging-in-Publication Data

Benedict, Helen.
    The lonely soldier : the private war of women serving in Iraq / Helen Benedict.
        p. cm.
    Includes bibliographical references and index.
    ISBN-13: 978-0-8070-6147-3 (hardcover : alk. paper)
    ISBN-10: 0-8070-6147-6 (hardcover : alk. paper)   1. Iraq War, 2003—Personal narratives,
American.   2. Women soldiers—United States—Interviews.   3. Women soldiers—United
States—Biography.   I. Title.
    DS79.76.B445 2009
    956.7044'34092273—dc22   2008036228

For the war dead, and the living wounded

War happens to people, one by one.

—Martha Gellhorn, war correspondent, 1967

CONTENTS

THE LONELY SOLDIER

The Lonely Soldier

On a blustery night in March 2004, I joined a small crowd in New York City to honor the citizens and soldiers who had died in the first year of the Iraq War. Among us were children, Vietnam veterans, and a mother whose young soldier son had just been killed; she held his wide-eyed picture up throughout the vigil. Huddling together for warmth, we lit candles and read aloud the names and ages of the dead. After each name, a woman struck a huge drum, making a hollow thud that chilled us more than any cold.

We began with the soldiers: Christian Gurtner, 19. Lori Ann Piestewa, 23....

Once 906 American names had been read, a young man took the microphone and read the names of some of the many thousands of Iraqis who had been killed thus far: Valantina Yomas, 2. Falah Hasun, 9...infants and teenagers, mothers and fathers, toddlers and grand-mothers....

It took at least an hour to read all those names, and afterwards the young man explained why he knew how to pronounce them: "I'm a soldier just back from Iraq," he said, "and we're being used as cannon fodder. We're being sent into war without body armor or decent vehicles to protect us. And most of the people who are dying in this war are civilians."

I was taken aback. This was the first anniversary of the U.S. inva-sion, and it was unpopular for anyone to criticize the way the war was being run, let alone someone who had fought in it. Surely this young soldier was going to be called a traitor by his comrades. So I began to follow the other few veterans who were speaking out like him, curious to see what they were up against, which is how I found army specialist Mickiela Montoya and learned about women at war.

I first saw Mickiela in November 2006, standing silently in the back of a Manhattan classroom while a group of male veterans spoke to a small audience. Sentiment had shifted by then, and a poll had just been released showing that the majority of soldiers were now highly critical of why and how the war was being fought. Among women serving in Iraq at the time, 80 percent said they thought the United States should withdraw within a year, and among men, 69.4 percent agreed.[1] Wondering how this young woman might feel, I approached her. "Are you a veteran too?" I asked.

"Yes, but nobody believes me." She tucked her long red hair behind her ears. "I was in Iraq getting bombed and shot at, but people won't even listen when I say I was at war because I'm a female."

"I'll listen," I said. And soon I was listening to all sorts of female soldiers from all over the country who wanted to tell their stories.

In the end, I interviewed some forty soldiers and veterans for this book, most of them women. The majority had served in Iraq, but a few had been deployed to Afghanistan or elsewhere. I included a variety of ranks, from privates up to a general; all military branches except the Coast Guard; and soldiers on active duty as well as those in the reserves and the National Guard. I thus use the word *soldier* to mean members of the Marine Corps and air force as well as the army.

Some women had only positive things to say about their service: it had given them a responsibility they never would have found in civilian life, and they were proud of what they'd accomplished. This was particularly true of soldiers in medical units. Captain Claudia Tascon of the New Jersey National Guard, who immigrated to the United States from Colombia at age thirteen and served in Iraq from 2004 to 2005, was one of these. "Because I'm more in the curing business than the killing business, I've seen the good of what we've done. We had dentists and doctors put themselves in harm's way to help kids in villages. I was in charge of a warehouse, supplying medical and infantry units all over northern Iraq, and I was also supplying the Iraqi army, who had nothing for wounds except saline solution. So I can't say anything bad about the war." Then she added, "In the civilian world, you'd never have a twenty-three-year-old in charge of people's lives and millions of dollars worth of supplies like I was."

Marine Corps major Meredith Brown, who comes from New Orleans, was so proud of her service in Iraq that she said she would go back in a flash if called, even though she'd had a child since her return. "If I got killed out there, my son would understand that I'd died to protect him and other Americans from terrorists coming to our backyard."

But most of the Iraq War veterans I talked to were much more ambivalent. Some praised the military but considered the war disastrous, others found their entire service a nightmare, while yet others fell in between.

From all these women, I chose to feature five whose stories best reflected the various experiences of female soldiers in Iraq, although I have included the stories of others as well. As different as these soldiers are, they all agreed to be in this book because they wanted to be honest about what war does to others and what it does to us. Above all, they wanted people to know what it is like to be a woman at war.

More American women have fought and died in Iraq than in any war since World War II. Over 191,500 women have served in the Middle East since March 2003, most of them in Iraq, which is nearly five times more than in the 1991 Gulf War and twenty-six times more than in Vietnam. And by September 2008, 592 American female soldiers had been wounded in action and 102 had died in Iraq, more than in the Korean, Vietnam, first Gulf, and Afghanistan wars combined.[2]

Yet even as they increase in numbers, women soldiers are painfully alone. In Iraq, women still only make up one in ten troops, and, because they are not evenly distributed, they often serve in a platoon with few other women or none at all. This isolation, along with the military's traditional and deep-seated hostility toward women, can cause problems that many female soldiers find as hard to cope with as war itself: degradation and sexual persecution by their comrades, and loneliness instead of the camaraderie that every soldier depends on for comfort and survival. "I was the only female in my platoon of fifty to sixty men," said army specialist Chantelle Henneberry, a Montanan who served in Iraq from 2005 to 2006 with the 172nd Stryker Brigade out of Alaska.

"My company consisted of fifteen hundred men—marines, navy, air force, and army—and under eighteen women. I was fresh meat to hungry men. The mortar rounds that came in daily did less damage to me than the men with whom I shared my food."

This problem is not unique to Iraq, as Sergeant Sarah Scully of the army's 8th Military Police Brigade discovered in Korea. "I found two female soldiers who looked as though they'd been battered mentally. They had the dead eyes of abused women. I learned that one of them had been living by herself with about thirty men—Americans and Koreans—and had to have a guard placed in front of the shower each morning."

The view of women as sexual prey rather than as responsible adults has always been part of military culture, making it hard for female soldiers to win acceptance, let alone respect.[3] It is the main reason why women weren't allowed near a battlefield up through World War II unless they were nurses, and why they were forbidden to carry weapons until after Vietnam. It took the end of the draft for these rules to change, when the Pentagon became desperate for soldiers, but even then women were still barred from ground and air combat, warships, and submarines. Between Vietnam and the Panama crisis of 1989, the Pentagon loosened its rules again, reclassifying military jobs into complex categories that continued to ban women from ground combat but allowed them to provide "combat support" instead, a dodge that effectively drew women into battle without acknowledging it.

A year later, in the first Gulf War, forty-one thousand women were deployed, fifteen were killed, and women became prisoners of war for the first time since World War II. In the aftermath, President Bill Clinton expressed admiration for how well women soldiers had performed and pressed the Pentagon to open more jobs to them. By 1993 women were allowed to serve in several branches of combat aviation and on all military ships except submarines. By 1995 even more jobs had been opened to them, and between 1996 and 2001 women were serving in Haiti, Bosnia, and Somalia, where they were exposed to as much danger as men.

These days, women comprise 14 percent of all active duty forces, 11 percent of soldiers deployed to the Middle East, and over 17 percent of the National Guard and reserves.[4] They are indispensable to the military but are still banned from ground combat.

The Iraq War has made a mockery of this ban. Because its battle-fields are towns and roads, there is no frontline, and the U.S. military is so short of troops, women are frequently thrown into jobs indistinguishable from those of the all-male infantry and armor divisions. They are handling eighty-four-pound machine guns as turret gunners atop tanks and trucks, guarding convoys by hanging out of vehicles with rifles, kicking open doors and raiding houses, searching and arresting Iraqis, driving trucks and Humvees along bomb-ridden roads, flying helicopters and bomber planes, and killing and being killed.

But as the visibility of women combat soldiers is increasing in Iraq, so, it seems, is the hostility of their male comrades against them. This is happening for several reasons to be discussed in this book, but among them are these: War always fosters an increase in the sexual violence of soldiers.[5] Many men resent women for usurping the masculine role of warrior. And the military is still permeated with stereotypes of women as weak, passive sex objects who have no business fighting and cannot be relied upon in battle. As Sergeant Sarah Scully said, "In the army, any sign that you are a woman means you are automatically ridiculed and treated as inferior."

Mickiela Montoya put it another way: "There are only three things the guys let you be if you're a girl in the military—a bitch, a ho, or a dyke."

Not all military men see women soldiers this way, of course, but too many do. Some show their hostility by undermining women's authority, denying them promotions, or denigrating their work. Others show it through sexual harassment, assault, and rape.

"People worry about their loved ones' encounters with the enemy, but for females, sometimes the enemy eats, sleeps, and works right next to them," as air force sergeant Marti Ribeiro said to me.

To clarify exactly what so many women soldiers are facing, here are some definitions:

Sexual harassment is the use of sexually demeaning remarks to degrade and mark a person as an unwelcome outsider. Harassment is often dismissed as mere teasing, but studies have found it can cause the same rates of post-traumatic stress disorder (PTSD) in women as combat does in men.[6] Specialist Henneberry came back from her year in Iraq so destroyed by sexual harassment that she tried to kill herself.

Sexual assault is any physical sexual act short of rape committed by force or threats. In the military, the threat is usually to demote the victim, ruin her reputation or career, or put her in danger. Most military sexual assault victims are women, but 27–30 percent of military men say they receive "unwanted sexual attention" from other men, including rape.[7]

Rape is best defined as a form of torture. It can be committed by physical force or with the use of threats or rank. Under military law, any soldier who uses his rank to coerce a junior into sexual intercourse, whether with threats or bribes, is guilty of rape, yet this is the most common type of assault in the military. In the army, nearly 90 percent of rape victims are junior ranking women, average age twenty-one, while most of the assailants are noncommissioned officers or junior men, average age twenty-eight.[8] Rapists are not motivated by desire, but by a mix of anger, sexual sadism, and the need to dominate and destroy (many do not ejaculate), which is what is meant by the oft-repeated but little understood phrase that rape is about power, not sex. Just as the torturers in Abu Ghraib used sexual acts to degrade their captives, so do rapists with their victims.[9]

From the victim's point of view, rape is torture because it is a painful and violent attack on the most intimate part of your body and an attempt to destroy your dignity and autonomy. Rape and sexual assault by someone on whom you depend—whether a parent, partner, or comrade-in-arms—is more traumatizing than assault by anyone else.[10]

Rape is often committed with threats of murder or mutilation, so those who survive also have to cope with the trauma of having been almost killed. Women soldiers have been punched, knocked unconscious, slashed with knives, and threatened with guns by soldier rapists.[11] They have also been murdered, just as rape victims sometimes are in civilian life. In December 2007 the burnt corpses of marine corporal Maria Lauterbach and her unborn baby were found buried in the backyard of a senior officer she had reported for raping her.[12] During the Iraq War, four women soldiers who died of non-combat-related injuries had earlier been raped, and at least fifteen have died in such suspicious circumstances that retired army colonel Ann Wright and Congressman Ike Skelton have called upon Congress to compel the military to reopen the cases and investigate.[13] One of the most shocking of these cases is that of nineteen-year-old LaVena Johnson, whose dead body was found on her base in Iraq in July 2005. Her face was battered and she had been stripped, raped, burned, reclothed, dragged across the ground bleeding, and shot in the head. The army initiated an investigation, then suddenly closed the case without explanation and labeled her death a suicide.[14]

Women who survive rape or sexual assault can take years to recover. They feel depressed, ashamed and terrified, blame themselves in irrational ways, and find it hard to trust anyone again. Like combat veterans, they tend to feel emotionally numb, helpless, and fearful, and to have flashbacks and nightmares. They may also develop medical problems such as diabetes, arthritis, asthma, chronic pelvic pain, irritable bowel syndrome, eating disorders, and hypertension.[15] Some become dependent on drugs or alcohol and lose control of their lives: 40 percent of homeless female veterans say they were raped while they were in the military.[16]

The sexual persecution of women has been going on in the armed forces for generations, as decades of studies have revealed.[17] In 2003 a survey of female veterans from Vietnam through the first Gulf War found that 30 percent said they were raped in the military. A 2004 study of veterans from Vietnam and all the wars since, who were seeking help for PTSD, found that 71 percent of the women said they were sexually assaulted or raped while serving. And a 1995 study of female veterans of the Gulf and earlier wars found that 90 percent had been sexually harassed.[18]

The Department of Defense (DoD) shows much lower numbers, but that is because it counts only those rapes that soldiers have been brave enough to officially report. Having the courage to report a rape is difficult enough for civilians, where unsympathetic police, victim-blaming myths, and the fear of reprisal prevent 60 percent of rapes from being brought to light.[19] But within the military, reporting is even riskier. Military platoons are enclosed, hierarchical societies riddled with gossip, so any woman who reports a sexual assault has little chance of remaining anonymous. She will probably have to face her assailant day after day and put up with resentment and blame from other soldiers who see her as a snitch. She risks being persecuted by her assailant if he is her superior and punished by any commanders who consider her a troublemaker. And because military culture demands that all soldiers keep their pain and distress to themselves, reporting an assault will make her look weak and cowardly. For all these reasons, some 80 percent of military rapes are never reported at all.[20]

These barriers to reporting are so well recognized that in 2005 the Defense Department created the Sexual Assault Prevention and Response (SAPR) Office, and a year later offered the option of anonymous reporting to encourage women to come forward. The DoD insists on the success of these reforms, its proof being that the number of reported military sexual assaults rose by 40 percent in 2005 and 24 percent in 2006. "The success of the SAPR program is in direct correlation with the increased numbers of reported sexual assaults," Cynthia Smith, a Defense Department spokeswoman, wrote to me in February 2007. In fact, nobody can tell whether increases in reported rapes reflect more reporting or more rapes. The only way to accurately measure military sexual assault is to rely on veterans who are no longer afraid to report it, and those studies indicate that nearly one in three women soldiers is sexually attacked by her comrades, while harassment is virtually universal. This means the rate of sexual assault is now at least twice as high in the military as it is among civilians.[21]

Of course, a one-in-three rate still means the majority of female soldiers are *not* assaulted, nor do they all feel persecuted. Yet, if that many soldiers were dying of AIDS it would be considered an epidemic, as it would if that many rape victims were men.

A NOTE ON LANGUAGE

In this book, I have avoided the military jargon with which most tales of war are written. I've done this to make the book accessible to civilians as well as soldiers, but also because military language is notoriously obfuscating and euphemistic. Sometimes its euphemisms are designed to make something mundane sound important: *MOS*, or Military Occupational Specialty, is merely a job; and *FOB*, or Forward Operating Base, is a military camp. More often, their purpose is to disguise the fact that war and weapons are about killing: *IED* stands for Improvised Explosive Device—a homemade bomb; *friendly fire* means being killed by one's own side; *collateral damage* means the killing of civilians; *OIF*, which stands for Operation Iraqi Freedom, is the Pentagon's phrase for the invasion and occupation of Iraq; while *OEF*, Operation Enduring Freedom, is the war in Afghanistan.

But military language has another purpose, too, and that is to maintain a secretive culture that shuts out civilians. The rift between civilians and soldiers is so deep already that both sides regard the other with suspicion—a dangerous state of affairs in a democracy where the military is supposed to be carrying out the will of the people. I've heard too many soldiers characterize civilians as lazy and ignorant, and too many civilians speak of soldiers as brainwashed thugs. Military culture is steeped in secrecy; it fosters contempt for outsiders, imposes a gag rule on its soldiers to stop them from being candid to the public, and cloaks itself in myths of glory and machismo. Many a war history and military memoir perpetuates this culture with a style filled with acronyms and jargon that most civilians cannot comprehend. (In fact, some soldiers don't comprehend them either. I've talked to several who never knew exactly what the acronyms for their jobs or units actually stood for.) I have tried to avoid repeating that mistake here.

If the Defense Department invents euphemistic language to hide what it does, soldiers do the opposite. As in prison and high school— and much about the military resembles a combination of these two institutions—members deflect the hardship of their circumstances with wit and colorful argot: The onomatopoeic *chopper* means helicopter. *Brig* means a military prison, evoking the horrors of a locked hole in the bottom of a ship. *GI* stands for Government Issue, something few people remember anymore. *FOBette* is the term for a soldier who never leaves base. *POG* (Personnel Other than Grunt) means anyone who isn't a combat soldier. The *sandbox* is Iraq. I will translate this slang only when its meaning is not obvious.

The stories I tell here are based on many hours of recorded discussion with the soldiers in this book, corroborated by their colleagues where possible and bolstered by news accounts, their own letters, diaries and photographs, and military records of their service. All but one of the soldiers who had already separated from the military allowed me to use their real names. Among those still on active duty, two asked me to change their names to protect them from reprisals.

Each of these stories is, of course, unique, yet the tales of other soldiers echo them again and again. In some ways, these are the stories of individuals. In other ways, they are the universal stories of war.

PART ONE

Before

TWO

From Girl to Soldier

Life before the Military

MICKIELA MONTOYA

Mickiela curled up on her grandmother's couch, tucked her feet under her, and stroked her belly. Her long red hair was pulled into a high ponytail and her pretty freckled face was free of makeup. She was twenty-one, a year out of her tour in Iraq, and pregnant.

She was staying with her grandmother in California because she needed looking after. The day before she had been rushed to an emergency room with premature contractions and kept there overnight. Her grandmother didn't want her going anywhere until they knew what was wrong.

"She's so strict!" Mickiela whispered. "She won't even let me walk."

Mickiela was the first female Iraq War veteran I met, and when I found her she was living in New Jersey, working and going to school. Once she discovered she was pregnant, though, she moved back home to Rosemead, which is in East Los Angeles, and had been shuttling between relatives ever since. She seemed unconcerned. She had been bounced around like that all her life.

When I visited her in California, I discovered her grandmother's apartment complex nestled within a carefully tended garden shaded by eucalyptus trees. I climbed an outside staircase to her door and knocked, waking Mickiela from a nap. She greeted me in loose gray sweatpants and a skimpy green halter top that showed the modest slope of her belly. Her face looked a little puffy, although as freckly and fresh as all the other times I'd seen her. When I'd first met her three months earlier, I'd thought she looked achingly young for a war veteran, her wide brown eyes as clear as a child's. There, flushed with pregnancy, she looked younger than ever.

She led me into a dark room decorated in brown, and we sat on a long chocolate-colored couch. It was early January 2007, so Christmas decorations still hung about the room. As she nestled into some cushions, her grandmother and two of her many aunts busied themselves in the kitchen behind us.

Mickiela is strikingly self-possessed for her age. She shifts every now and then as she talks, but is never fidgety. Her laugh is full-throated and her smile bunches up her cheeks merrily. She always seems on the verge of a chuckle.

"This place is really nice," I said.

"No, it's not," she replied quickly, pulling a face. "Hey Gramma, she thinks this place is nice." Mickiela found my comment funny because, to her, Rosemead is a dump full of bad memories.

Rosemead is a Mexican neighborhood that looks like a typical L.A. suburb. The houses, mostly small cement cubes painted in pastels, squat in neat rows along tidy streets, their tiny front yards stamps of parched grass and cacti. The wide boulevards that crisscross the area are lined with the usual chain stores and banks, and from the tops of the hills one can see palm and eucalyptus trees stretching all the way to the mountains—at least if the smog isn't too thick. But the neighborhood is deceptive, for beyond the pretty houses and sun-blasted boulevards lie lives derailed by poverty and the woes of the unwelcome immigrant: gangs, crime, dead-end futures, and the long-reaching shadow of prison.

Mickiela's own family is entangled in gangs. Her father and many of his relatives are in one, her cousins in another, and because the gangs are rivals it's too dangerous for her to say which they are. She herself is the product of generations of teenage mothers: her mother had her at eighteen, her grandmother gave birth to her mother at fourteen. As a result, her complicated family is full of aunts younger than their nieces and grandmothers in their forties. "I have so many grandmas you can't count!"

Her own mother was a drug addict, so neglectful of Mickiela and her sister that Child Protective Services took them away when they were small. Her father was out of the picture, so Mickiela was raised by her maternal grandmother, her favorite, the one she calls Nana. "Me and Nana, we were the closest," she told me in her Spanish-inflected accent. "I'm Mexican but I don't look Mexican, I look white, and she was like me. She dyed her hair red, so we always looked the same. I could talk with her about anything. She always understood."

Mickiela was happy with Nana, but when she turned twelve and her sister was thirteen, her mother demanded them back, mostly to make them look after their little brother. For the next three years the family kept moving from one home to another, the sisters sometimes staying with their mother, sometimes with other relatives. In one house, the sisters' room was a closet just big enough to hold a single bed, so they had to take turns sleeping on the floor. Mickiela's mother liked to punish her by locking her in that tiny room for days at a time, only letting her out to go to school. "I have these crazy long diaries I wrote in that room. I would write things like, 'I wanna kill myself!' Then I found out that my mom was reading my diaries, so I learned how to write in my own little language so she couldn't understand."

When Mickiela was fifteen, her mother was evicted for not paying rent, and the family was out on the street. The sisters returned to Nana once again, but this time they only found more trouble. Nana had developed gallbladder cancer, which had metastasized. Soon she began losing weight and her red hair. Gradually, she also started losing her mind.

Just as Mickiela was in the middle of this crisis, and at the end of her junior year in May 2002, she and all her classmates, most of whom were also Mexican, were sent to the school auditorium to take a test called the ASVAB. No school officials bothered to explain what it was, but Mickiela soon found out. It was the Armed Services Vocational Aptitude Battery test, the test you take to get into the military.

Military recruiters were a common sight in the hallways of Rosemead High. They would set up tables covered with alluring pamphlets promising money and adventure and call out to students as they walked by. With their clean, pressed uniforms and flashy smiles they were such a seductive presence that Mickiela can't even remember the recruiters who were offering other careers.

Since 9/11 and the start of the Afghanistan War, the military has been targeting schools like Mickiela's—schools in communities where jobs are scarce and the students are poor or the children of immigrants—and promising glamorous careers and citizenship to those who join. But by the time Mickiela was in eleventh grade, the government had given recruiters another advantage as well: the No Child Left Behind Act of 2001.

The act stipulates that no public high school can qualify for federal money unless it gives the address and telephone number of every student to the military and allows recruiters access to the school. Any family that wants to keep its address private has to submit a form saying so, but most people don't know this. Once recruiters have this information, they court the students like basketball scouts, calling them at home, taking them out for meals, and making any promises they want. Recruiters can do this because the enlistment contract that every recruit must sign states that none of these promises have to be kept—something else most people don't know.[1]

The main reason the government smooths the way for recruiters like this is because after 9/11, enrollment in the military dropped drastically, especially in the army. Between 2000 and 2005, recruitment declined 20 percent among noncitizens, nearly 7 percent among Hispanics, 10 percent among whites, and 58 percent among African Americans.[2] This made recruiters so desperate to meet military quotas that they grew reckless; the army reported a 60 percent rise in "inappropriate actions" by recruiters between 1999 and 2005. They were helping high school students forge diplomas and cheat on drug tests, threatening to arrest students if they didn't sign up, and lying.[3] In 2006, two news stations equipped students with hidden cameras and sent them to recruiting offices. "Nobody is going over to Iraq anymore?" one student asked a recruiter. "No, we're bringing people back," he replied. Another was filmed saying, "We're not at war. War ended a long time ago."[4]

Mickiela's recruiter was a white man in his mid-thirties who was married with children. He would drive up to the school in a new car, blasting hip-hop out of the window, and take her out for nice lunches. "He said that if I signed up with the National Guard I wouldn't have to serve outside the country. National—that means *in* the country, right?" He told her the army would give her $3,000 just for enlisting, pay for college, train her in the job of her choice, and enable her to travel abroad, all of which sounded dazzling to the sixteen-year-old. But what actually happened was that the $3,000 came in increments over the next four years and was taxed, she never got any money toward college, she was trained in the one job she asked not to do, and she didn't get to travel anywhere abroad—except to the war in Iraq.

Mickiela said the recruiter was "really, really flirty," too, and when she introduced him to a seventeen-year-old friend who was also interested in enlisting, he began dating her. "I don't know if they ever had sex, but I know when they were supposed to go out on a date, he would just drive off to some place and make her give him head and that was it. She told me about it later." Mickiela pulled a disgusted face.

In 2005 a press investigation found that over a hundred young women were sexually exploited like this by at least eighty recruiters from the army, marines, navy, and air force. Some were raped in recruiting offices, some assaulted in government cars as they were driven to military test sites, and others intimidated into sexual relationships, like Mickiela's friend. Recruiters have a power that makes teenagers afraid to reject them or report their assaults, for they control whether the teen will get into the military at all, which for someone who can see no other way out of a dead-end life is power indeed.[5]

In spite of her recruiter's pressure, Mickiela resisted the military at first. The only part of the life that appealed to her was the physical challenge, for she had always been athletic. But when she went to her career counselor to discuss alternatives, all he said was, "When you're seventeen you'll be old enough to sign up."

Then Nana grew worse. She became addicted to morphine and turned delusional, accusing her family of trying to poison her, and she was wasting away in front of their eyes. Mickiela couldn't bear it. In an effort to numb herself, she took to ditching school and partying all the time. She joined a graffiti crew and got kicked out of one school, then another. "My boyfriend lived right opposite my school, so I'd go see him instead of going to classes. I was smoking a lot of weed. I was really messing up."

And then, on June 24, 2002, the day before Mickiela's seventeenth birthday, Nana died. She was fifty-two.

"I knew she was sick, but you never actually expect it," Mickiela said quietly from her other grandmother's couch, pulling a cushion over her belly. "If I cried when I was little, Nana would always say, 'Save your tears for when I die.' But she could say that 'cause death was such a distant thing, you know?"

After Nana's death, Mickiela was left alone with her stepgrandfather, who made it clear right away that he couldn't cope with raising her on his own. "He made me feel like he wasn't my grandpa anymore. I felt so vulnerable. I didn't know what to do."

For a time she continued to slide downhill. Nana had always been the one to get her to school, make her do her homework, keep her organized. With no one to look out for her, Mickiela didn't care anymore. But after a summer of partying, she grew disgusted with herself. Not knowing where else to turn, she went back to the recruiter. "I wanted to do something to be proud of. I imagined telling my grandchildren one day that I'd done something to protect the country." After all, it was September 24, 2002, by then, a year after 9/11.

The recruiter was delighted. He told Mickiela that all she needed was her mother's signature because recruits under eighteen cannot enlist without signed permission from a parent. Mickiela hadn't seen her mother in months by then, but she called her anyway and explained. "If you wanna join, forge my name, I don't care," her mother said, and hung up.

Mickiela forged her mom's name right under the recruiter's nose. "We do this all the time," he told her. "Don't worry about it."

So, at the beginning of twelfth grade and exactly three months after Nana died, Mickiela signed up with the California National Guard for what her recruiter told her would be six years. In fact, anyone joining any branch of the military for the first time is committed for eight years, or longer, if the military wants. But Mickiela didn't know that yet, just as she didn't know the country had been at war with Afghanistan since October 2001 because she never watched the news. Nor did she know the National Guard could send her to war whenever it needed to. She still thought she would be fighting forest fires, helping with floods, and protecting her country from terrorist attacks, all at home in California.

By the time Mickiela graduated from high school in June 2003, the United States had invaded Iraq, and National Guard members were being turned into combat soldiers for the first time since the Korean War.

ELI PAINTEDCROW

Eli (who pronounces her name *Elly*) was forty-six when I met her, had been home from Iraq for three and a half years, and was retired from a twenty-two-year career in the army. She is fully Native American, Mexica-Apache on her mother's side, Yaqui on her father's, and her bearing reveals her pride in this. She looks statuesque, although she is only five feet three, for her back is straight and her shoulders square. She also has the patient manner of someone who has seen a lot of life and listened to a lot of people. She calls the women she likes "sister" and had spent most of her civilian years helping others as a social worker and by conducting Native American healing ceremonies. Yet as mellifluous as her voice is and as gentle her movements, she has a quality both stern and fierce. "You don't mess with Sergeant PaintedCrow," as she likes to say.

Her fierceness is well earned, for she has endured a life of Faulknerian hardship. In no way does she seem beaten down by this, but she does seem weary. She can sound as tough as a street fighter when she talks about injustice, but certain subjects will make her slump in her chair and drop her voice to heart-wrenching tones. Sometimes her memories drive her out to her garden for a cigarette, where she stands blowing the smoke into the sky, her face raised and still as if listening to a whisper.

Like Mickiela, Eli lives in California, only further north, in Merced, a place of empty skies, golden hills, and almost no trees. The house she was living in when I visited her was her own, which she said sometimes felt like a ball and chain and other times like a welcome cave. It was a modest, one-story building of beige stucco in a row of similar houses that resembled the adobe dwellings of a pueblo. A small porch overlooked a front yard of yellowing grass and a flowerbed full of cacti as tall as a man.

Inside, her house was indeed cavelike, its walls painted in rich earth colors—umber, brown, rust—save for the kitchen, which was all a cheerful bright red, including the toaster and kettle. The rest of the dark house was also spotted with color: the bright blankets she'd bought in Iraq and spread over her furniture; the Native art on her walls; and the blanket draped over her ceremonial drum, which stood in a corner. Two large paintings on black velvet, given to her by Iraqi artists, hung in her little dining room. One was of a Native American woman dancing; the artist copied the image off a Hallmark card. The other depicted a veiled Iraqi girl with huge black eyes lined in kohl.

Eli had also ringed her dark eyes in black on the day I visited her, which made them look striking and intense. She was wearing a long green skirt, brown boots, and a sage-colored sweater. Her black hair was cropped short, framing her round, high-cheeked face; and her lips were bold with deep red lipstick. She wore dangling silver earrings and silver rings and bracelets on both hands.

We settled into her cozy living room, the front door open to let in the air, and she began her story. Outside, we could hear the occasional lonely hoot and rumble of a train or the shout of a child. Otherwise, all was quiet.

Eli was born on October 16, 1960, and until she was ten never lived in one place long enough to finish out a grade of school. Her father moved the family every six months—once they stayed in a motel for half a year—following what work he could find. But he was also running away from his drinking, hoping a new place would make him stop. It never did.

Eli's entire family was alcoholic: her father, Alvino; her mother, Victoriana; and all her grandparents, aunts, and uncles. "You know drinking is a problem for Native people," she told me frankly. "Well, it was no different for my family."

She was only able to finally stay put in fifth grade, when her father moved back to San Jose, where she had been born, and bought a house. Yet, in spite of this peripatetic life, she always did well at school, which pleased Alvino, especially as she was his first child and only girl. Because both her parents worked—Victoriana in canneries and nurseries, Alvino at whatever he could find—Eli was left in charge of her two little brothers most of the time, but she still managed to earn good enough grades to dream about becoming a teacher.

But Alvino was always getting drunk, and sometimes he beat up his wife. He had led a rough life himself, leaving his Arizona reservation at twelve, selling gum on the streets of Mexico, never learning to read or write. He was inventive and a skilled mechanic: he made earrings, fixed upholstery, built up a tire business, and eventually became a truck driver. But he carried with him the stigma and frustrations of the illiterate, which made him prone to explode into violence. And he took to collecting guns, which he liked to keep in the house.

When Eli was thirteen, her mother, who was two months pregnant with her fourth child, shot herself in the head with one of her husband's guns when she was drunk. She survived, but the baby was born with a heart murmur, a tumor in his eye, and so many health problems that he was kept in the hospital for two months, his mother with him. Eli was left to cook and clean for her father and brothers alone.

Not long after her mother had left, Alvino hired a young man named Eddie to help him fix cars. This was in 1973, and Eddie was twenty-four and just back from Vietnam. He was a surly, hard-drinking white man with one leg shorter than the other, and he horrified Eli. She heard rumors that he'd raped girls in Vietnam and thought of him as a loser and an outcast.

She was at home with a school friend one afternoon when she looked out her window and saw Eddie drinking and quarreling with a group of men. The argument escalated until the men jumped him and beat him up, leaving him to stagger, drunken and bloody, into a nearby park. Eli and her friend felt sorry for Eddie then, so they went after him to tell him to run away before the police arrested him for drunkenness. But he only spat curses and swung at Eli as if to hit her.

A few days later, she heard a knock on her front door. She opened it and there was Eddie. "Hey, I wanna say thanks and sorry," he said. "It was real nice to have somebody care what happened to me."

After that he began to pay attention to this thirteen-year-old girl who'd tried to help him, complimenting her, confiding in her. She was flattered—a grown man interested in her? Eddie courted her, acting gentle and interested, and then seductive. Eli wasn't sure what to make of it. She was half pleased and half afraid.

One night, Eddie took her to see a movie at a nearby drive-in. While they were sitting in the darkness, he persuaded her to drink with him and share a joint, and soon she was woozy and drunk. Then he pinned her down and raped her.

She told no one. She was too ashamed, for wasn't it really her fault? Hadn't she let Eddie get close to her, hadn't she encouraged him? She hated Eddie now, her flesh shrunk from him, but there he was, working with her dad every day, and she couldn't get away from him. Then one morning she woke up and vomited. The same thing happened the next morning, and the next. She had no idea why.

But her father did. He took her to the doctor and confirmed what he already suspected: Eli was pregnant.

Alvino was furious. He saw the rape as entirely his daughter's fault. He didn't care that she was only thirteen. All he minded was that she had dishonored him by losing her virginity to a lowlife white man, and by throwing away all her chances to become a teacher and make him proud.

As soon as they left the doctor, Alvino took out his car and went looking for Eddie, ready for murder. It didn't take long to find him—Eddie was standing outside a friend's house, chatting. Alvino pulled up with a screech. "Get in the fucking car," he said icily. Eddie did as he was told. Alvino was six feet tall and broad-shouldered, with a thick moustache and a stern, proud face. He was the kind of man people obeyed.

Alvino drove back to the house, sat Eli and Eddie at the kitchen table, pulled out one of his guns, and placed it in front of them. "You have five minutes to decide," he told Eddie, staring him down. "You either marry my daughter or die. Go in the back room and talk it over." The only reason he refrained from killing Eddie there and then, Eli's mother told her later, was because Eddie was now going to be the father of his grandchild.

"All I could think was, 'If my dad shoots Eddie he's going to go to prison, then all of us are going to be without a dad, my mom's going to be without a husband, and it'll all be my fault.'" So Eli told Eddie she would marry him.

"I really hated him," she said to me in her house, sitting quietly in her armchair, looking down at her hands. "My oldest son is the product of that rape, so he's very distant from me. I love him, but he knows the story and he feels pretty alienated from my family. He hates having an Indian mom because he sees no honor in that."

From then on, Eli's life grew worse. Eddie beat her up all the time, but her father wouldn't stop him and her mother was too sick to interfere. She knew of no shelters to go to, nobody to help. So she did what her parents and her grandparents had done before her: she turned to drink.

"Then one day, when I'm seven months pregnant, Eddie gets drunk, comes to this place where I'm babysitting for friends, knocks down their door, and beats the crap out of me. I call my dad and he comes, ties Eddie up, calls the cops, and they put him in jail for a year."

While he was locked up, Eli had the baby, a son she named Eddie Jr., and tried to go back to school. But in 1974 teenage mothers weren't welcome in high school and her teachers were so hostile that she dropped out. She enrolled in an adult school instead—they only let her in at fourteen because she produced a marriage certificate—and managed to earn her GED. But she was still drinking. Then Eddie got out of jail and came back to live with the family, and soon he was beating her up again. This went on for two years.

One night, when she was sixteen, she was driving with friends to a local youth center when a gunfight broke out in front of her car. Too drunk and disoriented to know what to do, she sat there helplessly until a teenaged boy pulled her to safety. He was nineteen, a handsome Mayo Indian named Joe.

She and Joe became friends, then lovers. Seeing a way out of her nightmarish life, Eli took her baby and ran off with him. But before long, he too turned abusive. "He put me in this immigrant housing place that was literally a shack, with two windows and boards that made a table that were attached to the wall. He would lock me in the house and go to work. I wasn't allowed to talk to anybody."

Soon she became pregnant again, this time by Joe. "Birth control—nobody told me about it. And I had so much trauma in my life, who thought about that? At sixteen, you still don't think it could happen to you, even when it happens, you know?"

But one lucky day Joe left for work and forgot to lock her in. She grabbed Eddie Jr., escaped to a phone booth, and called a taxi to her grandmother's, where she spent the next few months until her father relented and allowed her to move back home; he was always swinging between blaming Eli and protecting her. In 1977 her second son was born, whom she named Angel. Not long afterward, Alvino persuaded Joe to join the military and get out of her life.

"So here I was on my own with two children. Time goes on and I'm in and out of my dad's house. He kicks me out, he brings me back. He kicks me out, he brings me back." Eddie was in and out of the picture as well. Some days he was willing to be a father to both boys. Other days he was beating up Eli, drinking, and disappearing.

In spite of Eddie's abuse, Alvino kept pushing Eli to stay with her husband for the sake of the children and because he believed marriage was sacred. It wasn't Eddie's fault that he was violent, he would tell her; it was that he'd been wounded twice in Vietnam, had spent an entire year in the hospital, and wasn't quite right in the head. "So Dad decides to move us to Lake Tahoe. He figures this is going to solve all of our problems. Well it doesn't. I'm still an alcoholic, taking care of my kids at home. Eddie's still an alcoholic-addict, beating the crap out of me. But now I really have nowhere to go and no place to turn." By then Eddie Jr. was five and Angel three.

"Then one day, I just can't take it anymore. So I decide to kill Eddie. I try to come up with a plan of how to kill him and dump him in Lake Tahoe, but he's such a big man I can't figure out how I'm going to get his body there. I'm going to have to put him on a boat alive and then kill him, and he's a really strong guy. So I think, 'Okay. That isn't going to work.'" Eli laughed and pulled a face, although we both knew it wasn't really funny.

By the time Eli was twenty, Eddie had landed in jail once again for attacking her, and she had divorced him at last. "So there I was, living in a one-bedroom, cockroach-infested apartment in San Jose with two kids, on welfare, and I'm thinking, 'What am I going to do?' That's when I decide to join the army."

Her decision was not unusual, for a startling number of women and men enlist in the military to escape abuse. Among army soldiers and marine recruits, half of the women and about one-sixth of the men report having been sexually abused as children, while half of both say they were physically abused. These rates are considerably higher than those among civilians.[6]

But Eli explained that her decision to enlist also reflected a time-honored tradition among Native Americans. "It's something that Native people find great honor and pride in, and it's very hard to find things that bring honor to your family for Natives nowadays. The military is our way of holding on to the idea of being a warrior, of being a provider and a protector." Indeed, on a per capita basis, more Native Americans serve than any other population, overrepresented by 300 percent: they make up 0.75 percent of the population at large but 2.6 percent of the military. In some tribes nearly 70 percent of the men are soldiers.[7]

Having made her decision, Eli went to see an army recruiter, but he told her she couldn't enlist unless she had a husband with whom to leave her children. "Come back with a marriage certificate," he said. "I don't care how you get it, but that's what you need to get in."

Eli was distraught. Who would understand her predicament? The only solution she could come up with was Eddie. "So I go back and say, 'Eddie, will you marry me? I need a piece of paper that says I'm married so that I can join the army.'"

He squinted at her. "What do I get out of it?"

"I've saved up a thousand dollars. I'll give it all to you if you marry me with no strings attached."

"Okay, I'll do it."

Eli's father took the couple, in T-shirts and jeans, to get remarried in Lake Tahoe, with one of Eli's brothers as a witness. They didn't bother with a ring.

The very next Monday, September 24, 1981, only three days after the recruiter had sent her away, Eli returned with her marriage certificate in hand and enlisted. She hurried home to tell her father, hoping he would be proud of her, but he only laughed. "You won't last two weeks," he scoffed. "You never finish anything you start." She fled to the bedroom in tears. Her mother followed her.

"Don't you listen to him, *mi hija,*" she said. "You go do it, show your dad that he's wrong about you. We'll keep an eye on Eddie and the kids."

And so Eli left her children with her ne'er-do-well husband and went off to be a soldier.

JENNIFER SPRANGER

Jen grew up with none of the family dramas Eli and Mickiela had to bear. Her mother was a nurse, her father a firefighter, and she was raised in a white and solidly working-class neighborhood in the middle of America, with one younger brother and a lot of cats and dogs. "I was incredibly happy. I have a very supportive family. They were real proud of me."

She was particularly close to her father as a child, always eager to please him by earning good grades and going in for sports, but the subject that most drew them together was their love of the military. Every Memorial Day, he would take her to the parade and point out the female soldiers. "Look at those women there," he'd say. "You can do that too." He talked often about how he had wanted to go to Vietnam when he was young but had been prevented because the war ended just as he finished high school. This filled Jen with a longing to realize his ambitions for him. "I knew ever since I was twelve that I was going to join the army. I went to some recruiters before I was even in high school and I said, 'You'll be seeing me in a couple of years.' And they did."

She told me all this in her childhood home in a housing development just outside Racine, Wisconsin, a small industrial town on Lake Michigan surrounded by open fields. She wasn't home when I arrived to meet her, so I took the opportunity to look around. When her family had moved there, the housing development had been brand new, but twelve years later it still looked as bland as if it had just been built, its trees short and spindly, its houses painted in washed-out colors. Her house was the largest and most colorful on the block, yet even it was a muted gray-green. The whole place appeared unsure of itself, a suburb in search of a character.

Jen drove up and got out of her car, sweet-faced and young—it was only two days after her twenty-third birthday. We shook hands. Despite the snowy February air, her palm was sweating.

Like Mickiela and Eli, Jen defies any stereotype of a female soldier as masculine or Amazonian. She is barely five feet one, slender and buxom. She has a round face that tapers to a little chin, a small sharp nose, and wide hazel eyes. Her golden hair hangs straight and glossy, curling under her jaw. Some days she wears quite a bit of makeup, but the day I visited all she had on was brown eyeliner, barely visible behind her glasses.

She led me through the garage, stepping over a yellow Labrador and into a spotless kitchen with a white linoleum floor. Beyond was the living room, occupied just then by her Chihuahua, two cats, and her eighteen-year-old brother, James, watching TV on the couch.

Jen gave me a soda and sat at an oval kitchen table, her back to the sliding glass doors that overlooked the yard, which that day was covered in snow. Despite the weather, she was wearing jeans and a summery white smock, cut low to reveal a long gold chain with a cross—she was raised Catholic but says the Church's doctrines no longer interest her. As the hours went by it grew cold, so she pulled on a gray sweatshirt and hugged her knees to her chest. She never made any hot drinks or food for the entire six hours we talked, only drank from a giant pink plastic glass of water, lifting the cup to her lips with a shaking hand.

Jen speaks about her life with a sardonic honesty, enhanced by the flat tones of her Midwestern accent. At one point, she said, "When I get anxious I lose my train of thought, so I'm sorry if I jump around a lot. I hate being the way I am, I really do."

She often says she hates the way she is, just as her hands often sweat and tremble. These are the legacies of war.

In certain ways Jen is typical of the young soldiers who are fighting in Iraq today. Most are white and from rural areas, like her, and grew up in places that offer few jobs or careers. The average household income for recruits at the start of the war was $42,822, which makes any family of more than two what sociologists call "near poor."[8]

Jen's hometown of Racine is also typical of the kind of place that produces soldiers. Once it was thriving, with several factories and a lively downtown, but the death of manufacturing in the United States closed down the factories in the late 1990s, downtown grew empty and drab, and now Racine has the second highest crime rate in Wisconsin after the nearby big city of Milwaukee. "There's nothing to do here, no work," Jen said. "Everybody just wants to leave."

Jen was oblivious to all this in high school, however. She ran track, played golf, became the first girl in school to join the wrestling team, and found friends among the older students. She knew little of the outside world and that didn't bother her. She was beating boys at wrestling (she was in the lowest weight category at 103 pounds) and appearing in the local papers as a star. "Occasionally people still recognize me and say, 'Oh, you're that blond girl wrestler. I saw you wrestle back in '99 and you just beat the heck out of that little boy!' "

Once her older friends graduated, though, she became more aware of the blank facing her after twelfth grade. She had a boyfriend but not many friends, and began to fixate more than ever on the military. "My dad was a big part of that, but I don't want to say it was just him. The military was absolutely what I wanted. I was so excited about it. I could barely wait until I turned seventeen."

But she had another reason for wanting to enlist as well: her parents were fighting. This had been true for a while, but she hadn't quite recognized it before. Now it seemed worse than ever and Jen wanted out.

So a mere two weeks after her birthday, she went to her local army recruitment office, ready to sign up and fly off to an exciting life as soon as possible. Fine, said the recruiter, but first you need permission. Like Mickiela, she was too young to join without a signature from a parent.

Jen's mother, Joyce, didn't like the idea at all. This was February 2001, six months before the 9/11 attacks, but nevertheless she wasn't happy with sending her only daughter off to be a full-time soldier who might be deployed overseas. Jen's father, John, was more enthusiastic, although he wanted her to go to college first. He offered to pay her tuition so she wouldn't need to enlist for that reason. "But she said she wanted to go into the army full-time at eighteen; she was real adamant," he told me.

Jen's view is different. "I knew my dad would be so proud of me if I signed. He wanted me to be a soldier." Finally, the two of them went to see the recruiter together, where John persuaded his daughter to sign up with the military police instead of a construction unit, as she'd planned. "I wanted to be an electrician, but my dad's always wanted me to be a cop, and he's very persuasive."

So she signed up for the military police reserves to give herself time to finish high school before going on active duty, and spent the weekends of eleventh grade at drill. "From the first time I put that uniform on, I was so proud I could've been walking on air. Everybody else was going to the mall on weekends, but I was going to play army. I thought I was great." She read army manuals every night and wore her army T-shirt to school as often as possible. "The army was all I was looking forward to at that point. I was only going to school because I had to in order to get to the next place I wanted to be."

She never suspected that place would be war.

TERRIS DEWALT-JOHNSON (*The names of Terris and her husband have been changed to protect her career.*)
Terris is the only one of the five soldiers featured in this book who grew up in a big city. An African American, she was raised in a rough neighborhood of Washington, D.C., and, like Eli, her childhood was torn by violence—or, as she prefers to put it, "My life was a little drastic." But you would never know this to meet her. She laughs all the time; has a teasing, affectionate way with her four children—gentle but firm; and calls her husband, whom she's known since she was nine, "a gentleman and a sweetheart."

A veteran of sixteen years in the U.S. Army Reserve, Terris works as logistics manager at the Centers for Disease Control and Prevention (CDC) in Atlanta, Georgia, a job that frequently sends her traveling on business around the country. She lives in a spanking new development in the Atlanta suburb of Duluth, its streets so safe that children drop by to play all the time. Her sunny, two-story house has white carpets, huge plate-glass windows, and a spacious garage. And she and her husband, Terrence, an auto mechanic, who have been married for twenty-one years, have two girls and two boys who bubble with humor and confidence. Much of this, she would be the first to point out, is thanks to her career in the military.

I first met Terris in March 2007, a week before her thirty-seventh birthday, when she had been back from her year in Iraq for eleven months. She greeted me at her door wearing her camouflage fatigues, having just returned from a morning of the drill that soldiers on inactive duty must attend once a month. The uniform, which made her look much taller than her five feet six, was one of the digital models issued at the end of 2006: a wash-and-wear polyester and cotton mix, its pockets, patches, and stripes stuck on with Velcro. (The design is different than the old "chocolate chip" desert camouflage uniform, which was tan with jagged brown blobs on it. This one is a busier design in gray, pale green, and beige, with a matching beige T-shirt beneath.) Her desert combat boots were sand-colored suede and new—she was still breaking them in. And her hair, which she sometimes wears in feminine cornrows, was pulled back tightly that day and crammed under her army beret, making her face look square and mannish. No uniform could disguise her high cheekbones and generous mouth, however, nor the beauty of her huge, light hazel eyes.

She welcomed me into her spotless house, which Terrence and the children were in the middle of giving a thorough scrub, and showed me to a small white parlor by the front door, outfitted with white furniture and a white cast-iron coffee table. The room was pristine but for one thing: the table's glass top was missing. She waved a hand at it as we sat down. "The glass is gone 'cause I threw a vase at it when I was angry one day and smashed it. I can get pretty mad sometimes."

Taking a seat beside a set of glass shelves displaying framed photographs and two ornate urns, she leaned forward, elbows on her knees, and began her story.

Terris enters her story like an actor. She talks directly to those involved, points and gestures, and reproduces facial expressions and dialogue like a one-person movie. Her voice rises in anger or drops to a whisper, her body strains forward—the effect is mesmerizing. This was the way she told me about her stepfather, Frank.

Back in D.C., when Terris was four years old, her mother, Bunny, separated from her father and married Frank, who turned out to be a violent drunk. Fueled by alcohol, he would fly into rages and beat up the children, but he saved the worst of his violence for his wife. He hit her with a hammer, broke her arm, lacerated her legs, and once he stabbed her thirteen times with a long kitchen knife until it sank in so deeply he couldn't pull it out. Bunny only survived, Terris said, because she was so fat.

Like both Eli and Jen, Terris was the eldest girl, only in her family there were eight other children. She spent much of her childhood trying to protect the little ones from Frank, locking them in a bedroom when the fights started and calling the police. But because Bunny always refused to press charges, the police eventually stopped coming, which left Terris and her oldest brothers to defend themselves and their mother alone.

Terris was close to her brothers, especially the three eldest, Andre, Roland, and Ronald, because she shared the same father with them and they were each only a year apart in age. Andre, the oldest, was a talented musician, but also street-tough and determined never to let anybody beat him in a fight. He taught Terris how to play basketball and softball and how to box and stand up for herself. The second brother, Roland, whose nickname was Chucky, was always getting himself into trouble, but he was Terris's favorite. "Chucky wasn't very smart—I would always help him with his schoolwork. But even though he was a troubled kid, he had a big heart." And then there was her younger brother Ronald, the brains and comedian of the family. "They all, in their own way, taught me about survival."

Terris's fear of Frank began to change one June day when she was thirteen. It was the day before Ronald was to graduate from elementary school, and the children were looking forward to the celebration. But while they were at school, Frank drank himself into a rage, hit their mother in the head hard enough to split open her skull, and ran off. "When I got back from school, my mom was lying in a pool of blood. We had to call the ambulance to come get her. This was the night before my little brother was gonna graduate, and now it was ruined— I was enraged! So me and Ronald decided to stay up and wait for Frank. We knew he would come back because he always did. He would do his dirt and come back."

Terris and Ronald each armed themselves with a baseball bat and sat on the neighbor's porch to wait. Sure enough, in the wee hours of the morning, Frank returned. "Where'd your mom put the car?" he growled.

The car was across the bridge, but Terris told him it was down an alley, so he started toward it. Terris and Ronald crept up behind him, bats at the ready. Frank looked for the car, realized it wasn't there, and turned around. "And before he could get completely around, I swung, I swung with everything I had for my little thirteen-year-old arms, and I hit him square in the center of his head. Boom! And when he hit the ground, I was just on him, wailing. I zoned out just thinking of all the things he had done to my mom.

"Then my brother was shaking me because he was scared. I mean the first time I'd hit Frank, I'd knocked him out cold, so everything I hit, like a limb, it just bounced. My brother shook me till I woke. 'I think we killed him,' he whispered.

"I looked at Frank just lying there, and I thought, 'Oh God.' Because you think you want to kill somebody, but really you don't."

The children went back in the house and called an ambulance. "Then I go back out and Frank's still laying in the same spot. So I smack him around, *slap slap*. 'Hey Frank!' Slap him around some more. And finally he comes to. Talk about relief! 'Oh Lord, okay, I ain't killed him!' His head was hurting him and I had broken his arm. He says, 'What happened?'

"'I don't know. You was just laying out here...'

"So we got him back in the house and laid him on the couch. The EMS came—the same paramedics who'd picked my mom up. They're looking around and they're like, 'Didn't we come to this house a little earlier?'

"Me and my brother are sitting on the couch, looking at him all big-eyed and innocent. 'Uh huh.'

"'Didn't we pick up a lady from here?'

"'Uh huh.'

"'This is the guy who did that to your mother, right?' the paramedic guy says. 'Did you all do this to him? Because if you did I don't blame you. If a man hit my mother like that, I'd do the same to him.'"

Terris laughed triumphantly when she said this, reliving the moment of vindication.

Frank's violence continued, but the older Terris and her brothers grew, the more they fought him. "It was, 'I got to kill this guy or he's gonna kill my mom—it's either him or her.'" By the time she was eighteen Frank's violence had mostly stopped.

Terris once asked her mother why she stayed with Frank, as they are married to this day. "And you know what she said? 'Love is powerful.'" Terris shook her head. "Ain't no love powerful enough to keep me in that situation. No, never."

Tough as she was, Terris could not protect her family from the streets once they were grown. Andre, the oldest, went to prison for manslaughter and drug dealing. The middle brother, Chucky, her favorite, became a crack addict and was killed when he was twenty-seven; Ronald, the smart, funny one, was murdered a few years later; and Andre followed him the same summer. All three were shot to death in drug deals gone wrong or cycles of senseless revenge.

"I loved all of them dearly and miss them," Terris told me sadly. "Not having them here has torn our family apart." She pointed to the photographs and urns on the glass shelves beside her. "Those are pictures of my brothers. And the urns there, that's where I keep their ashes."

Her three little sisters, too, succumbed to alcohol and drugs. Of all the children in the family, only Terris and one of her youngest brothers, who is also in the military, managed to stay sober. In her case, she attributes this to her great-grandmother and great-great-aunt, to whom she was able to flee for peace and safety throughout her childhood.

Terris was the only one of her siblings who liked spending time with their elderly relatives. Almost every weekend she would take a series of three buses to stay with them, and she spent a month every summer with them too. "At home I was a kind of Cinderella. I had to look after everybody and never got any acknowledgment. And there was all that domestic violence going on. Looking after two old ladies was easy compared to that." Thanks to these women, she learned to have the faith in God and confidence in herself that she felt she needed to avoid trouble and despair.

Soon after finishing high school, Terris moved in with Terrence. (She hyphenated her surname with his to honor her dead brothers.) She had their first daughter, Shawntia, when she was seventeen, and their first son, Alexander, two years later. By the time she was twenty in 1990, Terris was working two jobs: one at McDonald's, the other selling tour tickets at Washington, D.C.'s Union Station.

"Then one day this recruiter comes up to me, and he says, 'You ever thought about joining the military?' And he starts telling me about how I could travel, pay for college, all that stuff. And I got interested."

So after consulting with Terrence, who supported her interest, she signed up with the Washington, D.C., Army National Guard. She had just changed her life forever.

Terris's decision made her part of a striking demographic: From 1990, when she enlisted, to 2000, African Americans made up the majority of women in the army, about 48 percent, while whites hovered at 40 percent, and the rest were mainly Hispanic and Native American.[9] (By contrast, all minority men together made up only about a third of male soldiers.) But, as mentioned earlier, by 2005 black enlistment had dropped 58 percent, more than any other population. The main reason, military analysts say, was opposition to the Iraq War: 83 percent of African Americans were against it by 2005. As one young man from Philadelphia told a reporter, "It's not our war. We got our own war here, just staying alive." By 2008, African American women were still over-represented in the military compared to their population at large, but their ratio among women deployed to the Middle East had dropped from nearly half to under a third.[10]

ABBIE PICKETT

When I first met Abbie in January 2007, she was twenty-four and had been home from war for nearly three years. We met in England, where she was spending a year as a student, and when she arrived at the London house where I was staying, I found a tall and slender young woman at the door, with green eyes, thin lips, and a narrow, delicate face. Her wavy blond hair was tied up in a scarf, and she was casually dressed in jeans and a sweater, her face bare of makeup.

We sat in the chilly kitchen with mugs of hot tea and slipped quickly into conversation. Abbie speaks quietly, her voice high and soft, and weighs her words with care. She barely moved as we talked, except to prop her face in her hands once in a while, elbows on the table. Thoughtful and sensitive, she has the gentle manner of a nursery school teacher—which, indeed, she was before she went to war. It was extraordinarily difficult to imagine her wielding a gun, let alone enduring the horrors she saw in Iraq.

Ten months and many telephone conversations later, I met up with her again, this time in Madison, Wisconsin, where she was living with her boyfriend and going to college. She drove me to meet her parents in Darlington, the town where she grew up, which was about an hour away and so small that its downtown was only four blocks long. Nestled amid gentle hills and patches of woods, Darlington is a quiet, friendly place. Most of its 2,500 residents are conservative, Republican, churchgoing folk over fifty years old, who are fiercely patriotic and have a history of sacrificing their youths to war. Abbie's father, Steve Pickett, who like Abbie was born and bred in Darlington, told me that even though the town and its surrounding Lafayette County are sparsely populated and among the poorest areas in Wisconsin, more young men from there died in World War II and the Vietnam War than from most other counties in the state.

Abbie's parents go to church, too, but are neither conservative nor Republican. Steve is a locally elected county clerk, and Deb, Abbie's mother, is the owner of a small art gallery and print shop. They are both practicing Catholics and liberal Democrats who believe in the responsibility of citizens to do their part in the world.

Abbie grew up in a white clapboard house (now painted blue) at the top of a steep hill on the edge of town, not far from the local cemetery. She was the second of four children: her sister, Kristen, was three years her elder, while her brother and little sister were younger by eight and eleven years, respectively. Her closest childhood friend was a boy from down the road named Jeve, whose mother was the local district attorney and whose father was the town doctor. She and Jeve spent hours playing outside and talking about what they wanted to be when they grew up. "We were humanists," she said in her quiet voice as she drove me past his house. "We both knew we wanted to help people." Jeve grew up to work for a nonprofit organization in Eastern Europe. Abbie's path would be quite different.

Abbie became something of a rebel once she entered her teens. "She had a different hair color every week," Deb told me with a rueful smile. At school Abbie tried to fit in with the popular cliques, but at heart she couldn't stand the backbiting gossip of the other girls. "It just hurt to see people being so mean." She was also religious like her parents and wanted people to behave with proper Christian generosity. So although she tried—too hard, she thinks now—to look and act like a popular high school girl, running track and dressing in the latest styles, she felt like a misfit.

At home, she also began butting up against the formidable will of her mother, who has the quick wit and plainspoken manner of a woman who knows what she thinks. "I had a lot of classic teenage fights with my mom. There was a lot of 'you don't understand me!' and slamming of doors," Abbie said with a laugh.

Deb chuckled in agreement. She, Steve, and Abbie were sitting with me in the local diner, eating huge slices of cake and discussing the mysterious motivations that had led Abbie to the army. "She wasn't one for taking orders," Deb said with a bemused expression on her freckled face. "She wasn't exactly noted for liking to be told what to do, either, or for being on time or getting up early. So why would I ever think she would join the military?" Steve, a quiet man with a white moustache and small, kind eyes, nodded.

But Abbie was searching for a way to define herself in the world. Feeling out of place at school and irritated at home, she also felt overshadowed by her older sister, who seemed to be perfect at everything she did, from athletics to scholarship. "Kristen impressed people wherever she went. That's what I've always had above me. Now she's going to be the first doctor in our family. I'm real proud of her, and we're close now. But I did feel rivalry with her at school. All the Pickett kids had to have something special. I was looking for mine."

One older girl at school Abbie admired, the prom queen of two years earlier, had joined the military, and this caught Abbie's imagination. "This was something my sister had never done. It was my own path. And if you really want to rebel in a political household of liberal Democrats, you join a Republican institution like the army. I was very green about it. I wanted to give something back to society, wanted the honor of doing something for my country. But, really, it was a rebellion." She was seventeen and this was 1999, so she had no reason to expect war.

Recruiters were easy to find in Darlington High. Their presence would be announced over the intercom in the mornings, and they would often join the students during lunch in the cafeteria. The military is the main way for Darlington youths to pay for college, as the recruiters well knew. And there was so little work in the area that young people were eager to earn the extra $200 they would be paid for drilling one weekend a month.

Abbie chose the National Guard because she wanted to do good works in her home state, and because, unlike the Army Reserve, the National Guard offers state benefits. But her parents were horrified.

They didn't want their daughter in the military and refused to sign the papers permitting her to join. Back during Vietnam, Steve had seen the damage the war had done to soldiers, and several of his friends had been killed. "We knew the possibility of war was ever-present, but kids don't take that seriously," Deb said.

Abbie argued that they had always promised to support her in whatever made her happy. Anyway, she told them, if you don't sign, I'll just wait till I'm eighteen and do it alone. "I kind of had them in a box," she admits now.

"She argues like a lawyer," Deb said. "She made us feel if we didn't sign, we weren't being supportive parents. What could we do?"

Finally, they told her that as long as she did enough research to know what she was getting into, they would sign. Abbie did the research, but when she makes up her mind about something, her parents said, there's no budging her. Sure enough, she remained undeterred.

Defeated, her parents reluctantly agreed, and Steve went with her to the recruiter, just as Jen's father had with her. "We sat and interviewed him because I wanted to make sure this seventeen-year-old knew what she was getting into," he told me. "The recruiter had made it sound as if joining the army was like going on a world tour. He had to be quizzed until he told the truth. I wanted her to know they own your soul once you sign, and that they can send you to war."

But Abbie still would not be moved. So, at last, and with many misgivings, Steve signed the permission papers. Abbie was now a member of the Wisconsin National Guard.

"When I joined the military I got an overwhelmingly good response from my community. If I went downtown or to the supermarket in my uniform, people were proud of me. And all the people in my school were intrigued by where I was going when I went to drill one weekend a month. I finally felt like I belonged."

She paused and added softly, "After all, it was pre-9/11. We all thought differently then."

THREE

They Break You Down, Then Build You Back Up

Mickiela Montoya

Bomb the village, kill the people
Throw some Napalm in the square
Do it on a Sunday morning
Do it on their way to prayer.

Ring the bell inside the schoolhouse
Watch those kiddies gather round
Lock and load with your 240
Mow them little motherfuckers down.
—*Marine basic training song*

The first thing Mickiela did to prepare for boot camp was cut her hip-length red hair. She didn't chop it all off—it was still long enough to put up in a ponytail—but as the tendrils dropped around her feet she felt liberated, as if with her hair she were shedding the wild girl who now only embarrassed her. She had just turned eighteen and graduated from high school, and she was ready to move on—away from her grandpa's grief, from Rosemead and the troubled kids she knew there, and from her own ache for Nana.

Mickiela was to train at Fort Leonard Wood, Missouri, and she was excited about going because she had never left the West Coast before. She bought the requisite duffle bag, packed the few clothes her recruiter had told her to bring, and waited for him to pick her up as promised. Instead, a female recruiter she didn't know arrived. Mickiela was disappointed and nervous. What had she let herself in for?

She flew into St. Louis on a hot evening in June 2003, then took a long bus ride to the base, arriving, as virtually all recruits do, late at night. There she was told to wait in a large bare room, made to stand in one line after another, and then sent outside to a parking lot to wait again in the unfamiliar mugginess of the Missouri summer. She sat on the ground with the other new and bewildered recruits until nearly three in the morning, swatting mosquitoes and sweating, afraid to go to sleep because she was so unsure of what would happen next.

Fort Leonard Wood sits on 71,000 acres of land and would look like a vast college campus, were it not for the tanks and military trucks lying about like giant toys. Because it's surrounded by woods and is so humid and buggy, soldiers call it Fort Lost-in-the-Woods and Little Korea. As the recruits were soon to find out, it did not in the least resemble the dry and dusty environment of Iraq.

Mickiela wasn't thinking of the four-month-old war that first night, though; she was too tired. From the moment she arrived she was either waiting in confusion, being ordered about without explanation—or running. As she put it, "The minute you get there, they treat you like crap."

She told me about all this on an autumnal Sunday in 2006—six months before I saw her in California—in her little rented house in Jersey City, New Jersey. She was taking political science classes at the Brooklyn branch of Long Island University then, and working in midtown Manhattan, a mere twenty-minute commute from her house and not far from Fort Dix, where she had to drill one weekend a month. Her job was computer accounting for a retail company, a skill she'd learned in the army. After recruits take the ASVAB test, their scores determine the jobs they can choose: cook, driver, supply clerk, chaplain's assistant, or engineer, for example. "When my recruiter asked me what job I wanted, I said anything but computers. I hate computers. So they trained me on computers," she said with a chuckle.

She was sharing the house with a young female soldier she'd met on the way to Iraq, but their friendship was not going well. Her roommate was drinking, taking drugs, and getting into fights; even while I was there, someone out in the street was screaming threats and obscenities up at the window. Mickiela shook her head, embarrassed. "That's the girl she got into a fight with last night. My roommate's getting into a lot of trouble."

But Mickiela had her own troubles because she had just found out she was pregnant by her soldier boyfriend. She wasn't showing yet, though, and when she greeted me at the door she looked as trim and fresh as a gymnast. "Hi, come in!" she said in her friendly way. "Are you cold?" She shivered. "I can't get used to this climate." She led me through the house into an almost empty but spotless kitchen. Later I came to see that soldiers often carry their military habits of order and cleanliness into their homes. Some of their places don't even look lived in.

She made us mugs of hot tea and led me into the tiny front parlor, which served as the TV room. Sitting in a hard chair, she pulled a sweatshirt around her compact body with a shiver and began to talk, interrupted occasionally by the beep of her cell phone. It was her boyfriend, pleading with her by text message not to keep the baby.

It is easy to see why Mickiela was a party girl in high school, for along with her ready smile and natural grace, she has an open, sunny manner. She says the army stole that side of her, along with her femininity, but in fact she is still very feminine, which made it all the more startling when she showed me photographs of herself in her battle fatigues. Almost nothing transforms a woman as much as military garb. Men may have to shave their heads, but their uniforms do not dramatically alter their bodies. But women look immediately sexless—which, of course, is the idea—and if the women are short, like Mickiela, the effect is even more dramatic, especially if they are wearing the bulletproof vest known as a flak jacket and a Kevlar (the helmet).[1] They look like little boys in men's clothing with a bowl on top of their heads. After all, the uniforms may have been adjusted for women, but they were designed for men.

The military has a profoundly muddled approach to women's uniforms. On the one hand, women must wear the unisex combat fatigues, on the other, their dress uniforms are not pantsuits, as one might expect, but skirts to be worn with "flesh tone nylons" and jackets tailored in an exaggerated hourglass shape. Until recently, army women also had to wear a small, folded cap with their dress uniforms known as "the cunt cap" in army vernacular. They now wear the same beret as men.

After the long wait in the parking lot that first night at Fort Leonard Wood, Mickiela was sent to a huge room full of metal bunk beds. She had just fallen into an exhausted sleep on her hard mattress when she was woken by a shout. She and the other recruits were ordered to stand at attention and then make their beds, even though they were about to get right back into them. The recruits were roused twice more that night, and awoken for good at five the next morning. Every night from then on they were jolted awake at least twice and made to perform a senseless task, such as buff the already buffed floor or fold their already folded clothes. In the mornings they had to do an hour of exercises before breakfast.

Mickiela's first order of business was to buy the supplies her recruiter had neglected to tell her to bring. She was given a smart card, a debit card that automatically deducted $100.00 from her first paycheck (she was earning $270.50 a week), and sent to the fort's shop to buy her equipment: regulation brown towels and washcloths; toilet articles, foot powder and tape (to protect her feet as she broke in her tough new army boots); physical training shorts and T-shirts known as PTs; the required white underwear; and clips and hair bands to keep her hair in regulation shape. Women don't have to shave their heads like men, but they do have to keep their hair tidy and off their shoulders. (Female marines must spray and gel their hair to make it lie flat.) Meeting these regulations takes so long that many women just cut their hair short, as did Eli PaintedCrow. In Iraq, where conditions are so harsh, a good many women are shaving their heads too.

Once Mickiela had bought her equipment, she was given her uniform of green camouflage (the digital version had not yet been issued) and ordered to get her shots. This was another matter her recruiter had neglected to tell her about. "I have a huge phobia for shots. Before the army, every time I would get a shot I literally passed out!" No matter. She had to join the other recruits in a human assembly line, while two medics worked methodically through them, jabbing each person in the arm with five vaccines in a row. "Then they told the females to go in another room, turn around, and drop our pants. And they went around tapping us on the shoulder and sticking us in the butt, over and over." The worst was the controversial anthrax vaccine (discussed in the next chapter), which burned painfully and made her arm hurt for hours.

By the end of her first day, Mickiela was in a daze. Filled with shots, sleep-deprived, her ears ringing from being shouted at and ordered about, she felt disoriented and exhausted. And the women who shared her barracks weren't helping: most of them had arrived together from their very white hometowns in Kentucky and Kansas and seemed to want nothing to do with a Mexican girl from L.A.

She collapsed onto her bunk bed, aching and lonely.

THROUGH THE LOOKING GLASS

After Mickiela had finished being processed through reception, which in her case took three days, her nine weeks of training started in earnest. Basic combat training is divided into three phases called Red, White, and Blue. Anyone who falls sick, is injured, or fails a test must cycle through the entire training period again, something every recruit dreads. (Boot camp lasts twelve weeks in the Marine Corps, which is the only branch to continue the original practice of segregating men and women. In October 2007 the army announced it was expanding basic training to ten weeks.)

At the start of basic, recruits are given a fitness test to make sure they can survive the challenge. If they fail, they are sent to a fitness training unit (FTU), or what Mickiela called "fat camp." (Other soldiers call it the Fat Turd Unit.) There, they are put on strict diets and exercised into acceptable shape. Mickiela had no such problem. She passed the test easily.

The first day of basic is called Day Zero, when recruits meet their drill instructor, the person in charge of what soldiers call "breaking you down, then building you back up again." Her Day Zero began with the drill sergeant flicking the lights on and off and yelling at the recruits to wake up and get into line. "You walk, you go to parade rest, you go to attention, and then you walk one step, and you go back to parade rest, over and over." After that she was told to run with her packed duffle bag clutched to her chest and get into a chamber truck, which is like a cattle truck with seats around the inside edges. "Put your head on your duffle bag!" the sergeant shouted, and all the recruits had to bury their heads so they couldn't see where they were going. When the truck stopped, the sergeant yelled again, "Everybody out!" and they had to jump down and run.

"There's hundreds of people running out at the same time with these bags, so everybody's falling down and tripping over each other," Mickiela said, laughing at the memory. Then began a charade like something out of a Marx Brothers movie, which would be repeated throughout basic training. "You go into this other room and they yell at you, 'Line up! Drop your bag! Line your bags up!' You line your bags up, but lining them up is never straight enough for them, so they make you drop and do push-ups, and then you have to empty out your bag, and the drill sergeant inspects everything in your bag, which is packed really tight. So first you have to empty it, then you have to throw it all back in there, and people are trying to roll their stuff the way we've been told, but now they don't want you to roll anything up, they just want you to throw everything back in. And it's embarrassing cause we had male drill sergeants and you have three days of dirty underwear they can see."

The women were sent to the upstairs floor of their new quarters, the men to the ground floor. "We had to put our bags in our lockers, and everything in your locker has to be exactly the same. Your pants have to be folded with the fly to the back, with your uniform on top and every-thing buttoned and facing the other way. The hangers have to be exactly two fingers apart, with four fingers in the front of your PTs. In the front is your towel, folded to the right with the washcloth on top with the middle folding to the left, and then your PT uniform folded flat with the army logo out. And your underwear has to be three-folded, three inches here, one inch wide there. Everything is, like, exact."

Mickiela chuckled, raising her eyebrows at me. She had never de-scribed basic training to a civilian before, and it made her see how odd it all sounds—the maniacal rules, the constant yelling, the getting up three times a night to polish the already polished floor. In retrospect, she thought it was funny, but she admitted she'd spent most of boot camp in a rage.

Mickiela's rage was intentionally provoked. Drill instructors scream commands and insults all the time, often right into recruits' faces, and recruits are supposed to take it without a blink. "They figure out your weak spots and try to get at you like that," she said. "Like, if you have crooked eyes, they tell you. They call it 'constructive criticism.' It does make you lose some of yourself." And although drill sergeants are not supposed to hit recruits anymore, they do; a dozen marine instructors were recently prosecuted for assaulting trainees.[2] (In training for the all-male special forces such as Navy SEALs and RECON Marines, violence and torture are still used on recruits, the rationale being it prepares them to handle capture.)

Marine corporal Lydia Sanchez, who served in Iraq from 2004 to 2005, told me about the harsh approach at her boot camp at Parris Island, South Carolina, where she trained in 2001 at the age of twenty. "The first month they really try to break you down. They yell at you all the time, although they try not to use racial insults or curses. And there was shoving. I heard some drill instructors were getting in trouble for hitting recruits, and one was accused of breaking a guy's hand.

"And the drill sergeants bully people. There was this one woman who kept peeing in her bed at night and they would tell her she was disgusting. She told me she'd never had that problem before, but she had a really intense bladder infection. She'd asked to go to the doctor early on, but she was told she had to come right back and that she couldn't miss the training. It gets so you're afraid to go to medical. You just try to handle problems on your own. So it had got to the point where she couldn't control her bladder." (Lydia Sanchez is not her real name. She asked that her name be changed because she is still in the marines and fears reprisals.)

Mickiela said that although the insults sometimes got to her, the yelling didn't. "I was used to being yelled at because of my mom. I could deal with it. The only time I broke down was when the drill sergeant said, 'All of you guys are used to your mom and dad tucking you into bed,' and it made me think that my grandma had just died, and I don't have a mom and dad to do that. That's when I started to cry. But if you cry, you get into a lot more trouble, so I hid it. I had like one tear." She ran a finger down her cheek. "But I was really mad the whole time."

A typical day of boot camp lasts about sixteen hours and in that time every task is made as grueling as possible. Recruits have to run everywhere and do constant pushups and sit-ups. They practice running while carrying another soldier on their backs. When standing in formation or in line, they must hold their arms or rifles in some way that is a strain. And if one recruit does something wrong, the whole platoon is "smoked" (punished) by having to do something painfully strenuous, such as perform a large number of pushups or squat with arms held out until they tremble.

"We would form up in front of the building to be inspected, and they'd say, 'Okay, get into your PTs, you have five minutes.' But only the guys could use the front door—females had to use the back door. So we had to run all the way around, up the stairs and down the hall to where our things were. And then we had to change and hang everything perfectly and be back downstairs in five minutes. Nobody would ever do it in five minutes, so it was this constant cycle of punishment."

After a time, some recruits learn to regard all this yelling and punishment as a game, but some crack and strike back. Any recruit who does this and resists reform through punishment and recycling will be dismissed from the military for "failure to adapt." But few are released this way anymore. The Pentagon is too desperate for bodies.

As the war has dragged on, recruits have been ever harder to find and keep, even though certain enlistment bonuses have risen to $40,000. Among high school seniors, 60 percent have no interest in joining the military now, a rise of 20 percent from before 2001. And among men between seventeen and twenty-four—prime recruiting age—seven out of ten are disqualified because of health problems such as obesity, being openly gay, or having a "moral" issue such as belonging to a gang.[3] In its consequent desperation, the army has softened basic training and taken to recycling trainees who fail instead of kicking them out; the number of recruits who flunked out dropped by two-thirds between 2005 and 2007.[4] The army is also accepting more high school dropouts, easing its test standards, and taking people with flat feet, asthma, high blood pressure, attention deficit disorder, and men who are only five feet tall (women have to be four feet ten): conditions that used to be certain disqualifiers. Virtually every soldier I talked to had stories of fellow recruits who were sickly, fat, weak, or couldn't shoot their guns. Mickiela said she had a friend who refused to even fire her rifle. They shipped her out anyway.

THE RED PHASE: WEEKS 1–2

In this first phase, Mickiela spent most of her time working out, but she also had to memorize and swear to uphold seven "army values":

Loyalty: "Bear true faith and allegiance to the U.S. Constitution, the Army, your unit and other soldiers."

Duty: "Fulfill your obligations."

Respect: "Treat people as they should be treated." (On the Fort Jackson Web site, this ambiguously phrased "value" is illustrated with a photograph of a male and female soldier together. The man is at the top of the picture and the woman is sitting just below his crotch level; a pose with more than a hint of sexual subservience.)

Selfless Service: "Put the welfare of the nation, the Army, and your subordinates before your own." (This self-sacrificing "value" is the only one illustrated with a prominent picture of a woman.)

Honor: "Live up to all the Army values."

Integrity: "Do what's right, legally and morally."

Personal Courage: "Face fear, danger, or adversity." (Only men illustrate this one.)

In addition, recruits must memorize the Warrior Ethos: "I will always place the mission first." "I will never accept defeat." "I will never quit." "I will never leave a fallen comrade."

Mickiela also spent a lot of time at "D & C," drill and ceremony practice. To drill means to stand, march, and reflexively obey orders, and is derived from the age-old practice of training soldiers to load and fire weapons in precise coordination. Critics say drill is obsolete and wastes the time that could be used on more specific weapons and combat training, but most commanders defend it, saying it prevents military units from degenerating into murderous mobs.[5]

By the end of her first two weeks at boot camp, Mickiela was passing her tests well and had found a few friends. But she still missed Nana and mourned her lack of family, especially when the mail came. There was never a letter from her mom.

THE WHITE PHASE: WEEKS 3–5

In this middle phase, Mickiela had to learn to fight hand-to-hand, throw grenades, and clean and shoot her M-16 rifle, which is three and a quarter feet long and weighs eight and a half pounds. "I was scared at first. They teach you to balance the weapon on your shoulder—you aren't allowed to call them a gun in the military. And I forgot to put my earplugs in and it was so loud! I know a lot of people who are deaf now in one ear. My ears still hurt a lot too. But the first time I shot my weapon, I felt powerful. It changed me forever."

She also practiced thrusting a bayonet into human-shaped sacks while screaming "Kill!" at the top of her voice. "And they make you shoot at targets the shape of little men. They taught us chants to march to, as well. I remember one":

What makes the green grass grow?
Blood, blood, bright red blood
What makes the pretty flowers bloom?
Guts, guts, gritty grimy guts.[6]

Mickiela must have seen a startled look on my face when she said that, because she quickly added, "You say these words so much they lose their meaning. It felt unnatural at first, but you do it so much you don't even think what the word *kill* means after a while."

I asked her if she was ever disturbed by screaming "Kill!" while stabbing a human-shaped target. "Yeah!" she replied quickly. "But it's the army, so you can never say so. But I don't know, it was fun. They build you up to it: 'One, two, three!' and you hear one loud *kill*! It's just a word." She hesitated, looking uncomfortable. "Talking about it here in my civilian clothes—it feels funny that I said that. But if I was to talk about it in my uniform, it wouldn't."

"Does this mean the training works?" I asked. "It makes you numb shouting 'kill' and shooting at human-shaped targets?"

She nodded. "The training works. I never met anyone who said they wouldn't kill somebody."

The part of the White phase that was not fun was the gas chamber. The gas is CS gas, similar to pepper spray.[7] "Have you ever heard about the gas chamber? Oh my God. You know how we have our NBC [Nuclear Biological Chemical] mask? Well, to show you appreciation for the mask, they make you put it on and go into the gas chamber. Then you hear a voice telling you to take your mask off, and you take it off, and you feel everything burning, like little needles. And you start snotting. Your eyes burn, you can't breathe. Then they come in with their masks on, and they're like, 'What's the last four of your social [security number]?' and you have to say it, and if you don't say it loud they make you say it again. And then they open the door and you walk out. And once the air hits you everything starts burning even more. It's terrible!"

For the first few months of the Iraq War, the military command was so afraid of a chemical attack by Saddam Hussein, they made their soldiers don the mask constantly, along with the hot and uncomfortable plastic and carbon-lined chemical-protection suits known as MOPP (Mission-Oriented Protective Posture) gear, which look like puffy camouflage fatigues. These precautions, it turned out, were totally unnecessary: Saddam had no chemical weapons.

By the end of the White phase, some of the recruits around Mickiela, both male and female, were breaking down. "We had three girls try to kill themselves. Two went to sick hall and got some Motrin or Advil, and they ate the whole bottle, both of them, on the same night. When they found them, the girls were delusional. Then the other girl tried to burn herself to death. They found her in bed with matches in her hand, and the bed was made tight around her."

The three women were put on suicide watch, which meant they were guarded twenty-four hours a day, had their shoelaces and metal belongings confiscated, and had to wear bright orange vests all the time, like a sort of scarlet letter. All three had failed a test and faced being recycled through basic training right from the beginning. Mickiela thought this was why they had become so desperate.

All recruits are under intense pressure during boot camp, and it is not uncommon for some to crack like this, but many women have the additional pressure of sexual harassment. When they run obstacle courses, men line up to ogle their bodies. When they walk into the food hall, hundreds of eyes undress them. When they reach or bend to pick up something, men whistle, groan, and stare. This can go on every hour of every day, and creates an excruciating sense of oppression that few men ever experience. (Although men who are labeled gay or emotionally weak are sometimes humiliated this way too.)

Air force sergeant Marti Ribeiro, a young wife and mother whose family has been in the air force for two generations, was harassed like this throughout her eight years of service, both in training and during her deployments in 2003 and 2006. "I ended up waging my own war against an enemy dressed in the same uniform as mine. I had a senior noncommissioned officer harass me on a regular basis. He would constantly quiz me about my sex life, show up at the barracks at odd hours of the night, and ask personal questions that no supervisor has a right to ask. I had a colonel sexually harass me in ways I'm too embarrassed to explain. Once my sergeant sat with me at lunch in the chow hall, and he said, 'I feel like I'm in a fish bowl, the way all the men's eyes are boring into your back.' I told him, 'That's what my life is like.'"

During her second deployment, in Afghanistan, Ribeiro decided this time would be different. "Excuse my language, but I decided to be a 'bitch.' So I stepped off the plane into my own personal hell. Yes, I was able to put up a wall, but at a price. I'm tall and blond, so I stuck out like a sore thumb. I couldn't go anywhere without being watched by a million eyes. My wall became thicker and thicker. I'm normally a very bubbly person, but that disappeared behind the wall, and to this day I don't know if I've ever regained that part of my personality."

Mickiela also had to change her personality to cope with harassment, which is why she said the army robbed her of her femininity. She altered the way she talked, and even the way she walked. "There's so many guys watching you walk, so I had to learn to do it with no girlyness at all." Like Ribeiro, she felt she'd lost her real self.

As well as having to cope with sexual harassment, female soldiers are up against a military that demands they perform on a par with men while simultaneously assuming they are inferior. This drives many to become obsessed with proving themselves, especially in the face of the differential standards of physical fitness. "We're all trying to prove ourselves bad enough to play with the boys," said Miriam Barton, an army sergeant from Oregon who served in Iraq as a heavy gunner with an engineering unit from 2003 to 2004. "You gotta be twice as bad as they are in order to get half the recognition." (Barton asked that her name be changed to protect her while she battles the military and government for her veteran's benefits.)

The different standards for men and women have been a subject of controversy ever since sex segregation in boot camp ended under President Clinton in 1994. In the army, for example, both men and women must be able to do eighty sit-ups, but men also have to complete seventy-five pushups, while women are only asked to do forty-six.[8] Some argue that these easier measures for women bring down fitness standards for all soldiers. Women's answer to this is that every unit has women able to meet the male standards; that if you adjust for size and weight the regime is equally challenging; that some women are stronger than some men; that women can shoot as well as men, if not better; and that much of modern warrior prowess isn't about strength anyway but about quick thinking and technological skills.

A recent study discovered that women sustain twice as many injuries as men in basic training, especially in stress and bone fractures. Yet the study found the injuries were less related to height or strength than to women's relative lack of fitness when they begin boot camp.[9] It seems likely that the injuries are also occurring because women are trying so hard.

THE BLUE PHASE: WEEKS 6–9

This last phase is marked by more physical training and an obstacle course, culminating in a weeklong camping and marching trip designed to test the recruits' skills. "We went on a 15K march and I'd wrapped my feet in tape to help my arch, but I didn't know how to do it right," Mickiela said. "The tape sliced my feet and my entire heel was a blister, so it felt like I was walking on bone. But you have to finish the march or you get recycled. It was the worst ever! I was limping all the way." (Mickiela referred to the march in kilometers because, somewhat oddly, the American military uses the metric system for all measurements.)

At the end of that week, in September 2003, her basic training was complete. She and the other recruits put on their dress uniforms and attended a small ceremony to receive their diplomas. Some had family there to cheer them on, but nobody came for Mickiela. Yet on her very last night she was handed the first and only letter she'd received from her mother. "Sorry for not saying goodbye," it said. There was not a word about the fact that Mickiela had just finished training to go to war.

Mickiela's experience of basic training does not reflect everybody's, as boot camp is many things to many people. For some it is a satisfying challenge, for others a grueling test. For many it is hell. But however it's experienced, and however much the military portrays it as being about building discipline and esprit de corps, the bottom line is that boot camp is about training people to kill.

This may seem obvious, but killing has not always been as easy for soldiers as one might assume. In World War II, only 15–20 percent of soldiers were shooting to kill; most were either deliberately missing or not shooting at all. Military historians decided this was because no amount of conventional drill could overcome a human being's revulsion toward murdering his own kind, even in the face of life-threatening danger to himself or his comrades. What was needed was training that would condition soldiers to kill reflexively and dispassionately. So the military concentrated on developing a psychological approach to achieve just this, and it seems to have worked. By the Korean War, about

55 percent of soldiers were firing to kill, and by the Vietnam War the rate had risen to over 90 percent.[10]

Now, this deadly training is being used again, with a mix of technology that distances and facilitates killing, discussed later, and the psychological approaches described above, some of which are old, some new, but all of which bear a close resemblance to what most people would call brainwashing. This is how it was done to Mickiela:

She was deprived of sleep to make her susceptible to suggestion and keep her too exhausted to rebel. She was screamed at by her superiors and made to shout, "Yes, sir!" in reply to humble her and accustom her to functioning in an atmosphere of constant aggression. She was humiliated, made to obey capricious commands, and to endure arbitrary punishments to stoke her anger while prohibiting her from venting it, thus building up aggression. She was treated like a child to give the drill sergeant the authority of a parent. She was kept from the news to keep her ignorant and malleable. Her uniform, rules about hair, and the fact that she was no longer called by name but only by rank, "recruit," or the last four digits of her social security number, were all designed to erase her civilian identity. She was made to sing bloodthirsty songs and chants to inure her to killing. She was kept in constant physical pain to break down her will and accustom her to the harsh conditions of war. And while she was punished for independent thinking, such as asking questions, she was rewarded for complying with group behavior or sacrificing herself for others. In the words of Jen Spranger, the soldier from the dead-end town of Racine, Wisconsin, "A single soldier is nothing. It's all about the group."

It's worth pausing here a moment to ask who, exactly, this "group" is. As others have pointed out, a military group defines itself through contempt for and hatred of the enemy. But this enemy is not only, say, Iraqi rebels or the Taliban; it is also the outsider: the "soft" or nonconformist soldier, and those age-old butts of military contempt, women and homosexuals.[11] Military language reveals this contempt all the time. Even with a force that now includes women, gays, and lesbians, and rules that now prohibit drill instructors from using racial epithets and curses, instructors still denigrate recruits with words like *pussy, girl, bitch, lady, dyke, faggot,* and *fairy;* the everyday speech of ordinary soldiers is still riddled with sexist and homophobic insults; and soldiers still openly peruse pornography that humiliates women and sing the misogynist songs that have been around for decades: "This is my rifle, this is my gun [penis]; this is for killing, this is for fun." Or, to the tune of "The Candy Man":

> Who can take a chainsaw
> Cut the bitch in two
> Fuck the bottom half
> And give the upper half to you?[12]

This misogynist language is so deeply engrained in military culture as to be reflexive. Yet it serves as a constant reminder to women that, even as they are winning honors and advancing in numbers and positions in the military, when it comes to the group, they are alone.

ADVANCED TRAINING

The very morning after Mickiela graduated basic, she was shipped off to Advanced Individual Training, or AIT. Most soldiers are allowed to go home between the two phases, but not Mickiela. Instead, she and her comrades were ordered onto a bus and driven straight from Missouri to Fort Lee, Virginia. The trip took a day and a night, so long she lost track of time. But all she could think about was how angry she was at her mother for not writing until the last minute and for never acknowledging that Mickiela was now a soldier.

AIT lasts about twelve to fifteen weeks, depending on the soldier's job and the branch of the military, and its purpose is to train soldiers in a specific duty, or MOS (Military Occupational Specialty). This is when many find out that the job they chose when they enlisted has been replaced with whatever the military needs.

Mickiela found AIT much easier than boot camp, although she still had to wake early, exercise for an hour before breakfast, and clean the barracks till they shone. For most of the day, though, she would take classes in weapons training and computers until early evening, and then she was free until bedtime at nine. As she no longer dropped into bed exhausted every night, she had more time to make friends with the other women. "We would talk about basic and how much we hated the officers, but it was all light conversation. We didn't talk about politics or the war."

The drill instructors did, though. "They never spoke about it until we got to AIT, but then they were like, 'Half of you are going to Iraq.' Up until then, I'd had no idea."

Mickiela finished training the first week of 2004, after which she went home to stay with Nana's husband, with whom she had reconciled by then. She'd intended to go back to school until she was deployed, but it was too late to enroll, so she spent the next six months working in retail and having fun. "After a while my grandpa decided I was going out too much, so he kicked me out of the house." This forced her to move in with a friend, which only led her back to the weed-smoking lifestyle she had hoped to renounce. Thus, it was almost a relief when, the following summer, shortly after her nineteenth birthday, she was ordered to Fort Dix, New Jersey. She was about to be sent to Iraq.

"My grandpa had been in Vietnam and when he found out, he didn't want me to go. He warned me I'd be raped. But the army makes you feel like you've abandoned the country if you don't go. They make you lose your self-respect. I felt like I had no choice." She didn't. The only legal way out would have been to find a doctor to testify that she was mentally or physically unfit, which she had neither the means or know-how to do so.

Mickiela arrived at Fort Dix at the end of August 2004, by which time an estimated ninety-eight thousand Iraqis had died in the war, and the number of U.S. soldiers killed had just hit one thousand.[13] But these were matters she and most of her fellow soldiers tried hard not to think about. They preferred to concentrate on the training and to party as much as possible before shipping out to war.

Some of the training was a refresher course for soldiers being brought out of inactive duty, but much of it was the first training Mickiela received specifically for Iraq. "They put us in this foxhole thing and there was this little hut far out to the left, and inside the hut were Iraqi people. We had to bomb them. I don't know if they were real Iraqi people or if they were military personnel dressed up, but they all had the little turban thing and the dress thing, and they had women. They told us you couldn't shoot a woman."

The military does use Iraqi and Arab immigrants, whom it calls cultural role players, for training, most of them hired by private corporations. It also uses nonwhite and women soldiers.[14] Eli PaintedCrow commented on this. "They never use white soldiers to do the role-playing, but they could. Kurdish people are pretty light-skinned. But we're not supposed to be bombing white people, I guess."

Mickiela bombed and lobbed grenades at the pretend Iraqi village and practiced kicking open doors, raiding houses, and searching and arresting the inhabitants. Yet even though she was told, like most other soldiers at the time, that she was going to Iraq to give the people freedom and help them recover from Saddam Hussein's brutal rule, the only training she was given on Iraqi culture were two briefings and a DVD, which she forgot almost instantly. She was taught no Arabic and was not even given a map.

At this stage of training, soldiers in combat units learn to use the latest war technology I mentioned earlier: radar guns, Night Vision goggles, computers, and the electronic communication devices that became known as "Nintendo warfare" in the 1991 Gulf War because they make war look so exactly like a video game. (In fact, video games are used in training to simulate combat.) Night Vision goggles, which soldiers call NVG, use thermal imagery to read the heat emitted by a body as if it were light. This makes it possible to see through fog, rain, smoke, and the dark, as long as there is a little light to help. But military psychologist Dave Grossman argues that as efficient as these devices may be, they encourage careless slaughter because they make people look like featureless green or white blobs. Shooting them down seems as harmless as knocking over a row of toy skittles.[15]

These devices, coupled with the powerful automatic guns soldiers use now, have resulted in the killing of thousands of innocent civilians in Iraq. Many soldiers and journalists have described how gunners commonly react to a single lobbed grenade or sniper by mowing down everyone in sight, either with the .50-caliber belt-fed machine gun that sits atop tanks and Humvees, or with the Squad Automatic Weapons (SAWs) that can fire one thousand rounds a minute.[16]

Mickiela was herself to be a tank gunner, although she didn't know that yet. But when she wasn't bombing pretend Iraqi houses and taking classes, she had time to party and flirt. Even though soldiers are officially forbidden to *fraternize*, the bizarre military term for dating, one of the most striking results of integrating women has been the blossoming of romance. This is what happened when Mickiela met Joseph.

"I met him the night I arrived at Fort Dix and we immediately started talking. We were never flirty with each other, but our conversation was just really good. He said, 'Give me your number,' and later he texted me and said, 'What's good?' Just like that." She smiled at the memory.

Mickiela was instantly smitten, and soon she and Joseph were a couple. "Joseph's black but he's light and looks kind of Dominican. He's real cute. He's six foot, a big, muscular guy." He came from New York, which is why he was at the New Jersey base.

Because of the rules, she and Joseph had to keep their relationship secret. This wasn't easy. "Everybody would gossip about each other all the time—it's worse than high school! You work with these people; you sleep and eat with them. We had twelve girls in bunk beds all in one room. They would gossip about how everybody would sleep with everybody except me and him. He was a sergeant and I was a specialist, so it couldn't be known. But they knew."

A few weeks later, in October, Mickiela awoke feeling sick. She went to the medical unit and took a pregnancy test. It came out positive.

Federal law prohibits the military from offering either the "morning after pill" (Plan B) or abortion. In 2002, Department of Defense health officials approved Plan B and ordered it to be stocked at military medical facilities, but before that could happen, Bush's appointees overruled the decision.[17] So, although Mickiela was barely nineteen and at the beginning of her military career, hardly ready to have a child, the army gave her no choice but to keep the baby.

The medical personnel at Fort Dix and Mickiela's superiors immediately assumed she'd become pregnant on purpose to get out of going to war—the usual assumption about pregnant soldiers—but this was an injustice in Mickiela's case. "They treated me so bad! It made me really hate the army." Still, partly because of her Catholic upbringing, which made her reluctant to have an abortion even if she could, and partly because she loved Joseph so much, she grew excited about the baby. Joseph also seemed pleased, and soon she found herself dreaming of how the two of them would make a family.

While her unit continued to train, Mickiela was kept on medical hold at Fort Dix under a cloud of disgrace. In November 2004, Joseph's unit shipped out to Iraq, followed by hers two weeks later. She was left behind, surrounded by strangers.

For the whole of her first trimester, while she was held at Fort Dix working an office job, she felt horrible. She couldn't stop vomiting and sharp pains kept shooting through her womb. As weeks of this went on, she began to worry about all the vaccines she had been given, especially the anthrax, which she'd heard has dangerous side effects. Was that what was wrong with her? And what if her baby turned out to be damaged?

When she was three months pregnant, in January 2005, she went home for a leave of nine days and sat in her grandpa's house, worried and depressed. She missed Joseph terribly and felt guilty about her friends going off to war without her. And she was still bleeding and cramping. Two days before she was due back at Fort Dix, the pains grew so bad she checked herself into a local emergency room.

The doctors examined her. The pregnancy was not viable, they said. She would have to have the fetus removed.

FOUR

They Told Us We Were Going to Be Peacekeepers

Jennifer Spranger

Two years before Mickiela went off to boot camp, Jen, the young recruit who was so eager to please her firefighter father, also trained at Fort Leonard Wood. She spent the summer after eleventh grade there, when she was just seventeen. It was August 2001 then, a month shy of the 9/11 attacks, so she had no idea what was in store. She only knew she was proud, a little scared, and dazzled by all the attention she was getting from men.

"I mean, when you're standing there with a hundred guys and ten girls, the guys are going to want to talk to you," she explained in her flat Wisconsin accent, her hazel eyes large behind her glasses. "But—and it took me way longer to realize this than it should have—it was just a game to see how many girls they could sleep with. Not all the guys were like that, but most were."

The women in her unit were another matter. "They were kind of unapproachable and tough. I've always been shy, so it was hard for me to meet all these new people. There was this woman, Sergeant Martinez, who took me under her wing, but other than her I was real intimidated by the girls in my platoon."

Apart from her shyness, Jen enjoyed herself. She liked the physical challenges, which she found quite easy after her high-school athletics, and as for the dehumanizing songs and shouts of *kill,* she didn't take them any more seriously than did Mickiela. "We had songs about blood running through the streets and this and that, but nothing seemed real." It wasn't the songs that made people ready to kill, she believed, it was the bond between soldiers. "The training makes you depend on everyone else. You become such a tight-knit group that the thought of anyone hurting someone you care about is enough to make you instantly want to kill them."

Abbie Pickett, the young woman who had enlisted to rebel, said the same thing. "I think the real reason we kill on the battlefield isn't because we stuck a bayonet into a dummy on the assault course. It's because your best friend is sitting next to you and you want to save his life."

Sadly, what many women find out, Jen and Abbie among them, is that although they may feel this bond with their fellow soldiers, not all those soldiers feel the same bond with them.

Right after Jen came home from boot camp to start twelfth grade, the World Trade Center and Pentagon were attacked, which made her surer than ever that she had been right to enlist. At home, though, life had become more difficult. Her parents' quarrels were escalating, and soon she and her beloved father were fighting as well. The main source of tension was that Jen and her boyfriend wanted to move in together, but her parents thought them too young. Yet as soon as Jen graduated in 2002, having completed her senior year in one semester, she defied them and rented an apartment with her boyfriend anyway. This not only upset her parents more than ever but also devastated her boyfriend's mother, who believed the couple was living in sin and threatened to disown her son unless he married Jen right away. So Jen and her boyfriend waited for her to turn eighteen in February, and the next month they married. Her parents did not attend the wedding.

"I thought I was all grown up and smart. I just wasn't," she said as she shivered in her mother's house four years later, pulling her knees up in her chair. "I'm not proud of myself for this. It was an incredibly stupid decision."

Jen often reprimands herself like this. She will speak of people who have wronged her with bitterness, but she is never as hard on anyone as she is on herself.

Although Jen's husband was also a soldier, and would eventually deploy to Afghanistan, he neither wanted her in the army nor to leave for the rest of her training. "You're just going so the guys will hit on you," he kept saying.

"I thought I was in love, so I listened to him for a little while. I was supposed to go to AIT right after I graduated high school, but I put it off for months." She enrolled in a local college and took courses in civil engineering. "And then something snapped. I thought, 'Why the hell am I listening to this guy and putting everything on hold?' So I moved back home." The marriage hadn't even lasted the summer.

Once she was back at her parents' house, Jen spent one weekend a month at drill, as all reservists must, during which time she became the unwilling object of an obsession. The man was a sergeant, older and married with children, and at first she had thought of him as a father figure. "I was so young and I wanted so badly to be a part of everything. He would ask me to go rock climbing with him—he lived on the navy base where my unit was doing some work—and I thought, 'Great, he's in his forties, I'm eighteen, nothing to worry about.' I was so naive."

One night on the base, while Jen and some other soldiers were having a barbecue, the sergeant turned up drunk and declared he was going to kill himself. "He said that he loved me, and his family would be taken care of when he was dead. I was scared he really would do it, so I called the navy police. He was put in the psych ward of the hospital for two days."

Unluckily for Jen, this same sergeant was in charge of promotions in her unit, and she soon found her every attempt at advancement blocked. "I tried to change units to get away from him at least twice, but they wouldn't let me. I put in the paperwork to go on active duty—they threw it away." She wanted to report that he was pulling strings to prevent her from escaping him, but in the end she didn't dare. "I wanted to fit in, and you can't fit in if you make waves like that. You rat somebody out, you're screwed. You're gonna be a loner until they eventually push you out."

Despite this setback, Jen was still thrilled to be in the army and happy to return to Fort Leonard Wood for her military police training at the end of October 2002. Bush was already planning to invade Iraq by then, but she knew nothing of this. She thought she was being trained to police unruly soldiers on home bases. "I learned how to ride around in a police car, handcuff people, break up a bar fight, things like that." It turned out, however, that her unit's mission was EPW: Enemy Prisoner of War operations. "I didn't even know what EPW meant!" None of her training would apply to her job in Iraq.

GUINEA PIGS

Jen graduated from AIT in early January 2003 and shortly afterward was ordered to meet up with her unit at Fort Dix, New Jersey, the same base from which Mickiela would deploy two years later. There, Jen's company was to join the 822nd Military Police Battalion out of Arlington, Illinois, and fly to Kuwait. Why they were going was not made clear.

At Fort Dix, she settled into a routine similar to Mickiela's, and all went well until the time came for her vaccinations. Soldiers bound for war areas in the Middle East are typically inoculated for meningitis, polio, tetanus-diphtheria, yellow fever, hepatitis A and B, typhoid, and, depending on when they signed up, smallpox and anthrax. Some are also vaccinated for measles, mumps, and rubella in one shot, as well as for the flu, cholera, and chickenpox (varicella).[1] Most receive these vaccinations all at once.

The medical effects of injecting a person with so many vaccines at the same time have been inadequately studied, but side effects of the smallpox and anthrax shots are known to be dangerous, especially for women. In 2003 a young recruit named Rachel Lacy and a nurse named Deerheart Cornitcher both died at Fort McCoy, Wisconsin, of complications caused by these latter two vaccines. Three days after Cornitcher's death, the CDC issued a warning that the smallpox vaccination is dangerous to those with heart conditions.[2] But the official reaction to the anthrax shot was murkier.

The anthrax vaccine is given in a series of six injections, which are notoriously painful, as Mickiela discovered. Abbie Pickett fainted each time she had hers. But Jen, who received hers later in Kuwait, had the worst reaction of all. "It gave me a really high fever. I remember walking around the camp completely out of my mind—I didn't know where I was. I lost my hearing for a week and a half; I thought it was never going to come back. I'm pretty good with pain, but almost as soon as you got the anthrax shot it burned like fire. It made a lot of people really sick. They told us it was okay, but anything that makes you that sick can't be okay."

She was right. By 2001 there had been so many reports of adverse reactions to the anthrax vaccine that Congress directed the Defense Department and the CDC to establish a Vaccine Healthcare Centers Network to monitor reactions and research safer ways to administer vaccinations. Four such centers were set up, the leading one at Walter Reed Army Medical Center, the military's primary veteran hospital, but in all the years since, none of these centers have made their findings public.

Dr. Meryl Nass, an expert on anthrax at the Mount Desert Island Hospital in Maine, has been following the military's handling of anthrax vaccines for years. She found that military medical providers had been instructed not to report adverse reactions in their patients unless the patient was hospitalized, missed twenty-four hours of work, or an entire batch of the vaccine was contaminated. She also found that even after a Congressional investigation forced military leaders to demand that the four research centers file reports, so little was done that this demand had to be repeated in three different years. Her findings were echoed by a newspaper investigation in 2005, which discovered that the Pentagon had failed to report to Congress a staggering twenty thousand cases of soldiers who had been hospitalized after receiving the vaccine between 1998 and 2000.[3]

Anthrax is an acute infectious disease caused by the bacterium *Bacillus anthracis,* and it is most familiar to people from the scares of October 2001, when four Americans died after handling envelopes containing anthrax powder. Humans are infected in three ways: by getting the bacteria in cuts, by inhaling it, or by ingesting it. Infection through the skin is the least severe and can be treated with antibiotics, although about 20 percent of untreated cases result in death. But inhaling or ingesting anthrax is often fatal.

Although anthrax occurs naturally in animals, it can be used as a bacterial weapon, so the military instigated mandatory vaccinations against it back in 1998. Since then the vaccine has been given to over 1.8 million service members and civilians.[4] When Jen, Mickiela, and Abbie were in training, they were threatened with military prison if they refused the shots.

Then, in 2004 a federal judge ruled that the military was acting illegally in forcing the anthrax vaccination on its personnel because the U.S. Food and Drug Administration had not yet approved the vaccine's use for inhaled anthrax, only for anthrax absorbed through the skin. The military stopped giving the vaccinations for a few months until the FDA approved the shots in 2005, although the judge allowed only voluntary injections. By then so many soldiers were leery of the side effects that half of them declined.[5]

Now the vaccine is mandatory again. In October 2006 the DoD cleared the way, and in March 2007 the military resumed the shots for all soldiers serving in the Middle East or Korea, maintaining the vaccination is well studied and safe.[6] Yet Dr. Nass has documented a long list of adverse reactions to the anthrax vaccine, including pains in muscles and joints; short-term memory loss; periods of confusion, accompanied by fatigue and insomnia (Jen had all these symptoms); inflammatory bowel disease; autoimmune disorders, including lupus; multiple sclerosis; reactive arthritis; rashes; and thyroid disorders.[7]

Women have all these risks and more. Studies found a whopping 39 percent rise in birth defects for pregnant women who take the vaccine within their first trimester, a side effect that even the military acknowledges, as well as a rise in the likelihood of miscarriage.[8] (Mickiela's fears for her baby were well founded.) Benign breast lumps leading to hospitalization occurred nine times as often after anthrax vaccinations as before. Breast and genitourinary cancer hospitalizations occurred more than three and a half times as often, and abnormal Pap smears led to hospitalization more than five times as often.[9]

Dr. Nass says these findings are so alarming that they should be enough to halt the use of the anthrax vaccine immediately. But she also opposes it for another reason: the DoD has never even been able to prove it protects anyone from an anthrax attack in the first place.[10]

She is not alone in her opposition. In May 2006 the Government Accountability Office, the investigating arm of Congress, issued a report that called for a "better, alternative vaccine" to anthrax, saying the "vaccine has not been adequately tested on humans; no studies have been done to determine the optimum number of doses; the long-term safety has not been studied and data on short-term reactions are limited."[11]

Nonetheless, the military is still forcing anthrax shots on every soldier going to Iraq or Afghanistan.

Women also have to contend with another problematic shot, one that men never get: the Depo-Provera birth control injection. "I wouldn't say they really pushed the shot on us, but they kind of did," Jen said. "They told us it's not going to be sanitary over there. They never said it was about not getting pregnant, 'cause you're not supposed to be having sex anyway, but they said it would keep you from having your period. That sounded good to me. I've always had heavy periods. But instead, it made me bleed for three months straight. I became anemic. I had to be on iron pills for about two months."

A shot of Depo-Provera must be taken every eleven to thirteen weeks to stay effective, which is easy to miss in the chaos of war. ("The result of my Depo shot is running around my living room right now," one soldier told me.) Jen's nonstop bleeding is a documented side effect, but irregular bleeding is more common, with menses often stopping altogether, especially in women who have been on Depo for some time. The shot also causes bone thinning, which never reverses.[12] Yet soldiers are never told of these or any other side effects of the many vaccines forced upon them.

The question of what all these shots are doing to soldiers will be raised again as more troops return from Iraq, especially now that so many are women. And soldiers are worried, for themselves and their future children. Most of the women I interviewed were aware of earlier carelessness with soldiers' health—the exposure of Vietnam War soldiers to the toxic herbicide Agent Orange, the experimentation on them with LSD, the manifold problems that have come to be known as Gulf War Syndrome—and told me they don't trust the military to administer vaccines safely, to study them honestly, or to compensate adequately those who suffer their consequences. "We knew they were experimenting on us, but we couldn't do anything about it," Jen said. "We knew we were guinea pigs."

By the time Jen's last round of training at Fort Dix was completed, it was February 2003 and President Bush was ratcheting up his threats against Saddam Hussein. He had already accused the Iraqi dictator of hiding his weapons of mass destruction (WMDs), and on February 24, he and the leaders of Britain and Spain approached the United Nations with what amounted to a request for permission to invade Iraq. (They were voted down eleven to four.) In reaction, Iraqi citizens were either trying to flee or battening down for war: closing their shops, storing supplies, and watching their gas dry up and the value of their money plummet. It was clear to most of the world by then that the United

States was about to attack Iraq, even without the UN's permission, but when the drill sergeants finally told Jen and her unit they were going to Iraq, they never spoke in terms of war.

"They told us we were going to be peacekeepers. We were going to help these people who'd been oppressed by Saddam Hussein for so long. We were going to have medical supplies, school supplies for the kids, and we were going to help rebuild things. And I honestly thought that's what we were going to be doing."

The minute Jen finished at Fort Dix, she was flown to Kuwait. She was now Specialist Jennifer Spranger of the military police, and she had become part of the urgent push leading up to war.

FIVE

The Assault Was Just One Bad Person, but It Was a Turning Point for Me

Abbie Pickett

While Jen was training in Missouri, Abbie, the soft-spoken rebel from Darlington, was in Fort Jackson, South Carolina, waiting. She had arrived in such a flood of recruits there was no room for them all to start at once, so she was held in reception for two weeks with nothing to do but kick around in the Carolina heat. When Day Zero did finally arrive, however, the date happened to be September 11, 2001.

The morning began unremarkably, with the drill sergeant ordering Abbie and the others to stand in parade formation and swear their oath of allegiance: "I do solemnly swear that I will support and defend the Constitution of the United States against all enemies, foreign and domestic, so help me God. Amen." As soon as they finished, the drill sergeant said something about airplanes hitting towers, but Abbie was too far away to hear him properly. Suddenly people were crying and running toward their barracks. She looked around, bewildered, until finally somebody explained.

The rest of that day was chaotic. The sergeants pulled out anyone from New York or whose parents worked in the Pentagon and let them go, and then asked if anyone was Muslim. "One guy was, and they pulled him out, too, though he came back later. We didn't know what that was about."

All that week, rumors spread that basic would be sped up and the recruits sent to some sort of war early, but in the end the only break in routine was a ceremony to honor the people who had died in the attacks. "They told us if we wanted to cry it was okay, but then we needed to pick it back up and use that emotion to motivate us to get out there and fight. I remember thinking, 'They're telling me what I can and can't feel already?'" Otherwise, training continued as normal, with the recruits allowed no more contact with the outside world than before. Abbie was only permitted to call home three times during the entire twelve weeks she spent at Fort Jackson, which, as a small-town girl with a close family, she found hard. "And we were only allowed to keep a newspaper one night, then they'd take it away. No TV was allowed and we didn't get Internet. They want to cut you off from the world outside."

She was aware, however, that President Bush had retaliated against the 9/11 attacks by declaring a "War on Terrorism" and bombing Afghanistan on October 7. And one of the rare times she did get to call home, her mother told her she could now be sent to war, even though she was in the National Guard.

"If my country needs me," Abbie replied righteously, "I'll go."

"I was very altruistic in those days," she said to me in the London kitchen where we first met, sounding a little wistful. "At that point everyone was behind this. They told us there was no prouder time to be a soldier. It was true. When I was allowed to go home for Christmas, people shook my hand in the airport and thanked me. It was very humbling because I hadn't done anything yet. But I was ready to go to war in the name of 9/11. I felt that I'd do anything to protect Americans in a heartbeat." She paused. "I remember thinking that the government would never make me go to a war that isn't justified."

A TURNING POINT

Like Mickiela and Jen, Abbie found boot camp grueling but bearable, for at home she'd been running track and cross-country long enough to develop the strong, lean body of an athlete. "I never really felt like they broke me in basic. The only thing that was difficult was being away from my family."

Once she had finished basic and spent some time back at home, she was sent to Fort Lee, Virginia, for advanced training, the same place where Mickiela had done hers. By then it was the beginning of 2002 and the Iraq War had already been decided upon in the back rooms of the White House. But it was still a remote possibility to soldiers like Abbie, who assumed that if she went to war at all, it would be to Afghanistan.

At Fort Lee, she trained as a truck mechanic and refueler. She was attached to the Wisconsin National Guard's 229th Engineering Company, whose work was building roads, bridges, and military bases, and preparing ground for construction. This wasn't exactly what she'd expected to do in the army, but she saw it could be useful. When she was a girl, floods had once half-buried Darlington in mud and the National Guard had come to clean it up. That impressed her, so she hoped to be doing that sort of work with her unit too.

After Advanced Individual Training was over, Abbie went home again and worked as a nursery-school teacher until the opportunity arose to go to Nicaragua with her unit on a mission to build schools. She jumped at it. She might not have been a kid running around in the fields with her friend Jeve anymore, but she hadn't forgotten their dreams of doing good in the world.

When she arrived in Nicaragua, though, she was shocked. "It was the first time I was faced with such poverty and seeing children so young without shoes or anything to eat. It blew me away." Still, she loved the job. It was her company that turned out to be the problem.

Up until the first Gulf War, the 229th had been all male and virtually all white, and it still had what Abbie calls a "good-old-boys' club" character that mistrusted women. Abbie was one of only five women among forty or so men in her platoon, and soon the hostility and suspicion of her male superiors became only too evident. They so frequently assumed she would be incompetent, criticizing and checking on her all the time, that she grew self-conscious and clumsy, as if she couldn't help but fulfill their expectations.

Then something happened that made everything worse. Abbie told me about it in London, quietly and with hesitation, as the memory is still so painful she finds it hard to talk about.

"We'd all been out drinking, and this lieutenant colonel and another officer said they'd walk me back to my section of the camp. I knew something didn't feel right, but I didn't know what to do. We ended up in this isolated place by the water storage tank. There was no one around. Then the other officer lay down and pretended to sleep. And that's when the colonel started to do stuff."

The colonel sexually assaulted her, and she was so shocked and frightened she didn't know how to defend herself. "I was fresh out of AIT, I was nineteen years old, and he was an officer. For six months you've had it drilled into you how to talk to officers, how to follow orders. I'm not saying that's an excuse, but I felt really stupid after it happened.

"Later, another girl told me that he tried to pull the same crap with her. She was about the same age I was, the same rank [Abbie was an E-4 specialist]. I honestly believe the other officers there knew what was going on. I think he had a reputation, but they let him get away with it. It makes you feel even more disgusting that he'd brag about it."

Abbie's experience of being assaulted by a superior officer is only too common. Because the military is so hierarchical, and more than 88 percent of officers are male, it is packed with men who have power over women.[1] Many of them abuse it, either by using their rank to coerce women into sex or by punishing those who reject their advances. Women have told me of being forced to do pushups till they vomited, of being put on twenty-four-hour shifts with no sleep day after day, of being made to imitate the walk of chickens or march with clocks around their necks, and of being assigned to extra-dangerous missions, all by senior-ranking men whose advances they had refused. As one woman wrote to me, "I'm a female soldier who served in combat in Iraq in 2004 and was sexually assaulted. The VA [Veterans Affairs] didn't take me seriously till I became suicidal and started cutting myself. What made it so bad for me was that the guy who assaulted me, and who I managed to fight off, then proceeded to put me in places where I'd get injured—and did."[2] The use of rank to coerce someone into sexual relations, whether with threats or bribes, is legally defined as rape in the military, but the men who do this rarely face any consequences because their victims are too afraid to report the assaults, and because, as will be seen, the military protects them.

The lieutenant colonel who assaulted Abbie knew this very well. Because he outranked her, he could be sure she would find it hard to disobey him and even harder to report his abuse. And he was right. She had no idea who to tell or what to do, and she knew the other officer who had pretended to sleep would stand up for him if she complained.

"Two officers—you can't tell me that's not intimidating." All she could do was feel ashamed and disgusted with herself, a common reaction to sexual assault.

Abbie's one comfort was that she would never have to serve with that lieutenant colonel again, as he was attached to a different company than hers. But the experience wounded her and soured her idealism and trust in people. "The assault was just one bad person, not the whole unit, but it was a turning point for me."

DOUBTS

After coming home from Nicaragua, Abbie started college in September 2002 and tried to push the assault from her memory. But going to college between training and deploying for war can have a strong effect on an idealistic mind.

"I was in basic training at a very patriotic time, right when 9/11 happened, but by the time I started college things were changing. The mindset was turning from 'Let's rush in and get revenge' to 'Whoa, put the brakes on. What are we doing?' Colin Powell was asking the president to take a step back, and the UN was too. And President Bush was pushing further into Iraq, looking for those weapons of mass destruction and coming up with nothing. If there were WMDs, I wanted to make sure they were there; and if there was a link between 9/11 and Iraq, I wanted to see what it was. So I tried to educate myself through different types of outlets, and all of them were kind of wishy-washy, both the far left and the far right. Nobody really knew the answers."

On the left, Abbie was hearing that any war in Iraq would be a cynical grab at oil, that Saddam had no WMDs, and that Iraq had nothing to do with 9/11. On the right, Republicans were saying we must free Iraq from a bloody dictator, root out his hidden weapons, repress Islamic terrorism by introducing democracy, and squelch Osama bin Laden and al-Qaeda, proving to the world that the United States will not be defeated.

"I didn't really know where I stood. But when I asked, people would get really pissed off. 'You know we don't ask questions like that.'"

It was true that in the first year after 9/11, criticism of the government's hawkishness was not much tolerated. Anyone who suggested that Saddam and Iraq were irrelevant to 9/11 or America's safety was shouted down as unpatriotic. Even Commander General Anthony Zinni—who had been overseeing military operations in Iraq and its surrounding areas since 1991 and saw Saddam as weak, his army as decaying, and his connection with terrorism as nonexistent—went unheeded. Instead, Bush and Vice President Dick Cheney preferred to be persuaded by the then deputy defense secretary Paul Wolfowitz and his feverish view of Saddam as a Hitler who had to be stopped at any cost.[3]

Thus it was in February 2003, while Abbie was midway through her first year of college, that she received the e-mail her parents most feared: she was going to war.

"No one had any idea it was coming. In two days, everyone in the unit had to drop their lives, pack up, and go to God knows where."

In those two days, Abbie also had to take care of a grim job: filling out her will and the other paperwork soldiers must complete concerning what will happen if they die. This caught her up short, for she hadn't really thought about dying at war before. She gave away a lot of her possessions and felt horrible about how much her friends and family would fear for her safety. But the worst was writing what she called the "what-if letter"—the goodbye letter she would leave for those she loved in case she was killed. Even so, she couldn't truly grasp the danger she faced. She was young and vital, and she had yet to see the reality of war.

At the end of those two days, Abbie bade a wrenching goodbye to her family and caught a bus to Fort McCoy, a huge base in the middle of Wisconsin, for last-minute training before she shipped out.

After all that rush, she expected to leave any minute. But one week went by and nothing happened. Then another week passed; still nothing. The whole of February crawled by like this, with no mission and no information. March arrived, the invasion started, the bombs were dropped—yet still her unit didn't budge. The closest they got to war was watching it on TV in the chow hall.

As the wait dragged on, Abbie grew steadily angrier about the way her unit was treating her. "One day I'm in college, two days later I'm reporting for duty. You can imagine how confusing that was. I was in the middle of discovering boys, having a good time. Then you're expected to turn it off completely. But you're still a woman. Trying to find that balance between wanting to be tough, yet wanting to be a woman, was really hard. People think, 'You just can't be a woman in the military.' But you should be able to be. A guy can be a guy—why are you asking me to be stripped of all my sexual being? Guys can be as sexual as they want out there, but if a woman is, she gets called a slut."

She was also just as mystified as Mickiela by the lack of training in Iraqi culture. Like Jen, Abbie had been told she was going to Iraq to help people, yet the only cultural class she was offered was by some soldiers who had once taken a couple of courses on the Middle East. She found their information useless.

Jen experienced the same thing at Fort Dix. "They gave us a card that had about ten Iraqi words, and simple things like you're not supposed to show people the bottom of your feet. But otherwise nobody knew anything about Iraq to tell us. Either that or they just didn't want to. If we were really going over there to help those people, I think we would've gotten some training about their way of life."

Since 2004, the army and marines have been giving troops bound for Iraq a "smart card," the updated military version of cultural training. This is not the debit card Mickiela used to buy her underwear but a brochure that lists a few phrases and commands in Arabic, basic hand signals, rules of politeness, and a simple map. It also contains rows of crude cartoon faces with different features and skin colors, which soldiers are meant to use to help Iraqis identify insurgents. The card comes in several versions, but the advertisement for the one called the "Iraq Culture Smart Card" says it all: "Offers a useful guide to Iraqi history, culture and customs in one easy to carry, easy to use Kwikpoint."[4]

While Abbie was waiting at Fort McCoy, she was supposed to learn how to drive multiaxle trucks but never had the chance for reasons her father finds ironic. "You know why they couldn't teach her to drive those trucks?" he said to me in Darlington. "Because they ran out of gas. Fort McCoy out of gas! Then she gets to Iraq, and she's driving a truck full of fuel!"

What troubled Abbie most about her time at Fort McCoy, though, was that certain members of her unit were stealing, getting drunk, and illicitly trading in army property. "I've never been able to bite my tongue, so when I saw anyone do these things I'd tell. But anytime you bring out allegations, you automatically make enemies. There's this big good-old-boys' network that you don't even realize exists until you go up against it. It makes you lonely. You lose your friends and you start second-guessing everything you thought had value or weight. You realize everything the army's been feeding you is bullshit."

Feeling increasingly disillusioned and alone, Abbie slogged through the wait. It wore on past the first month of the war and the toppling of Saddam's statue, through April, and into May. "The wait was so long, they started letting us go home for weekends, and that was hard. We'd be telling our families goodbye six, seven times, never knowing if it was going to be the last. It got so I didn't want to go home after a while. It was too emotionally draining." That was a miserable time for everybody. Abbie's parents and older sister were so worried about what would happen to her that they couldn't sleep. And the two little ones couldn't understand why their beloved sister kept coming home only to leave again, over and over.

Meanwhile, on May 1, 2003, Bush made his infamous blunder of posing aboard an aircraft carrier under the banner MISSION ACCOMPLISHED. "Major combat operations in Iraq have ended," he announced, and thanked the troops for "a job well done."

Two and a half weeks later, Abbie and her unit were ordered onto an airplane. They were off to fight the war that was supposed to be over.

SIX

These Morons Are Going to Get Us Killed

Terris Dewalt-Johnson

The very same day Abbie was at Fort Jackson, learning of the 9/11 attacks, Terris, the soldier from Washington, D.C., was sitting in the Pentagon itself. She was in what she calls the sub-sub-basement, working on computer records for the Department of Military Support, when the first World Trade Center tower was hit.

"It was chaos! The monitors were going and the phones were ringing, and people were talking all at once." She was staring at the monitors in shock when she saw the second tower collapse. Once that happened, pandemonium. Everyone was rushing around, answering telephones, taking messages. But nobody realized that the Pentagon had been attacked, too.

"Then we heard the evacuation alarm. *Doop, doop, doop!* And the next thing you know someone says, 'The Pentagon's been hit!' And I'm like, 'Wait a minute, *I'm* in the Pentagon!'"

Luckily for Terris, the Pentagon is so huge and she was so far away from the damage that she saw nothing of the burned bodies and casualties caused by the attack. But when she was ordered to evacuate, she found terrified crowds outside and the air full of black smoke. Nobody was allowed to drive, so she joined the rush of people hurrying away over the nearest bridge. "I looked back and it was just a mess. Flames and smoke. And I'm thinking, 'Oh my God! The United States is under attack!'"

At that moment, a soldier beside Terris on the bridge looked over at her and said flatly, "We're going to war."

Terris had been in the National Guard for nine years by then, having completed her training in the early 1990s. She'd had two more children and had worked a series of civilian jobs, including becoming a prison guard in a privately run prison in D.C., with the redundant name of Corrections Corporation of America Correctional Treatment Facility. This last job became especially significant in 1998 when her favorite brother, Chucky, was murdered. She told me the story sitting beside the urn that contained his ashes, her hazel eyes filled with sadness.

"He got shot in his head four times, and his body was dumped on a railroad track right behind my high school. He was killed by two guys for stealing their drug stash—value around two hundred bucks." She shook her head, her rich voice dropping. "The value of life is just so crazy. He was only twenty-seven. It just about killed my mom."

Chucky's death so upset Terris that when the men who shot him were arrested, she could think of nothing but revenge. "The first thing I'm thinking is, 'These guys have got to come through my jail.' I was gonna either get them killed outside, or I was gonna kill them myself when they came through the system." She was serious about this. But then she had a dream, which she considered a message from God. "I was walking down the sidewalk and this figure came up beside me, dressed all in black. I looked over and it was my brother. He was bright, like a globe that glows in the dark. I looked at him and I'm like, 'Chucky, where have you been? I've fucking missed you!'

"He said, 'It's all right. Don't worry, I'm all right.' And then he was gone."

She woke up weeping. "I sat on the side of the bed and cried and cried. But then I started thinking about what Chucky told me and started laughing instead. I was like, 'Yes, he's all right.' He's saying just leave it alone. And that's when I decided to let it go."

A year later, in 1999, she left the prison job to return to active duty in the army, and that is when she was stationed at the Pentagon.

After the 9/11 attacks, Terris continued working at the Pentagon until December, when she was offered her job at the Centers for Disease Control and Prevention in Atlanta. She was enormously relieved at having the chance to escape the streets that had claimed Chucky's life, and even more so later, when Andre and Ronald were murdered in the summer of 2003.

"D.C. is such a poison place to me. All you've got is a bunch of drugs and killing. My oldest son got shot in a drive-by there when he was five years old. He was in my mother-in-law's yard, just playing, and he got shot. The bullet grazed both of his feet. I just about lost my mind. I couldn't stay in the operating room when they were stitching him."

For the next few years the family enjoyed their new life in Georgia, but Terris never forgot the prescient words of the soldier on the bridge; she knew the day would come when she would be summoned back to active duty. She watched the United States invade Afghanistan and then Iraq, waiting for the call. And finally it came. In October 2004 she was told to report for war.

The first challenge was to explain this to her children. Shawntia was eighteen by then, Alexander—the one who'd been shot—sixteen, Martrese twelve, and Ronald ten. All along Terris had been telling them she might have to go. "But we never really talked about what might happen to me, or about death. You don't want to think about it. I believe they were afraid I'd be hurt, but my kids know their mother's a little rough, a little hard core. So the only thing we talked about was keeping it together. I told them Daddy is gonna be stressed out, he's gonna miss Mommy, but he's gonna do his best to care for you, so please don't give him a hard time." She assigned each child a set of chores and made them all promise to help their father while she was gone.

On January 12, 2005, Bush announced that the search for weapons of mass destruction was over, having yielded nothing. A month later, in early February, just before Terris's thirty-fifth birthday and the second anniversary of the war, the summons came for her to leave. She kissed Terrence goodbye, told the children once more to mind their daddy, and left. As for the danger—1,500 American soldiers had died by then, over 10,000 had been wounded, and more than 100,000 Iraqis had been killed, most of them women and children—she couldn't let herself think about that.[1] All she could do was try to stay alive.

CHICKENSHIT

Terris was sent to a reserve center in Orangeburg, South Carolina, for processing, where she was attached to the army's 414th Transportation Company. She knew no one there because this wasn't her home unit, so she sat back and watched. "I wanted to see who's a good soldier, who's a troublemaker, who's a motor-mouth. I was sorting out the trustworthy companions from the losers." It didn't take her long to see that the sergeants and commanders were constantly jostling for power and bickering in front of their soldiers.

"Now you don't do that in front of lower enlisted. It's like a husband and wife having issues—you don't display it to your children." She felt this was particularly important because the majority of soldiers in the unit were under twenty-one. "All these kids just came out of school, and they haven't even learned to function in the civilian world, let alone in a war zone. But instead of the leadership saying we need to work together to get these soldiers back safe and sound, too many people wanted to be chief and not enough wanted to do the work. It was bad for morale."

A couple of weeks later the unit moved to Fort Bragg, North Carolina, for combat training, but matters did not improve. The sergeants were still quarreling and contradicting one another's orders, and they became obsessed with writing up soldiers for every little infraction, such as wearing the wrong T-shirt to drill. As Paul Fussell, the author of some of the most honest books ever written about war, would put it, Terris's leaders were immersed in chickenshit: "Chickenshit is so called—instead of horse- or bull- or elephant shit—because it is small-minded and ignoble and takes the trivial seriously. Chickenshit can be recognized instantly because it never has anything to do with winning the war."[2]

Chickenshit plagued Terris throughout her deployment, as it did most of the soldiers I talked to. It is something soldiers have complained about since the military was invented.

Terris's job was an 88 Mike, meaning a truck driver, but even though the war was two years old by then, she was taught nothing of how to drive on desert terrain and bomb-laden highways. Instead, she was given Vietnam-era training for the jungle. For example, she and the other soldiers at Fort Bragg were taught to react to attacks by stopping their vehicles in a herringbone pattern, jumping off and taking up a fighting position. "But in Iraq, if you come under attack you keep that truck moving! You don't stop for no reason 'cause that would stop the whole convoy." A stopped convoy makes a sitting target.

Even more absurdly, she and her comrades were trained to lie in the grass with their rifles at the ready and to use jungle plants for cover.

For the first few years of the war, much of the training was wrong-headed like this. Most boot camps are in lush or forested areas of the United States, which may be fine for simulating the fields of Europe or the jungles of Vietnam but are entirely inappropriate for Iraq. (Notable exceptions are Fort Bliss, Texas; the National Training Center at Fort Irwin, California; and the Marine Corps base in the Mojave Desert, Twentynine Palms.) But geography aside, many of the training methods themselves were wrong for this war too. Even as late as 2005, the training was still ignoring the realities of Iraq: the desert, the lack of cover, the heat, and the fact that the enemy is indistinguishable from the civilians who crowd marketplaces, drive the roads, or eat their dinners quietly at home.[3]

At Fort Bragg, Terris soon heard the soldiers around her grumbling about the irrelevant training and chickenshit. "They're not saying anything in front of the higher-ranking individuals, but among themselves—and I'm one of them—they're talking about how screwed up it is. 'Man, I can't believe I've got to go to war with these guys. They're gonna get us killed.'"

Then Terris had another of her dreams; only this time it was a nightmare.

"I was in a truck and it gets hit. The vehicle blows up and all I see is this big ball of fire above me—I could feel the heat in my dream. My sight goes black for a minute, and when it comes back, I'm floating up out of the vehicle and I look down and I can see smoke and fire. The next thing, I descend from the clouds to my mom's house. My mom is there, and she's going berserk because the news has gotten to her that I got killed. And that's what hurt me the most, my mom going through that."

The next morning, Terris was ordered to the firing range to practice shooting, but as she lined up to get her rifle from the supply room, the dream nagged at her. "I get my weapon and when I look up, the first sergeant and the commander are over there, and I'm thinking, 'These morons are gonna get me killed.' And all of a sudden anger just comes over me." She envisioned herself, with frightening clarity, shooting both men dead.

"Sergeant," she said abruptly, "I can't go to the range today. Somebody needs to take this weapon, please."

"You're going to the range."

"No, sir." She threw her rifle and helmet to the ground and walked off.

One of the few other women in the unit caught up with her. (Terris

was serving with 10 women in a company of 130. One woman was a lieutenant, and another the only other woman her age; most of the rest were
under twenty.) "You all right?" her friend asked. Terris told her about
the dream, then went back to the barracks and called her uncle, who
happened to be a bishop of a nondenominational church called Arise
Outreach Ministry. The dream, he suggested, was a warning about the
dangerous incompetence of her leaders. So she decided to speak up.

"Now, as a woman you have to create a force for yourself. If you
present yourself in a passive way, you're seen as nothing. You've got to
be direct and stern to make them listen."

What she said to her commander was certainly direct. "We've been
together now for about four or five weeks, sir, and for some reason the
senior enlisted still have not gotten it together. Now, none of these soldiers are going to tell you this to your face, but I will. We don't believe
that you are able to lead a horse to water."

This remark did not go over well. The commander wrote her up for
attempting to destroy government property—that is, for throwing her
rifle to the ground—and for "conduct unbecoming an officer." (Terris
was an E-5 sergeant by then.) Then he told her that between refusing
to shoot on the rifle range and mouthing off, she had made herself
conspicuous enough to be sent for a mental evaluation. He handed her
the agreement to sign.

She refused. "I've been in the military fourteen years, sir, and I've
never been sent for a mental eval. Just talk to me, sir, when there's a
problem. I know when I get tense, my brows kind of frown up, but it
really doesn't mean anything. I'm not as fierce as I look."

The commander relaxed and that seemed to be the end of it—at
least until two weeks later, when the unit flew to Kuwait.

SEVEN

This War Is Full of Crazy People

Eli PaintedCrow

Like Terris and Abbie, Eli also trained at Fort Jackson, only many years earlier, in 1981, when Ronald Reagan was president and the conflict on America's mind was not in Iraq but Central America. Her unit was one of the first to mix men and women, and the army was even less aware of its biases than it is now; her drill sergeant called her Taco because she spoke Spanish. But Eli was young and insecure, too relieved to be out of reach of her violent husband Eddie and too intimidated by the unfamiliar world of the military to do anything but keep her mouth shut. So she stopped drinking and concentrated all her efforts on making it through boot camp.

But life hadn't finished causing her problems yet. Her eldest son was staying with his grandmother while Eli was gone, but Eddie had insisted on keeping the little one, Angel. Three days before she was to graduate, Eddie called her. "I made a mistake," he said. "I was out looking for a job and your dad came and beat me up."

Instantly suspicious, Eli telephoned her father for his side of the story. He said he'd dropped in on Eddie at dawn to check on him and had found four-year-old Angel in the apartment by himself. "Where's your daddy?" Alvino had asked.

"Dunno," the little boy replied. "Some woman with dirty feet came and they went away."

Alvino waited for Eddie to come home, then beat him up so badly that Eddie couldn't see out of either eye. Hearing the ruckus, a neighbor called the cops, who took Angel to a shelter, where the social worker in charge refused to release him to anybody but his mother.

When Eli heard this she called Eddie back and cursed him out at the top of her voice. Unfortunately, soldiers never have any privacy. "I'm on the phone, saying, 'You motherfucker son of a bitch, I'm going to kill you when I get home!' I hang up the phone so hard I almost crack it. And everybody's like, 'Oh my God, what happened?'"

Eli's drill sergeant summoned her to his office and asked what was going on. She explained she had to go home to rescue Angel from the shelter. "The drill sergeant was this white guy looked like Fred Flint-stone, and he said, 'But Taco, you're three days away from graduation. If you go home now, you'll have to do basic training all over again.'"

Desperate, Eli asked her father to explain her dilemma to the social worker and plead for a reprieve. The social worker called her. "All right, I'll release your child to your father," she said. "But if you ever go back to your husband, I will take your children away."

"Don't worry," Eli replied. "That will never happen again." And it didn't.

Once she'd graduated from basic, her drill sergeant called her in to see him again. "Taco, what are you going to do when you get home?"

"I'm going to look for my husband, Drill Sergeant."

"Well, I want you to know you're a very good soldier and killing your husband is only going to put you in jail and take you away from your kids. So I don't want to read about you in the newspaper. You under-stand me, Taco?"

"Yes, Drill Sergeant."

"And that," Eli told me, "is how I graduated boot camp."

PREY

Not long after she had finished training, Eli's command belatedly real-ized that her ability to speak Spanish could be useful in ways other than as the butt of a joke, so she was sent to Honduras as an interpreter for the rear command. Reagan was shoring up the right-wing government in Honduras at the time, in preparation to fight the leftist Sandinistas over the border in Nicaragua, and the U.S. military was building bases and airstrips around the country. Eli spent eight months there in 1986 as part of this effort. She would mingle with the Hondurans when she could, curious to get to know them and uneasy about whether her government was in the right. But she had another problem to cope with: sexual assault.

"Two majors and a lieutenant assaulted me while I was in Honduras. One major called me into a tent and tried it there. I grabbed him by the collar and said, 'You touch me again, I will tell your wife.' The other major just kept making advances, but it was too subtle to tell anyone about." The lieutenant, however, she had to physically fight. "He was looking for prey and he thought I was weak because, with my hair cut short for the military, I looked about twelve. But sexual assaults happened to me several times in my twenty-two years in the military, a couple times that succeeded. I got even with them in my own way, but I never reported them because nobody believes you."

Eli's words about not being believed are equally true today. The prevailing attitude in the military, from women as well as men, is to regard a woman who reports sexual assault as a traitor, a weakling, a slut, or a liar, and soldiers often punish such a woman by ostracizing her: turning their backs when she walks into a room or refusing to speak or listen to her. Even Jen had this attitude in Iraq. "I would have been angry at a female for reporting sexual harassment and making waves. And it wasn't like anybody ever touched me—I wasn't one of those women you could push around in that way." These soldiers have bought the age-old myth that men rape out of lust, enticed by shameless women, only with the added twist that women soldiers should be able to handle abuse by themselves. And then, because any woman who says she's been raped makes other women feel vulnerable, they will often blame or disbelieve the victim rather than face their own danger.

Staff Sergeant Cassandra Cantu, a six-year veteran of the air force, told me about her encounter with this attitude in Afghanistan, where she served for half a year in 2006. "While I was there I was sexually harassed daily. I lived in constant fear for my life while doing convoys and feared being raped when I returned to base. I felt the eyes of the men on me all the time." One day her commander made a casual comment about some rapes on base, but when she asked to know more, he laughed and replied, "I don't understand how you can get raped when you carry a weapon around twenty-four hours a day." Later she indignantly reported this to her supervisor, but all he said was, "You're in the military, that's what happens. Deal with it." These men never paused to think that the assailants had guns, too, or that any woman who shot or tried to shoot a fellow soldier would be in a lot more trouble than any man accused of rape.

Marti Ribeiro, the air force sergeant who was harassed for all eight years of her military career, served in Afghanistan in 2006 as a combat correspondent with the army's 10th Mountain Division, an all-male unit. This is her story.

She had been given the extra job of guarding a post at night, not far from the prison where some members of the Taliban were being held. For several hours she stood there alone, looking out into the blackness, her rifle and radio by her side. But gradually an unbearable craving for a cigarette came over her—soldiers smoke or chew tobacco constantly at war—so she set her rifle and radio down and walked twenty feet away to the "smoke deck." She knew it was against the rules to leave her weapon and post even for a second, but nobody was around and she couldn't smoke at her guard station because the light of her cigarette would make her a target.

She had just taken a few drags when a U.S. soldier in uniform appeared out of the darkness, grabbed her in a chokehold and dragged her behind some power generators, where her screams could not be heard. She struggled and kicked, but he had such a strong hold on her throat that she could barely breathe. She fought with all her strength, but it wasn't enough. He pushed her to the ground and raped her. As soon as he'd done his deed, he fled, leaving her gasping for breath and icy with shock and pain. She pulled on her clothes and stumbled back to her post, where she remained for the rest of her shift.

"Then I did what every *Law & Order* show says to do: don't take a shower and go immediately to the authorities. I thought they would listen to me, but I was wrong. I was told that if I filed a claim I would also be charged with dereliction of duty for leaving my weapon unattended in a combat zone. So, I shut up and didn't say anything to anyone, not even to the women I shared a tent with, though I sensed the same thing had happened to one of them."

She was so traumatized and full of self-blame that she couldn't even explain to her own mother why she left the air force until six months after she'd returned home. "It makes me mad when I think about the fact that I let them get to me and left the military. I was third-generation air force. I had dreams of becoming an officer one day, like my father and my grandfather. Unfortunately, because I'm female, those dreams will not come true."

The military has long been using threats and punishments like this to silence and expel women who report sexual violence.[1] Some recent examples: In 2005, army lieutenant Jennifer Dyer was threatened with prosecution for desertion because she refused to return to her post with an officer she had reported for raping her.[2] In 2006, army specialist Suzanne Swift was court-martialed for desertion, demoted, and put in prison for a month for refusing to redeploy under a sergeant whom she had reported for repeatedly raping her.[3] That same year, Cassandra Hernandez of the air force was charged with indecent behavior after she reported being gang-raped by three comrades, which amounted to accusing her of her own assault.[4] And also in 2006, army specialist Chantelle Henneberry was denied a promotion after reporting a sergeant for sexually assaulting her, while he was promoted almost immediately.

The Defense Department claims that since 2005, its updated rape reporting options have created a "climate of confidentiality" that allows women to report without fear of being disbelieved, blamed, or punished like this. I will discuss the effectiveness of these reporting options in chapter 14, but the fact remains that all the cases I describe above happened *after* the reforms of 2005.

"It's taken me more than a year to realize that it wasn't my fault," Sergeant Ribeiro told me. "The military has a way of making females believe they brought this upon themselves. That's wrong. Yes, I made some bad decisions, but the guilt lies with the predator, not me. There's an unwritten code of silence when it comes to sexual assault in the military. But if this happened to me and nobody knew about it, I know it's happening to other females as well."

PROMISES

Eli too kept quiet about her assaults, even after she came back from Honduras. But meanwhile something happened to cheer her up: her father presented her with an eagle feather, a symbol of having achieved the status of warrior and a great honor. For the first time in her life, she felt he was proud of her.

The gesture was particularly poignant because he was dying of cirrhosis of the liver. As Eli stood by his sickbed, he asked her to make him a promise. He had just bought a new tractor-trailer, huge and shiny, but was too sick to drive it: would she learn to drive it so he could give it to her?

Touched and honored, Eli promised.

Over her career, Eli quickly rose to the rank of staff sergeant, became a drill instructor, taught others how to be drill instructors, and ran administration for a drill instructor unit. She hadn't forgotten her promise to her father, though, so when he died she went home to claim the truck he'd been so proud to offer her. It was gone. Her mother had given it to one of Eli's brothers, who sold it for nothing to buy drugs. "My mom was the kind of person who valued sons more than daughters. I tried so hard to be that son! But I didn't talk to her for many years after that because I was so hurt."

Eli still wanted to keep her promise, but now that she had no truck of her own and certainly couldn't afford to buy one, the only way she could learn to drive one was to change her job in the military, go back on active duty, and let the army teach her. At first she was reluctant because she wanted to stay home with her sons, but her mother said, no, finish what you've begun. "That value is very important to Native peoples, finishing what you've begun," Eli explained. So she left the boys with her mother and changed units from training drill instructors to transportation. And because she was a reservist, she also had time to go to school on the army's dime and become a social worker. She spoke about this in her house, standing by her open door. The sun was setting by then, casting a rosy light over her elegant, broad-cheeked face.

"People heal by healing others. I was an alcoholic; I became an alcohol and drug abuse counselor. I was raped; I counseled women who were raped. I was a teenage mother; I've worked with teenage mothers. I was beaten up; I've worked with battered women." She also held Native healing ceremonies and retreats for women. And for years she took battered women into her home.

Eli was so proud of her career in the military and all it had given her that, in spite of the racism and sexual assaults she encountered, she encouraged both her sons to enlist. Eddie Jr. joined the army when he was eighteen, and Angel joined the marines at seventeen. By the time Eli turned forty-three, her sons were grown and married, she was a grandmother of seven, and she had become a counselor in alcohol and drug abuse for Madera County, California, working with parolees coming out of prison. She was just about to be promoted to manager when the United States invaded Iraq, and she was called to war.

DRAGON LADY

Eli never believed the United States belonged in Iraq, sure that behind the talk of democracy and freedom lay racism and greed for oil. Nevertheless, she felt honor-bound to go, partly because she had promised her father to finish what she'd begun, and partly because she was still caught up in the Native admiration of warriors. And then she had only one year left before she could retire from the military and collect her benefits. How she would reconcile serving in a war she thought wrong was a dilemma she would just have to solve when she got there.

Now that she was a truck driver, she was separated from her home unit and sent to the 211th Transportation Company in Marina, California, which was supposed to prepare other units to deploy. When she arrived, she found the company in the same disarray as Terris later found hers. It was such a shambles that even preparing the soldiers to fly to Fort Bliss for training turned into a farce.

The army had paid for a commercial airplane to carry the soldiers directly to the Texas base, with the stipulation that no ammunition was allowed on board. "Well, we heard some guy put some ammo in his bag, which meant that me and the other sergeants had to search every bag right there on the airfield; two hundred and eighteen soldiers emptying bags and we had to look through every one!" By the time they found the bullets, the pilot had lost patience and left, leaving the entire company stranded on the airstrip with no flight and no plan.

The chaos continued even after the unit finally reached Fort Bliss. Eli had been promoted to sergeant first class (E-7) by then, making her the highest-ranking noncommissioned officer available, so she was put in charge of the female barracks, which turned out to be a thankless job. The soldiers were going wild, the men coming through the windows at night to sleep with their girlfriends, and everyone was getting drunk.

The commander told Eli to rein in these miscreants without kicking any out, as the company needed a certain number to deploy and was losing too many to medical and other problems already. Eli was just figuring out how to do this when she received another devastating phone call. This one too was about Angel, only it was from the Red Cross.

"Your son's been in a car accident. We're giving him his last rites." Angel was twenty-six.

Eli flew out to him immediately and found him in a coma. He'd been driving home from his marine base in Texas with a friend when they had skidded on black ice and hit an oak tree, which had slammed the front of the car right onto Angel's lap, crushing him. That he had survived at all was extraordinary, but the prognosis was bleak. The doctors said even if he managed to stay alive, he would be severely brain damaged and unable to walk. Eli stayed with him for four weeks, watching over him, insisting he get the best treatment, praying and heartbroken. But once her leave was over, she had no choice but to return to her unit.

When she got back, she found the female officer who'd been in charge in her absence hiding in her room. "The females are going to beat me up," she told Eli in a panic. "I overheard them planning it." Eli scoffed and stormed out to fix the mess. "The females were just nuts. I got dubbed the Dragon Lady because I had them out in formation at ten o'clock one night to scold them. You have to realize these are twenty-year-old privates and they're scared they're going to go to Iraq and die. It makes you do some pretty crazy things. It's a sort of 'I don't care; what are you going to do to me, send me to Iraq?' attitude. They really are teenagers in their thinking, so I'm looking like their mom and they're being rebellious. The commander's like, 'Oh, don't be so mean, Sergeant PaintedCrow.' And I'm like, 'We're going to war, and you want me to not be so mean? How do you think they're gonna shoot somebody if they start crying because I tell them they can't leave their room?'"

After that, the female soldiers did their best to wreak revenge on the Dragon Lady. "None of them would confront me directly; they'd do it in a group by yelling things at me. But when I tried to instill discipline, the first sergeant would come and change my orders and not tell me. So I was losing my power base. This happens to women all the time in the military."

While this was going on, Angel was still in a coma and Eli was terrified he would die.

Finally, the Marine Corps sent an official request that she come to her son, which won her a discharge from active duty. For the next seven months she stayed with Angel, doing all she could for him. He had what doctors call a closed-brain injury, which had put him in the coma, and when he awoke he sat in his wheelchair without moving or talking for weeks. His lungs were lacerated and his legs broken in several places. Eli helped him through every therapy she could find, and by the time six months had passed, he had metal bars in both legs and was walking and talking. "He's still brain injured, but he can do all the things they said he wouldn't do. They were getting ready to deploy him when the accident happened, so I kind of look at it as a gift. I might have lost my son for good out there."

Angel is still too disabled to work, but one would never know it to look at him. I met him in Merced when he dropped in on his mother to say hello. He looked stocky and healthy, and greeted me with friendly cheer. He had a new baby by his current girlfriend, a young wisp of a girl who hardly said a word, making Eli a grandmother for the eighth time.

Back in 2003, Eli wanted to stay with Angel, but the army had other ideas. In December she was called to duty again, this time with the 736th Transportation Company out of Bakersfield, California. Soldiers from across the nation were assigned to this unit specifically to deploy to Iraq, and because the military had a nationwide shortage of drivers, they needed Eli. Looking back on her promise to her father, she felt the irony of this. In asking her to learn to drive a truck, he'd never thought he would be sending her to war.

She arrived in Bakersfield to find her new company doing the same training she had already done at Fort Bliss, but when she offered her expertise the commander dismissed her. Like Terris, Eli said she often saw women ignored like this in the army. "It's because most women don't argue their points, they just accept the situation or complain about it. And when women do complain, it's seen as whiny. The problem is, we let the issue build and build until it becomes explosive. Then we make these big demands and the men don't listen."

Eli, however, was neither prone to keeping quiet nor to exploding with pent-up outrage. "I was taught to express myself by my father, and being a drill sergeant helped. I'm a very up-front person. People may not like me for that, but they certainly respect me for it."

This time the training lasted four months, and as the clock ticked toward deployment, morale in Eli's company grew steadily worse, largely because the leadership kept changing. "We end up with a commander who was a boat commander and knows nothing about trucks, with an acting first sergeant who doesn't want to be an acting first sergeant, and an E-7 sergeant who's so blunt about the things he wants to do to women that even the male soldiers are feeling disgusted and reporting it, though nothing is being done. And we have this commander—I don't know if he was bipolar or what—but at one point he's cussing at us, and then five minutes later he's crying and telling us how he doesn't want us to die.

"That's another thing they don't look at, the mental health of the person who's in charge. We've got some crazy people out there. We had an E-7 who was a homeless woman living in parks for two years till she got activated. An E-7 is very high ranking, high responsibility. She got it though the mail. She didn't even go to drill, and here she was. And then we got drug addicts. Nobody's testing. Or if they're being tested it's being overlooked because we have a shortage of personnel. And we've got gangsters who are doing deals with military stuff and everybody knows it but nobody's saying anything."

Mickiela too found criminals and drug addicts among her comrades, both in boot camp and Iraq, including the roommate in New Jersey who was getting into fights. "She was in rehab for cocaine when she was deployed, and they didn't give her no drug test, nothing. There was a crackhead there too. A lot of soldiers were caught with drugs in Iraq. We had four people got busted for weed and coke. And there's people who are alcoholics—they would have liquor sent to them."

Since 9/11 the military has been applying "moral waivers" to recruits, which means taking people with criminal records, something the Defense Department once abhorred. Rules on waivers vary with different branches of the military, but over 125,000 recruits with criminal histories enlisted between 2004 and 2007, including those with records in aggravated assault; in 2006, more than 1 in 10 army recruits had criminal histories, and by 2007, 350 marines were convicted felons. The use of waivers has risen 42 percent since the year 2000.[5]

This trend is dangerous, not least to women. Originally, the DoD listed sexual violence as a felony *not* waived by the military, saying that most of the crimes were burglaries, petty thefts, and drug offenses committed by foolish youths. Yet, in 2008, the DoD's own data showed that nine army and marine recruits had committed sex crimes, six had been convicted of manslaughter or vehicular homicide, and several dozen had convictions for aggravated assault, robbery, or domestic abuse, which almost invariably means violence toward women and children.[6] Steven Green was one of these. Green was the ringleader of the four soldiers who raped and killed an Iraqi girl of fourteen, Abeer Qassim al-Janabi, in 2006. They shot her parents and five-year-old sister to death in the next room while she was still alive, and then set fire to the whole family.

Green had a history of mental instability and violent misdemeanors, but the army had taken him anyhow.[7]

The current military policy of forcing soldiers to return to Iraq multiple times is making this situation worse. Iraq is now full of soldiers with physical and mental wounds from earlier tours. Some are put on powerful antidepressants and antianxiety drugs to keep them there; others have threatened suicide, been ignored, and then killed themselves or other soldiers.[8] How much gratuitous violence toward Iraqi citizens and female soldiers is committed by these unstable troops, nobody knows. But, as Eli put it, "This war is full of crazy people."

WALK WITH YOUR BACK AGAINST THE WALL

The problems among Eli's leadership quickly filtered down the ranks, resulting in constant chickenshit and racism. One example: "We had a sergeant who happened to be black, a truck master who was damn good—I'd follow that guy anywhere. But the reservists don't like him because he's black, so they won't do what he says. And the commanders are not backing him up, so he's losing his position."

The sexual harassment was also spinning out of control. One day Eli found a normally tough young specialist lying in her bunk, crying. Only at Eli's insistence would she explain why. "The guys are telling me that Sergeant W— said that he wants to, um, have sex with me anally, and I don't know what to do. I'm scared."

Eli immediately reported these threats to the first sergeant of her unit. "And you know what he answered? 'Tell her to walk with her back against the wall.'"

Eli filed a complaint after that, and in response the company held a quick sexual harassment class. She found it ludicrous. "That was just a way to cover it up. It didn't address the issue at all."

It has become standard for the military to react to reports of sexual violence by forcing soldiers to attend these classes, but many a soldier has complained to me that rather than explaining to men that sexual assault is criminal and traumatizing, the classes only caution women not to be provocative. Eli sat in a second session like this when she was in Iraq. "There was a rape when I was there and they sent a female, about twenty-one, to give a teaching about what sexual assault was about. Basically, she said that there's a bunch of horny guys and you have to be careful. If you know anything about sexual assault it's not about that at all; it's about power and control and internalized anger. And sexual assault training needs to be for men and women, but we only had women there."

Abbie also sat in on a sexual assault lecture and video when she was in training, and said the recruits saw it as a joke. "After it was done, everybody got up and slapped each other on the ass and said, 'Uh oh, I'm harassing you!'"

This is not to say that the reporting of sexual violence and other wrongdoing is always useless. Assailants have been reported, tried, and prosecuted in the military, and justice is sometimes served. In 2007, 8 percent of reported assaults went to court-martial—meager, but at least something. (In contrast, some 40 percent of men arrested for sex crimes in civilian life are prosecuted.)[9] Eli herself had some success at this back at Fort Bliss when she and a friend gathered up fifteen women with complaints about sexual harassment and racial discrimination and drove together to see the equal opportunity officer on another base. As a result, both the vulgar-talking first sergeant and the bipolar commander were removed from the company.

Unfortunately, instead of morale then improving, it grew worse. But not, this time, because of a man.

"We had a new white female commander, and the first thing she did was take the black E-7 female, the Mexican E-7 supply sergeant, and the black E-6 supply sergeant and relieve them all of duty for no reason. She didn't follow any of the proper procedures; she just said she's the commander and that's her reason."

Eli watched in horror. She was going to have to face the war in Iraq with a female commander who resented anyone who wasn't white or male and with a company in dangerous disarray. And there was no way she could get out of it.

PART TWO

War

EIGHT

It's Pretty Much Just You and Your Rifle

Jennifer Spranger, 2003

The stench was overpowering, strong enough to make Jen recoil as she stepped out of the military plane into the Kuwait night. She had no idea what it was. Rotting garbage? Burning oil fields? Dead bodies? She only knew it smelled nothing like Racine, Wisconsin. "The air was so thick that the inside of your nose, your ears was completely black. It was absolutely disgusting."

Cramped and exhausted from eighteen hours of flying, she and the other fresh soldiers filed down the airplane stairs and into a waiting bus. It was February 2003, the month leading up to the invasion, and they were to be driven to Camp Arifjan, a huge U.S. military base south of Kuwait City, to wait for the war. On the way, she huddled her small frame into her seat, her blond hair tucked under her army beret, wishing she could at least glimpse whatever there might be to see in the night outside. But the soldiers were forbidden to open the curtains or even peek out. She felt as if she were being delivered to war blindfolded.

When she reached the camp and climbed off the bus, she found herself in a vast complex of warehouses and tents, surrounded by coils of razor wire. To her surprise, the desert floor was as hard as a sidewalk, but covered with a layer of sand so fine it puffed up like baby powder at each step. Later, she learned that soldiers called the sand moon dust.

She and the other new arrivals were ordered into a long metal warehouse the size of an airplane hangar, stuffed with thousands of green army cots, almost every one occupied by a man. Jen was to sleep an arm's length away from her neighbor on either side, face to foot to minimize the spreading of disease. If she needed a bathroom, she would have to weave her way across the room with all those men watching her. She lay down and changed her clothes inside her sleeping bag, feeling a long way from home. The building reeked of sweat and feet and the musty tang of masculine bodies.

Jen was 1 of only 4 women in a platoon of 34 men, and 1 of 20 women in a company of 213. She was to live and work in close quarters with those men for the next seven months.

Camp Arifjan is known as one of the most dangerous bases for women soldiers in the Middle East. Built by the Kuwaiti government for American troops, it held about ten thousand service members and private contractors when Jen was there, almost all of them male. "They call Camp Arifjan 'generator city' because it's so loud with generators that if a woman screams, she can't be heard," said Abbie, who passed through it on her way home from the war. "They were saying the number of rapes that were happening on base by soldiers were very high, and they told us not to travel anywhere without another soldier."

Jen heard these rumors of rape as well, for rumors are the bread and butter of the military. "I tried very hard not to pay attention to that stuff. I didn't want to believe it was happening. But I heard there were several rapes there, not even only of females—of guys too. But they never filed charges against anyone."

It soon became routine for platoon leaders to order their women soldiers never to go outside at night without a female companion, not just at Arifjan but on all bases. Many resented this, including Staff Sergeant Liz O'Herrin of Madison, Wisconsin, who was in Iraq with the Air National Guard in 2006. "They tell us (after we hit the deck from an incoming mortar shell) that we shouldn't walk alone at night on base. We, as in females. How am I supposed to track down another female to go eat when I want to? Shower when I want? Females aren't exactly crawling around this joint. Screw you, you deploy me here and tell me it's not safe for me to walk alone to get a bite to eat because I'll probably get raped by one of our own?"

When Jen awoke on her first morning, she hurried outside to see where she'd landed, blinking in the harsh desert light. All around her stretched miles of beige sand, blending so exactly with the dust-filled air that it obliterated the horizon. Aside from the occasional desiccated pale green bush and a herd of raggedy brown camels beyond the fence, everything was the same color—that is, she thought, no color at all.

The camps in Kuwait are places of waiting, and Jen's time there was no exception. She turned nineteen a week after she arrived, but otherwise the days were tedious and uneventful. "For about a month we just sat around or did a lot of shopping at the PX [Post Exchange, the on-base shop]. They had a Baskin-Robbins there. There wasn't anything to do. We were just waiting, but nobody knew what for."

What they were waiting for was a decision from Defense Secretary Donald Rumsfeld on how to use them. President Bush had issued his ultimatum to Saddam Hussein by then—hand over your weapons of mass destruction or we bomb—and the might of the U.S. military was poised to strike. The Iraqis, meanwhile, were tense with dread, memories of past wars still painfully fresh. Iraq had once been modern and sophisticated, its citizens skilled, its middle class highly educated, and its cities beautiful. But since Saddam had taken over in 1968, the country had undergone thirty-five years of his brutal rule, two devastating wars, several air strikes by Britain and America, and thirteen years of economic sanctions that had destroyed much of the middle class and left the working class destitute. A whole generation of Iraqis had been traumatized by these events. Most had lost at least one family member to death or prison, and many, especially those not in the privileged circle of Saddam's Baath Party, had spent their lives struggling to survive. Now they faced invasion by America. Those who had suffered at Saddam's hands, particularly the Kurds, hoped the United States would bring relief from the dictator and a new start for the country. Many others were in favor of the United States getting rid of Saddam but wanted the Americans to leave quickly afterward. But some felt only that they were going to be victimized yet again, this time by an untrustworthy superpower.[1]

This was the Iraq that Jen was about to enter.

The waiting in Kuwait was miserable. All keyed up for action, the soldiers found themselves moribund instead. Bored and hot, their skin irritated by sand and insects, their lungs clogged with dust, they had nothing to do but think up practical jokes and squabble. Some soldiers developed walking pneumonia from the dust, others had constant eye

infections. A few went crazy. "There was this female who told her leadership she was gonna kill them if they didn't send her home," Jen told
me. "And we heard that a marine on another base in Kuwait blew up
seven people in his tent with a grenade."

After a while, the army found small missions for Jen's unit, one being
to guard a nearby port in Kuwait while U.S. ships unloaded Humvees
and tanks. "I think the missions were just to keep everyone occupied.
We spent twelve hours a day staring at the sand." But at least this en-
abled her to see more of Kuwait, and she gazed out of the truck curiously as her convoy rumbled along the roads. In the distance, smoke
stacks towered two hundred feet in the air, spewing flames and black
smoke. Abandoned tanks and artillery pieces from the first Gulf War
lay half buried and rusting in the sand. Twisted spikes of metal jutted
out of the desert floor. But strangest of all to Jen's Wisconsin eyes were
the Bedouin Arabs, standing still and expressionless by the side of the
roads, their long robes whipping in the wind.

A month of this listless existence crawled by until, on March 17,
Bush addressed the nation to say, "Should Saddam Hussein choose
confrontation, the American people can know that every measure has
been taken to avoid war, and every measure will be taken to win it." (In
fact, Bush had determined upon war at least eight months earlier.)[2] He
gave Saddam and his sons forty-eight hours to leave Iraq or face attack.
Saddam refused.

On March 19, Bush declared war.

On March 20, the United States bombed Baghdad.

On March 21, the United States hurled another 1,500 bombs and
missiles at Iraq in what it dubbed its "shock and awe" campaign.

On March 22, Jen drove into war.

LOST AND CONFUSED

At this point, Jen was neither questioning her role nor the purpose of
the war. She accepted that she was part of a mission to depose Saddam
Hussein, find and destroy his diabolical weapons, and bring freedom to
the Iraqis, and she also accepted the Bush administration's insistence
that Iraq was linked to 9/11. After all, this is what her parents and the
people in her town had told her, along with Fox News, the most popular
TV channel on military bases.

Jen was far from the only soldier who knew nothing about the real situation. In his memoir about the war, army lieutenant Paul Rieck-hoff described an astounding lack of knowledge about Iraq and politics among the young men in his infantry platoon. For example, when he asked them who was the vice president of the United States, answers included Joe Lieberman, Donald Rumsfeld, and George W. Bush. Sixty percent of the platoon got the answer wrong.[3]

Jen's unit belonged to the 822nd Military Police Battalion, and its task was to set up America's first prisoner-of-war camp in Iraq, just outside the city of Basra. Iraq is a nearly landlocked country shaped roughly like a triangle standing on one point, with its capital city, Baghdad, more or less in the middle. Basra sits at the border of Iraq's southeastern tip, where some of the country's poorest and bleakest areas lie. This was where the battalion was headed.

Moving a convoy of 175 or so hefty trucks and Humvees along sand-covered, bombed-out roads turned out to be a slow business, especially because nobody had been trained to drive on sand and nobody knew where the convoy was going. "The first thing we did was get lost. We didn't have any maps, and our radios were all old and broken—we didn't have nearly the equipment we should have. In fact, we got lost numerous times. There were gunfights going on all around us, and we were always having to stop and wait for the ordinance guys to come and deal with unexploded bombs on the road." Each time the convoy stopped, the soldiers had to jump out and take up battle positions by the side of the road, rifles at the ready. It was terrifying, for most of their traveling was done at night, when it was too black to see anything but the flash of bullets.

Jen was glad she at least had the protection of traveling inside a closed Humvee, even though it lacked any armor. "Some people had to sit on the back of a big truck, out in the open like the Beverly Hillbillies." A soldier's Humvee only slightly resembles the gas-guzzling Hummer we see on the roads of America. The military Humvee is slanted at the back, has a gun turret protruding from its roof, and is painted either olive drab or muddy tan. (Its name derives from high-mobility multipurpose wheeled vehicle, or HMMWV.) But ironically, the civilian Hummer is much more secure than many of the Humvees soldiers were driving during Jen's time at war. Those had only canvas roofs, or no roofs or doors at all.

The broken equipment and lack of armored vehicles Jen described were a direct result of the Bush administration's use of private corporations to provide the supplies and services the military used to provide for itself. These corporations included Blackwater Worldwide, Titan Corporation, CACI International, and Custer Battles, but the largest was KBR (Kellogg Brown & Root), a subsidiary of Halliburton, of which Vice President Cheney was once the CEO. Private corporations have always played a part in war, usually by manufacturing weapons at home, but never have they had a role as extensive as they have had in Iraq. During the first year of the war, Cheney and Bush awarded KBR more than $10 billion in noncompetitive contracts to provide soldiers with everything from food and water to vehicles, spare parts, and even weapons. This deal trapped soldiers between two mammoth inefficiencies: corporations interested only in profit on the one side, and an underfunded military unable to control its own supply lines on the other. KBR was buying shabby and broken trucks on the cheap, delaying deliveries to rack up billable employee hours, and sometimes threatening to refuse to deliver anything at all until it was paid, while the Pentagon was suffering chronic shortages.[4] This is why Jen and her fellow soldiers were driving into war in open, unarmored vehicles, with no body armor or only one decrepit Vietnam War–era breastplate, which wasn't much safer than driving into battle in a golf cart and a Hawaiian shirt. Thousands of soldiers were needlessly killed and maimed as a result.

When Jen wasn't huddled in the back of her unarmored Humvee, bumping along potholed roads and listening to enemy bullets whistling by and cracking against the roof, she tried to get a sense of what kind of country she was in. At night the most she could see was black sky, except when it was lit up with the distant flickering of oil fires, or bullet tracers, which looked like strings of white-hot beads. But even in the daylight, most of the time all she could see was the dun-colored desert stretching to the horizon, scattered with garbage and tire shreds. Occasionally, the carcass of a cow would loom into view, bloated to twice its normal size, its legs stiff as sticks; or a cluster of small yellow-brick buildings, pockmarked and crumbling from wind and war. But sometimes the convoy would drive through a border town that had just been bombed, where hardly a house was still standing, and she would see grotesquely blackened corpses stretched out on the ground, their skins split open, guts trailing; a dog chewing on a dismembered foot.

"Driving down the streets, you'd see bodies just left on the side of the road. It got to be kind of commonplace," she told me with a pained look on her small, round face. Yet, in the center of each village—and she found this unaccountably moving—there was always a small garden with maybe one tentative tree, like a flicker of hope.

Almost as shocking to Jen as the grisly sights of war was the hostility of the Iraqis. Like most soldiers at the time, she had been told the American troops would be greeted as heroes. Instead, children would pound on the doors of the soldiers' trucks and try to grab their rifles through the windows, or make gun shapes with their fingers and pretend to shoot the soldiers. "There were no smiles and waves, it was nothing like they told us it would be. After all, we went in right after the air war. If it was me, I don't think I'd be greeting us too happily either." Given that some ten thousand civilians were killed in those first days of the invasion, she had a point.[5]

Sergeant Miriam Barton, the army engineer from Oregon who talked about having to be twice as bad as the boys, was also driving in a convoy through the area at this time, and she had the same experience. "There was no throwing of candy and flowers where I was. We had people throwing rocks at us, shooting at us, taking frickin' potshots with flames and slingshots. It was real obvious we were not wanted."

As understandable as this hostility might have been, it was terrifying for the soldiers. "We didn't know what we were gonna run into," Barton said. "We didn't know if we were gonna get hit with chemical weapons or WMDs. For all we knew we were gonna get hit with a friggin' nuke at any moment, 'cause all we'd heard was these stories about how Saddam would sacrifice his own people to kill us. We would go into Saddam's bases and the Republican Guard would be running out the back. There would be food still cooking and uniforms everywhere, 'cause they'd be stripping their clothes off as they ran and just melting into the population. That's what makes this war so hard; you never know who's the enemy. Everybody's the enemy. And they all wanna kill you."

By the end of the first day, Jen's convoy was so lost it ended up at a marine base instead of the prison site where it was supposed to be. Once night fell and the sky turned its impenetrable desert black, the command told the soldiers to put on their Night-Vision goggles to spot oncoming danger. Jen and her team searched every inch of their Humvee. They had never been issued any.

The convoy pulled its vehicles into a circle like the pioneer wagons of the Wild West, and the soldiers settled down to sleep in their trucks. The base at least gave them a real bathroom to use—up until then, the women either had to hold up a poncho for one another or search for an all-too-rare bush, careful not to walk too far away in case they stepped on a mine or got shot. (Women soldiers soon become adept at urinating into empty water bottles or cups.) The men merely used the side of the road. American soldiers make their presence known in the desert with a trail of garbage and feces. Some clean up after themselves; some do not.

When dawn broke at last, the lost convoy pulled back onto the road and crawled along for the rest of the day, sometimes at barely nine miles an hour, for a convoy can only move as fast as its slowest vehicle. Soon, it began to fall apart. Sand clogged up engines; tires hissed flat; cumbersome trucks, already old and in bad shape, hit potholes and broke down. Any vehicles that couldn't move had to be left by the side of the road to wait for a passing engineer truck, and the soldiers inside were supposed to wait with them. (KBR exacerbated this problem by removing spare tires and tools from the trucks they delivered to the troops for reasons explained in the next chapter.)[6] Some soldiers were abandoned this way for hours, unprotected from attack.

Jen didn't know it yet, but that very day, March 23, 2003, and only a few miles off, army first private Jessica Lynch and her unit became separated from their own convoy because of this same sort of havoc. At the end of a mile-long line of trucks rolling into Iraq, Lynch's unit fell behind, lost radio contact, took a wrong turn, and drove into an ambush. Lynch became the most famous female soldier of the early Iraq War, not because she was hurt but because the U.S. Army staged a dramatic "rescue" of her from an Iraqi hospital. In fact, the Iraqi doctors, who were initially portrayed in the press as captors, rapists, and torturers, had actually done their best to tend to her wounds and return her to the Americans, at one point even putting her in an ambulance and driving her to a U.S. checkpoint, only to be turned away by gunfire. The Pentagon and the media later took much criticism for the way they spun the story, and Lynch has since set the record straight.[7]

Jen's destination was only a hundred miles away from Camp Arifjan, but her convoy was so lost it was still meandering through the desert forty-eight hours after it had left. Finally, it pulled into the site the command thought was its destination—an empty field. Just as the drivers formed another wagon circle, rain began to fall and a sandstorm whipped up, sending billows of dust hurtling around them. The sky quickly turned into a dense red fog, while the wind roared at fifty miles an hour. Within minutes the air had turned black, muddy, and suffocating.

As the radios were not working, Jen and her fellow soldiers were helpless to do anything but sit inside their vehicles and wait. The wind howled and whistled, pelting their trucks with rain-drenched sand and rocking their Humvees like toy boats in a bath. Jen was particularly worried because they were missing a young woman with whom she had trained and deployed. "She and another guy had some kind of mechanical problems with their truck and nobody knew where they were. They had no radio either, so there was no way for them to get help. We didn't see them for a day and a half."

The soldiers sat in that sandstorm for twenty-four hours, unable to see or hear anything but the wind and rattling sand. They strung a green cord between the trucks for anyone who needed to go out and urinate, but otherwise hunkered down to wait it out. Jen huddled in the back seat and tied a handkerchief over her nose, which at least kept the worst of the grit out of her lungs, but her eyes and nostrils were encrusted with it. She was sharing the Humvee with four men, although by army rules that was one too many—a space is supposed to be left open under the turret for the gunner to jump down should the team come under fire—and soon the tension got to them. "Those men did nothing but bicker with each other like little old ladies for hours and hours."

She took refuge in reading a novel by a little book light she'd brought with her. "They'd told us not to use a flashlight because it would make us a target, but the sand was so thick it didn't matter. I would've gone nuts without my book. It was *The Lovely Bones*. My mom sent it to me; it was very good." Many soldiers told me they turned to books for escape, and not only the comics and pornography favored by most. Corporal Meredith Brown, the gung ho marine mentioned in chapter 1, brought Jane Austen novels into battle with her. Airwoman Liz O'Herrin read short stories by Vladimir Nabokov.

The next day, March 24, the air finally cleared. Relieved, the soldiers climbed out of their vehicles, stretching and yawning and wandering about, when, with a shock, they noticed landmines embedded in the sand all around them. "You could see them everywhere!" Jen said.

"For those whole twenty-four hours everyone was walking around completely blind and not a single person got hurt!" The mines, she speculated, were mostly left over from the 1991 war.

Much of this mayhem—getting lost, parking in a minefield, not knowing how to drive on sand—could have been avoided if Rumsfeld had not been determined to run the war on the cheap. The wisdom within the Bush administration was that the Iraq War would be mostly fought in the air and won quickly, like the first Gulf War, so the soldiers on the ground were not only sent in without proper equipment but in inadequate numbers and with a lack of training that endangered all their lives.[8] This was bad enough for the regular army and marines, but Jen felt it was even worse for the "citizen soldiers" of the Army Reserve.

"I can't think of anybody who could have been less prepared than us. All the slip-ups, the getting lost and things like that don't surprise me. These people are civilians in their main lives, bankers and things like that, and they only train one weekend a month. They couldn't remember what they'd learned. It was a big problem for us that nobody was a career soldier."

Staff Sergeant Tom Dati, Jen's squad leader and friend, told me the same thing. "One of our commanders was the manager of a Bed Bath & Beyond at home. And he had to command a military police unit?"

NASIRIYAH

On March 25, Jen's battalion split up. Most of it headed to Camp Bucca, its original destination, but her unit was sent to a former Iraqi air base just outside of Nasiriyah, the city where Jessica Lynch had been ambushed two days earlier. The United States had just launched an extraordinarily vicious attack on Nasiriyah, blasting it for over thirty-six hours with explosive rounds that cut through concrete and steel, strafing it with at least two thousand rounds of rapid-fire bullets, and bombarding it with cluster bombs built to tear people to shreds. (This, even though the Geneva Conventions ban the use of cluster bombs in civilian areas.)[9] Then, only twenty-four hours before Jen arrived, RECON Marines, whose job is to draw enemy fire and expose ambushes, had battled their way through the city as well. Hundreds of Iraqis and several marines had died or been wounded in these attacks.[10]

Nasiriyah is an ancient city of squat, flat-roofed houses made of yellow mud or cement. Interwoven by narrow, twisting alleyways, it rests on the northern side of the legendary Euphrates River, one of the most fertile and picturesque areas of Iraq, with lush grass, waving palm trees, and grazing water buffalo. But when Jen got there it looked so much like a war movie she could hardly believe it was real. Buildings were smashed into heaps of smoldering rubble. Bodies lay in the roads, run over by so many trucks that they were flattened, their guts squeezed out of them. Skeletons of burnt cars sat by the roadside, their occupants charred and stiff inside. And although the remaining townspeople had been doing their best to clean up, Jen could still see rags of flesh, dismembered limbs, and mangled bodies—a little girl with half her face seared off; a man ripped open by gunfire; a dead woman clutching the corpse of her child.

The people who had survived were living in lean-to huts, pieced together with scraps of tin and cardboard. Garbage was piled head-high in the streets, its stink mingling with the gut-twisting stench of corpses. And nobody had lights, heat, or water because U.S. bombs had destroyed the infrastructure. "I remember seeing thirty women or so standing with buckets, trying to get water from this central well, and the water coming out gray and disgusting," Jen said. "As for the other stuff I saw, I can't think about that."

When her unit reached the air base, she and the other soldiers were ordered to set up their quarters in its former jail. "We had to clean it up, shovel out human feces. God, it was disgusting. There were electric torture devices hanging from the ceiling. One was a giant sponge mat lying on the ground with a metal hoop around it, connected to a wire coming from the ceiling. This is what they did to their own people, so I thought, well, maybe we are saving them." Jen was so spooked by the sight of these devices that she pleaded with her platoon sergeant to let her sleep outside. He refused.

She and the other soldiers cleaned up the building and moved their portable cots inside. "Luckily, I wasn't in the room with all the wires. We had maybe a couple of inches of space in between our cots, so it was pretty cozy. And I got my first shower since the war started! We even heated up water. We built a fire and had a big pot that looked like a witch's cauldron."

She showed me a picture of herself at this time, posing in front a huge mural on the air base, which depicted a gigantic Saddam in his military beret pointing to a black eagle and three soaring fighter jets. Jen was standing among her squad of five men, more than a head shorter than any of them but sturdy in her chocolate-chip battle fatigues and bulky green flak jacket. Grasping her M-16 rifle in one hand, she looked tiny, blond, and sunburned.

As strong as the sun is in Iraq, though, March nights can drop into the thirties, when the wind blows and the arid air of the desert no longer holds the warmth of the day. On one particularly frigid night, Jen's platoon sergeant ordered the soldiers to push their cots together and huddle up in their sleeping bags for warmth. They had just settled down like this when there was a blinding flash, followed by an ominous silence. Then, the loudest noise Jen had ever heard exploded around her, so loud it felt more like a physical shock than a sound, jolting violently through her body. She was terrified. It happened again and again, for the building was being barraged with mortars in what turned out to be one of the deadliest nights of the early war. (A mortar is a fat three-foot-long tube stuffed with a bottle-shaped explosive. When fired into the air, it arcs and falls down at a range of about three and a half miles. As it hits, it explodes into lethal daggers of flying metal called shrapnel, and the impact is enough to blow a truck to smithereens.) At the same time, the U.S. Army was blowing up stockades and munitions dumps all over the base, so it sounded to Jen as if she were in the middle of a catastrophic bombing. She huddled deep into her sleeping bag, rigid with terror. Then, right in the middle of the attack, she felt a man climb on top of her. "Get the fuck off of me!" she yelled in his ear, and pinched his thigh so hard he rolled away.

"It absolutely amazes me what pigs men are," she said when she told me about this. She knew who the soldier was. From then on, they avoided one another.

Nobody in her unit was hurt by the mortars, but every night after that the company was attacked with rocket-propelled grenades, RPGs, which are hand grenades set in a narrow tube with a rocket at one end. Sometimes the explosions were so loud that Jen's ears would still be ringing days later.

She and her unit stayed on the Nasiriyah air base for two weeks, seeking and arresting members of Saddam's army, whom they locked in a temporary prison. "I think we arrested more people during those two weeks than we did the entire rest of my time in Iraq. But there were also a lot of men that turned themselves in. I think they just wanted to go home to the families they never wanted to leave to begin with." As soon as the war started, droves of half-starved Iraqi soldiers did indeed turn themselves in for food and protection. Many had been forcibly conscripted into Saddam's army.[11]

CAMP BUCCA

After Nasiriyah, Jen's company moved on to join the rest of its battalion at Camp Bucca, a windswept, isolated base near the southeast border with Kuwait. There, they were supposed to take over the camp from the British and build it up into the first and largest U.S. prison in Iraq.

When Jen arrived, she found herself in a bleak moonscape of dusty sand shimmering under a red haze all the way to the horizon. Olive-drab tents were lined up in rows on either side of a dirt road and divided into four separate compounds by loops of razor wire. More wire circled the entire camp, along with a few wooden guard towers and a berm: a bulldozed sand dune meant to provide protection. And that was it, aside from dust and flies. The landscape was so featureless that the soldiers were soon joking about how they'd become experts on the different kinds of sand: the heavy deep kind that was hard to walk through, the moon dust that caked your face like powder, and the gritty kind that hurt when it blew against your skin. "We had one tree we could see from our camp," Jen said, "but for the most part it was a whole lot of nothing."

She set up her cot with thirty-three other soldiers inside one of the tents, which was twenty feet long and shaped like a droopy barn with no floor. ("After a while we stole some plywood from the engineers and made ourselves a floor to keep out the bugs.") Later, the tents were light tan, but for the first few months they were dark green, so soaked up the sun without mercy. They became so hot inside in the summer—over 140 degrees, some said—that soldiers would drag out their cots and sleep in the open, mortars and grenades be damned.

The sanitary facilities were even more primitive, with no toilets at all for the first few weeks. "There weren't even trees to hide behind. You were lucky if you could find a bush. There were times when I knew people were watching me, but I didn't care. Let those perverts get their jollies." But even once the toilets were built, they were only plywood Porta-Johns, which quickly began to stink in the heat. Men and women had to share them, and Jen said the women in her unit had constant bladder infections from trying to avoid those toilets, something I heard from many female soldiers. Because the camp lacked a sewage system, each morning certain soldiers would be given SBD (Shit-Burning Detail), the duty of pulling the metal waste barrels they called "burn shitters" out from under the latrines, dousing them with diesel fuel and gasoline, and burning the contents, which created stinking black clouds that hung in the air for hours.

For three months the soldiers had no showers either, so the only way they could wash was to pour a bottle of water over themselves. Between the salt from their sweat and the sand, their uniforms turned so stiff they could stand up on their own. As for food, all the soldiers had to eat were MREs (Meals Ready to Eat). Packaged in encyclopedia-size brown plastic bags, these consisted of a pouch of processed meat or spaghetti, crackers, a load of junk food and candy, a powdered beverage mix, and a plastic bag of chemicals to use for heating the food. (You added water to the chemical bag to create heat and plunged your meal pouch inside.) Few of the MREs were appetizing, and their low-fiber content was constipating, so the acronym quickly earned alternative meanings: Meals Rejected by Everyone, Meals Refusing to Exit, and "It's not a Meal, it's not Ready, and you can't Eat it."

Inside the tents, the cots were lined up parallel along both sides, an arm's length apart, and the soldiers would sleep with their feet pointing inward. There was no air conditioning, and the only way to get a fan was to find someone going to Kuwait who could buy you one. Nor was there any gender segregation, which meant that Jen had no escape from the ball-scratching, farting, tobacco-chewing ways of the soldiers around her.

"We all slept in one big tent, the four of us girls and about thirty guys, and each had about three feet of living space. There just wasn't the equipment to set up a girl's tent. After a while I put up my poncho to make a little wall so that I could stand up and change instead of changing under my blanket. I just wanted to be alone. I couldn't stand my team leader, and he was, of course, sleeping right next to me. I wanted to not look at him as much as possible."

Jen's team leader, a sergeant, was to become the bane of her time in Iraq. (He was not the same man who had threatened suicide over her at home, although that man too was at Camp Bucca.) Controlling and socially inept, he had already been removed from one platoon because his men couldn't stand him, and he wouldn't leave Jen alone.

"He'd always make sure that we were out together at the beginning, when we had to do guarding, and he would say disgusting things. He offered me two hundred fifty dollars for a hand job. I told him to kiss my ass." She took to nailing up dead snakes and scorpions on the tent post beside her bed to fend him off; several scorpion species in Iraq are poisonous, as are some of the snakes and spiders, and she knew he was afraid of them. The team leader then became vengeful, watching her all the time and trying to get her into trouble by reporting everything she did to the platoon sergeant.

The team leader wasn't the only man harassing Jen, but she told herself a good soldier shouldn't let this bother her. "The harassment got to be so commonplace that I didn't even think it was wrong. Anyway, it went up so high in the ranks there was nobody to tell." She also had another motive for keeping quiet, though: she didn't want her father to know. "I was always trying to make him proud. And I would have been too embarrassed to talk about it with him."

A tough-it-out attitude like Jen's is encouraged by the military, which makes it clear to women that they are on trial as soldiers and that trying to change the misogynist culture will only make them pariahs. Because of this, some women don't even realize how bad the harassment was until they get home. "Now, I think if someone said that stuff to any daughter of mine, I'd kill him!" Jen said in retrospect.

Sergeant Miriam Barton's solution was to deal out justice herself. "The military pretty much looks down on whistleblowers, but we had a couple semiheavy gunners like me who were female, so when we knew a male was trying to get into somebody's pants, we three would take care of it together. We duct-taped one guy to his rack [bed]. Another guy we tied up with dental floss when he was passed out, called everybody around, and then fired a shot and yelled 'Attack!' Public humiliation is a great way of getting your point across."

When Barton first joined her heavy combat engineering company, she was one of three women among 120 men, but by the time she went to Iraq, women made up 15 percent of her unit. Had she been as isolated as Jen, it would not have been as easy to act this tough. In general, female soldiers who serve with a good portion of other women tend to be less vulnerable to sexist discrimination of any kind than those who are vastly outnumbered. Claudia Tascon, the National Guard captain who served in Iraq with a medical unit, told me that 40 percent of the soldiers in her company were women, which she thought was the main reason she was never abused.

Jen's first job at Camp Bucca was to guard its entrance, which in her day consisted of nothing but a wooden shack and a watchtower. She had to stop every car that passed through to look for weapons and search the drivers and passengers. The job was nerve-racking because she never knew when she might be shot or blown up. Also, as she was one of the only women in her unit, and only female soldiers were supposed to search Iraqi women, she had to work there every night, while the men were able to rotate between the checkpoint and guarding the prison tents.

When Jen searched a woman, she would use mime to tell her to spread her arms and legs wide, then pat her down with the back of her hands. "They'd giggle. It was like they'd never been touched before, like it was a game. But some of them were very scared. You'd just smile at them and try to explain what you were going to do, that you'd never grab them. I don't think it was that big of a deal. But on the rare occasion when a guy searched a woman, that ended up being pretty traumatizing for them both."

Jen's job of searching women reflects a major role that female soldiers play in this war. Male soldiers are not supposed to search Iraqi women because it violates Iraqi customs and subjects the women and their families to shame and humiliation, whereas female soldiers can both search women and reassure them in the midst of raids or at checkpoints. Unfortunately, as Jen mentioned, this rule is not always followed, sometimes because of a dearth of women soldiers and sometimes becauses American soldiers are too hurried or angry to bother with cultural sensitivity.

The aspect of Jen's job that most disturbed her, though, was the hundreds of distraught Iraqis who lined up at the prison every day at dawn, clutching photographs of their missing relatives in the hope of finding them there. Only a handful of soldiers would be on duty at a time, and there was little they could do. They had no list of prisoners and no contact with them; they rarely even had translators. "We were told to promise these [Iraqi] people a list, but I never saw one, except a little handwritten list that wasn't even put in our hands. It stunk to have to tell them, 'We'll put out a list and you'll be called or have something mailed to you.' They didn't want to hear that. Most of them didn't have a house to mail anything to anyhow, never mind a phone. The same people would show up every morning to find their relatives, but we had nothing to tell them."

Jen was struck by one woman in particular who would arrive at sunrise every day with her husband. She was dressed in black and was so worn down that Jen couldn't tell whether she was forty or sixty. "At first she was calm and hopeful. Her husband spoke a little English and told us they were looking for their son. I tried to reassure the woman and say, 'There are seven thousand men in there. I'm sure he's probably in there too.' But somehow she found out he wasn't, and I guess she assumed he was dead because she just tore off her clothes. She was completely naked from the waist up. She was screaming and pulling out her hair, tearing at her face, her skin. Everyone just stopped and stared. No one knew what to do."

DEPLETED URANIUM

Along with the families looking for missing relatives, women would come to the checkpoint every day to find help for their sick children, seeking out Jen in particular as the only female soldier in sight. "Those babies had diseases I've never seen in my life, and pray to God I never do again," she said, shuddering at the memory. "Big, pus-y sores. The mothers wanted food and medical care, but we didn't have it to give to them. We'd been told that we were there to help these people, but we didn't have a damn thing to offer."

One day a woman thrust a baby into Jen's arms. "The baby wasn't moving, and it had sores all over it. I was holding an almost dead baby, and I wasn't able to help at all. That was the moment I started to turn against the war."

Jen was not the only soldier who told me about the diseased or deformed children she saw. When I visited army specialist Laura Naylor, who served with the 32nd Military Police Company in Baghdad from 2003 to 2004, she showed me a photograph of a baby girl she'd met in an Iraqi orphanage. The child was smiling and sweet, decked out prettily in a pink dress—only she had no arms or legs.

Some scientists believe these deformities and illnesses were caused by the depleted uranium weapons used in the first Gulf War. Depleted uranium (DU), a heavy metal almost twice as dense as lead, is a waste product from the manufacture of nuclear weapons, and the United

States and Britain use it in shells and armor because it's so hard it can slice through enemy armor and deflect bullets. But each time such a weapon explodes or an armored vehicle catches on fire (DU is highly flammable), radioactive particles are released into the air.[12]

Numerous researchers have tried to document the dangers of DU, with varying results. Some say Iraqi children exposed to DU in 1991 had four times the normal rates of birth defects and cancer, and that similar findings have been reported in the former Yugoslavia, where DU was used in the Balkan wars.[13] Others dispute these findings. But two recent studies have found dramatic increases in birth defects among the children of Gulf War veterans that mirror those seen in Iraq: female veterans were nearly *three* times as likely to have children with birth defects as is normal, while veteran fathers were nearly twice as likely.[14]

Most researchers do not question the rise in birth defects, cancer, and early deaths among Iraqis and first Gulf War veterans, only their causes. The U.S. and British governments, along with some scientists, blame malnutrition, lack of B vitamins, and other environmental pollutants, while maintaining DU is safe.[15] The UN does not agree. In 2002 it declared the use of DU weapons to be a violation of human rights, saying the substance will pollute the ecosystem of the Gulf for generations, and that "some 500,000 will die before the end of the century from the radioactive debris left in the desert."[16]

Recent studies back this up. In 2005, a significant rise in cancer was found among American workers who had been exposed to DU and none of the other factors present in Iraq.[17] In 2003, DU was proven to damage nerves.[18]

The United States and Britain are still using DU, which frightens Iraqis and coalition soldiers alike, especially those who plan to have children. Miriam Barton was covered from head to foot in DU powder at one point in Iraq. She also still had the anthrax vaccine in her when she became pregnant in 2003. She is now locked in a bureaucratic struggle with Veterans Affairs to find out why her son cannot hear or talk.

When Jen met those sick babies in Iraq, however, she was also witnessing effects of the first Gulf War. After Saddam invaded Kuwait in 1991, the United States retaliated by dropping enough bombs to destroy Iraq's infrastructure and electricity system, and even though Saddam restored some of it, the country's power remained weak and intermittent. This made the preserving of foods and medicines difficult, halted water pumps and sewage treatment plants, and turned people's houses into infernos. To further punish Saddam, the UN, backed by Britain and the United States, then imposed thirteen years of economic sanctions on Iraq, which blocked most imported parts, foods, and medicines; reduced all but the rich to poverty; and caused widespread illness and malnutrition. Between 1990 and 2002, mortality among Iraqi children under five years of age increased three-fold.[19]

This was what Jen was seeing when those women brought their sick children to her, begging for medicine and food. And the new war was only making it worse.

While she was working at the checkpoint, Jen came to realize that three kinds of prisoners were coming into Camp Bucca: Innocents who had been swept up by accident, which later reports put at 85–90 percent of all the prisoners.[20] Prewar criminals who had been transferred from other prisons—"You could tell the thieves because they were the ones without hands," she said. And the 10–15 percent who were genuine suspects, most of them resistance fighters who saw the United States as a hostile invader.

Jen and the other soldiers were told nothing of who the prisoners were, however, or why they were being held. Nor were they told much else about the war. They didn't know that in early April, Pentagon spokesman Lawrence Di Rita had enraged Iraqis by saying, "We don't owe the people of Iraq anything. We're giving them their freedom. That's enough." They heard nothing about how, when the fall of Baghdad on April 9 was marked by the toppling of Saddam's statue, many Iraqis reacted with less than the expected delight. And they were never told about the seventeen ministries that were destroyed by looting, the thousands of artifacts stolen from the National Museum, or the 341 tons of high explosives taken from the Al Qaqaa armory, soon to be used against U.S. troops.[21]

"That's why people started to go crazy, there were just so many things that didn't make sense," Jen said. "We had one compound that was just for Iraqi officers. To me, they belonged there because they were the masterminds. But we were told to treat them better than everyone else because they were going to be trained to rerun the country. They were the ones leading the army that was trying to kill us—okay, let's be nicer to them?"

After about three months, supplies began coming into the camp at last, and for the first time the soldiers had hot food, toilets, and shower trailers. They also finally had enough extra food and medicine to give to the Iraqis. But they still couldn't help with what the people needed most—the return of their sons, brothers, and husbands, cures for their sick and deformed children, and peace.

HATE AND FEAR

Jen worked the checkpoint for about two weeks, after which she was sent to guard the prison itself. At first she was relieved. "It made me so angry seeing those sick children. It's so much easier to see adults suffering than little kids who didn't do anything." But her relief did not last long.

Every morning she would be driven to the prisoners' tents and dropped off at the compound she was to guard. There, she either took up a position on the sand or climbed to a platform on top of a spindly plywood tower ten feet outside the razor wire. The tower offered no protection from the sun, heat, and wind but a flat wooden roof, and no shelter from the sandstorms that arrived with the spring and whipped around her for seven or so hours a day, driving dust into her eyes, ears, and mouth and through every gap in her uniform.

Each block of forty tents had only one guard on each side, although sometimes one or two extras would be positioned at the entrance, so Jen was usually the only soldier in sight. "You're pretty much sitting out there on your own for twelve to fourteen hours a day. Some of us had Motorola walkie-talkies that we bought before we left. Some of us had those little crank-powered phones, like the ones in *M*A*S*H*, but most of them didn't work. Most of the time we were completely cut off. It was just you and a chair and your rifle."

The prisoners were housed in the same sort of tents the soldiers slept in, only about twelve feet long rather than twenty, and because Camp Bucca was the only American prison camp in Iraq at that point, the tents were crowded. At the beginning, each was shared by roughly twenty-two men. Later, as more tents were built, the number dropped to ten or twelve. The prisoners slept in the tents when it was not too hot, but otherwise milled around outside in their loose shirts and trousers, or *dishdashas*—the ankle-length shirts soldiers derogatorily called "man-dresses"—with nothing to shelter them from the cloudless sky or the glaring desert floor. (The sand looked tan under the clouds, but turned blinding white under the sun.) Nothing was between them and Jen, either, except those rolls of razor wire. And the prisoners were angry.

"They would stand by the wire and mess with me all day, from saying that they were gonna hurt my family to taking out their thing and masturbating. And there was absolutely nothing I could do."

They hurled threats and insults at her all day long, and flung feces, scorpions, and snakes at her, too. "I heard rumors that the prisoners were even taking our letters out of the garbage and writing to our families, threatening to kill them and telling them we were dead. My worst fear was that something would happen to my family while I was gone 'cause of them. And there was one guy who would just stare up at me in the tower for a couple of hours every day. It irritated me worse than the guys who would expose themselves or yell things. He knew it got to me. There was a point when I couldn't look at him anymore 'cause I couldn't stand him staring at me straight in the eyes. I'd try to tell him to go away, but the more excited I got the happier he'd be just to stare at me. Actually, I wanted to shoot him. I couldn't, but I wanted to. It scared me to death that I could want to do that kind of violence."

Meanwhile, security was loose, and everyone knew it. "For the longest time there were riots every night. We'd fall asleep hearing them chanting and screaming. And they had all kinds of weapons; it's not too difficult to hide things in the sand." Sometimes the soldiers tried to quell the riots by using rubber bullets or batons. Other times they would just let the prisoners wear themselves out. "They'd chant and scream and throw things, but as long as they didn't escape, there was nothing we could do."

The prisoners did escape, though. "Later in the war they put up a chain link fence, but all we had were circles of razor wire, two of them side by side and one over the top, all wired together. There were big enough gaps where anyone could've gotten through easily. And after a while they would rust and not be as sharp. The ground was nothing but sand, most of it really soft. It didn't take any effort to dig it out." The blinding sandstorms and lack of manpower helped escapes too. "You're out there by yourself for hours; you're exhausted, you can't see, it's hot, and you have no communication. We got fed up; we were tired. There's only so far you can push your body."

Another problem was the chaotic leadership. "We would get different orders every day about what our level of force should be. One time they told us that even when the prisoners escaped we weren't allowed to fire at them. After that everybody just gave up. A lot of people started reading books, sleeping, 'cause there was just no way to win."[22]

All this and worse was confirmed by a Defense Department investigation in March 2004, triggered by the exposure of abuse at Abu Ghraib and released as the Taguba Report. The report declared that Camp Bucca was overcrowded, while the guard force was "undermanned and under resourced," and that it had cases of detainee abuse, escapes, and a lack of "clear standards, proficiency, and leadership" that led to "accountability lapses." It described the beating of prisoners by four soldiers on May 12, 2003, during Jen's third month there, and blamed Brigadier General Janis Karpinski, who was in charge of all military police brigades in Iraq, and Lieutenant Colonel Jerry L. Phillabaum, commander of Camp Bucca, for the problems. Karpinski was also blamed for the more severe abuses at Abu Ghraib.[23]

Karpinski, the first female general in America ever to command soldiers in combat, later wrote a memoir in which she defended herself.[24] She accepted responsibility for not having kept a close enough watch on the prisons, a grave mistake. But she also accurately pointed out that those responsible for the torture and abuse of prisoners were in Military Intelligence, which was not under her command, and were obeying directives from Lieutenant General Ricardo S. Sanchez (who had ironically ordered the Taguba Report), Donald Rumsfeld, and, in particular, Vice President Cheney, who had encouraged President Bush to dismantle the Geneva Convention protections for prisoners suspected of terrorism and clear the way for torture.[25]

I asked Jen if now, looking back in the light of the Abu Ghraib exposé, she might recognize anything she had seen at Camp Bucca as prisoner abuse. "Nothing," she replied. "The Geneva Conventions were being shoved down our throats all the time, especially by the Red Cross people. There were special little tents set up for interrogation, but we had no part in that. That was Military Intelligence. We would escort the prisoners there and back, and I never saw anyone coming out bloody or crying or screaming. There were always rumors, but nothing that keeps me awake at night."

Later, however, she told me something else. "I know that there were a few guys who lost it and beat up on a couple prisoners. Honestly, I didn't feel it was wrong at the time because I was so angry at them." When she was first at Camp Bucca, she added, prisoners were sometimes locked inside steel shipping containers and kept there for days in solitary confinement. "There were at least three or four CONEX[26] boxes being used like that, pure metal, and it was 100 degrees out there." She said the practice stopped when the Red Cross arrived at the camp.

In spite of this illegal treatment of the prisoners, Jen felt at the time that they were treated too well. They were fed chicken and rice while she and her fellow soldiers had to eat the much-detested MREs. They had showers months before the soldiers did. If they ran out of ice, the soldiers had to give them their own, much-coveted cups of ice chips. And the prisoners were living twelve to a tent, while the soldiers had to put up with thirty-five.

"It sounds dumb now—they were prisoners—but I was jealous. It was just so frustrating because nothing was the way it was supposed to be. We were taught that prisoners who behaved were rewarded with cigarettes and things. But everything was given to these guys, whether they were sitting there exposing themselves to us for hours or being model prisoners. And we were told that it was too hot for them to work, but we still had to go out after our shifts and build more compounds. There were a lot of very unhappy people when we heard it's too hot for them to work but not for us. And then we'd spent hours building these Porta Potties for the prisoners, and they would come out and dig a hole and squat down and do their thing right in front of you. It just got to me after a while. So I was happy getting up every morning, going to my tower, and yelling at the prisoners all day. I got known for having the loudest mouth, which is kinda surprising, 'cause I've always been a pretty quiet person. I never physically did anything, I would just yell and insult them. It made me feel better."

She did "physically" do something once, though, she confessed to me later. She had let the soldiers in charge know that if any of the prisoners who had been taunting her so relentlessly ever had to be subdued, she wanted to be part of it. One day, one of them began shouting and throwing himself at the razor wire, cutting himself on its rusty blades. So a couple of soldiers went into the compound, threw him down on the sand and tied his hands behind his back, then brought Jen in. She put her foot on his neck, knowing this was a deep insult. "It sounds terrible now, but I wanted him to have the humiliation of a girl doing that. He'd been masturbating in front of me, throwing shit at me. I wanted to push his face in the sand. I kicked sand in his face, and it felt good."

Another time, she was so enraged by the prisoners' taunts about the harm they'd done to Americans—one claimed he had raped Jessica Lynch and broken her legs—that she decided to play a dangerous trick on them. "They were always begging for our cigarettes, even though they had their own, so I took the chemicals out of the pouch we used to heat our MREs and sprinkled some in the cigarettes I gave them. I hoped something bad would happen to them. They'd insulted me; I wanted to get back at them. It sounds so childish now, but at the time nobody was thinking about consequences." The heater pouches contain magnesium, food-grade iron, and salts. Although they are highly flammable, they are not actually toxic, but Jen didn't know this at the time.[27] She never found out if those doctored cigarettes did the prisoners any harm.

She now says she was able to behave like this because she had come to think of the prisoners as less than human, just as soldiers have always thought of the enemy. Only, one day, something happened that shook her out of this delusion, at least for a moment.

She was listening to a Kuwaiti radio station up in her tower when a song came on called "Lady in Red." She never turned the radio up loudly enough for the prisoners to hear, because, as she put it, "I figured you're in prison, you make my life hell, so I'm not doing anything nice for you." But then a prisoner walked up to her tower and looked up at her. "Get the fuck away from me!" she yelled.

"I just wanted to listen to 'Lady in Red,'" he replied in perfect English.

"He spoke better English than I did! And that just scared the crap out of me. He could've been anybody from home! It got so easy to imagine them being animals. I mean, I'm not making a racist comment that I don't have some basis for—most of them were animals. They didn't even resemble human beings. But that guy, he could've been my next-door neighbor, he was so smart. I wasn't so scared of a dumb guy who'd go and be a suicide bomber, who is somebody else's pawn. But that guy spoke five or six languages. A lot of them did. It scared me how smart they were."

This comment sheds an interesting light on the age-old habit of dehumanizing the enemy in war. I have heard many soldiers refer mockingly to the fact that Iraqis don't speak English, as if they thought this alone made them deserving of death and destruction. Yet, as soon as a

soldier meets an Iraqi who is eloquent in English and clearly well educated, the illusion is shattered and the dehumanization reverses.

While Jen was telling me these stories in her mother's kitchen, her
voice began to crack and her hands shook even more than before. She
suffers from an anxiety disorder now and is prone to panic attacks that
make it hard to breathe. The subject of Camp Bucca invariably triggers
these reactions, even these many years later.

"I'm ashamed to say that I started to go crazy along with everyone
else," she said after a pause to calm her breathing. "And a lot of people
were going crazy—one guy began talking to his deck of cards. But I
started to *hate* those prisoners. I used to sit there and fantasize about
what I'd do to them. One time I had to put on very slow country music
and look down at the floor of my tower, 'cause I knew if I saw them
looking at me with that look like they're undressing you, I would put my
gun on fire and go nuts. Never in my life had I thought about hurting
anybody before that. But I truly wanted to kill them. And they didn't
do anything to me. I scared myself how much I hated those people and
how much I wanted to hurt them. That was the day I stopped feeling
numb."

Jen said all this hesitantly, her voice drenched with self-loathing,
her breathing panicked and shallow. But she seemed compelled to be
honest.

"In a twisted way I can almost understand the people at Abu Ghraib
acting out and wanting to hurt someone." She looked over at me, her
little body huddled on the chair, her young face somber. "I don't understand how weird they were with the abuse, that doesn't sit well with me.
But I understand them. It sickens me, but I can kind of relate."

Jen's words bring to mind British critic Cyril Connolly's comment,
"We hate what we fear and so where hate is, fear is lurking."[28] But Jen
knew perfectly well how afraid she was, although she would not admit
it to herself at the time. She knew that fear, along with the relentless
sexual harassment from the prisoners and her fellow soldiers alike, was
turning her into someone she could not even recognize.

"I wish I'd had a girl in my squad, somebody that I could talk to," she
told me wistfully. "But I didn't, so I had to deal with all this by pretending I was tough."

Without close female friends, Jen relied on the same devices as the
male soldiers to handle the stress of war. "We had little DVD players,

so we'd watch a movie and pretend we weren't in Iraq. We never talked about politics. Nobody understood what was going on anyhow, and everybody was so angry it was better not to talk about it."

She and the other soldiers also turned to booze, although alcohol is expressly prohibited in the military. "Alcohol was big. We would put it in our morning coffee. My grandma would send me vodka in a Scope bottle, dye it green and everything! [This was also a trick in the Vietnam War.] And people turned to prescription drugs, painkillers, whenever they could get their hands on some. It was a way to keep your mind off of it and pretend like you were having fun." (Other soldiers have said they were able to buy illegal drugs from Iraqis, even children.)[29]

Jen may have lacked female friends, but she did, at least, have her family, who sent her a care package and letters every week, and she did have some male buddies, including her squad leader, Staff Sergeant Tom Dati. "He was like a father to me. I think the world of him."

Dati, who is now a fireman in Chicago, having retired after thirty-three years in the military, said much the same to me. "I was about forty-five when I was in Iraq, with two daughters, and all the girls in my unit were the same age or younger than them. The women were much better to work with than most of the men. Like Jennifer—she was a good soldier. If I told her to do something, she just did it, while a lot of the guys would question and complain. Maybe the girls were just more mature."

INVISIBLE WOUNDS

Like many soldiers, during the entire time Jen was stationed in Iraq, she was struggling with her health. Early on it was her painful reaction to the anthrax shots, her nonstop period caused by the Depo-Provera injections, and the mandatory malaria pills that made her burn instantly in the sun.[30] Later, her food started going straight through her—something that happened to so many soldiers that they took to calling it the "Bucca bug." In an effort to kill whatever was causing this, Jen used so much hand sanitizer that the skin came off her palms. But it did nothing to stop her illness.

Miriam Barton had the same experience. "Everybody was sick the whole frickin' time. That was one of our jokes. You spend the first six months of your deployment pooping your guts out, then you spend the next six months puking your guts out, then you spend the next six months back in the States pooping and puking your guts out. Then you're deployed again."

Joking aside, Barton came back from Iraq seriously sick with liver failure. At first the army thought she had contracted hepatitis C and advised her to fill out her will, which shocked and frightened her, but that turned out to be wrong. "Nobody knows why, but a number of us had it. Some of them died in Germany, one died on the flight. We'd all been in the same area. But the army isn't even acknowledging there's a problem. I got told in Germany that I had 20 percent of my liver left and that I'd never have full function of it again. And it's true. I can't drink like I used to, and there's something wrong with my immune system now because I'm constantly sick. But because they lost my medical records from the point of my entering the military to the point of my leaving Iraq, they say nothing ever happened. I'm trying to get the VA to at least do a liver biopsy, but they won't consent to it. I think they're afraid of proving it's a problem."

Diseases like Jen's and Barton's are commonly caused by contaminated drinking water, and in Iraq the military water supply did eventually come under scrutiny. Like many combat support services, the job of supplying and cleaning the water belonged to KBR/Halliburton, and it was not doing a good job. In 2005, water purification specialist Ben Carter tested the water at Camp Ramadi marine base in Iraq and reported that of the sixty-seven tanks he examined, sixty-three had no chlorine and were dangerously polluted with malaria, typhus, and a long list of other microbes, including coliform bacteria from human and animal excrement, as well as a flesh-eating bacterium common in the region. He spoke of this in the documentary *Iraq for Sale* and began to weep as he said, "There's a lot of soldiers over there who might not come home with a bullet wound, but who will come home with pathogens in their blood because of Halliburton. And they don't even know to get tested for it."[31] Carter also found that KBR employees were giving soldiers the castoff wastewater from purifying units to use for laundry, showers, shaving, and brushing their teeth—stinky brown water that should have been thrown away and was twice as contaminated as the sewage-filled water from the Euphrates River that KBR was supposedly filtering.[32]

In January 2006, Carter and several other Halliburton employees testified before a committee of Democratic senators, accusing the company of serving contaminated water to the troops. The company denied every charge, but on March 7, 2008, a DoD inspector general's report confirmed Carter's findings, adding that soldiers at five different bases had come down with skin abscesses and infections, diarrhea, and other illnesses from the water.[33] Yet Halliburton is controlling the water supply for soldiers to this day.

Jen and Miriam Barton are among those soldiers never tested for these contaminants. It may take years for their illnesses to be properly diagnosed, if they ever are at all, because the water in Iraq contains parasites and pathogens that few U.S. doctors are trained to recognize. Meanwhile, scandals about the water supply to soldiers in Iraq continue to erupt. In February 2008 a former army official, his wife, and a businessman were indicted for taking half a million dollars in bribes on contracts to provide water to troops overseas.[34]

By the time Jen had been in Iraq for seven months, she had become perilously thin and was constantly fainting. She knew something was wrong, but for a long time couldn't get her leadership to listen. "I was too much of a bother. They had other things to do." Part of the problem was that sick soldiers had to be sent to Kuwait, but Camp Bucca was so understaffed the command was reluctant to let anyone leave.

Jen's weight dropped to eighty-seven pounds, which even for a woman of only five feet one is drastically thin. She began the shaking that has never stopped since, she was having the first of what she knows now are panic attacks, and her fingernails were peeling off. "Walking just the fifty yards to my tower, I would get so lightheaded that I would have to sit there with my head between my knees so I wouldn't pass out." She was so exhausted that she couldn't even face going to dinner most nights and would fall asleep on her cot instead.

Her leaders kept telling her it was all in her head, and for about a week Jen believed them. One of her friends thought otherwise, though. Every day he brought her snacks and pressured her to insist on seeing a medic. But when at last she did go, the medic found nothing except that her heart rate was unusually high. As for her platoon sergeant, his reaction was to threaten her with disciplinary action unless she ate more. "That's when I really started to lose it, 'cause I thought they were all against me."

Jen still held back from making a fuss about her illness because she felt so ambivalent about taking a medical leave. She didn't want to abandon her fellow soldiers in that hellhole while she flew off to safety, and she didn't want to be seen as a coward trying to get out of the war. Tom Dati noticed this about her. "She got real thin, but I didn't know how sick she was because she's not one to complain." But there was another reason she held back: she didn't want to disappoint her father by looking like a dropout.

For a time she struggled on, telling herself that at least she was functioning, but finally she became so sick that she called her parents after all and told them what was going on. They urged her to see a doctor at once. So she went above her difficult platoon sergeant's head to ask for permission to go to Kuwait. "It was a big deal to go, but I had to."

As soon as the unit heard she might leave, rumors spread that she was faking her illness to get out of the war, and most of her comrades offered no sympathy. It hurts Jen to remember this even now, for it reinforced the sense she had all along of being an outsider. "Most of the guys didn't take me seriously. They thought we women were there for their entertainment. That made me angry. I would've done anything for the people in my unit; I would've suffered for them. But I don't think the guys felt that way about me."

At last, in August 2003, she was flown to a hospital in Kuwait. There, the doctors said her heart rate was so high she was lucky not to have had a stroke, and they sent her to a military hospital in Germany.

"I felt so guilty about leaving people behind," she told me sadly. "I truly did not want to leave."

NINE

You're Just Lying There Waiting to See Who's Going to Die

Abbie Pickett, 2003–2004

By the time Jen had been at Camp Bucca for three months, Abbie was in Kuwait, having arrived in May 2003, two weeks after Bush had declared the war over.

If she had been frustrated at the "hurry up and wait" fate she'd met at Fort McCoy, she found it even worse in Kuwait. Like Jen, Abbie had been told that her purpose in Iraq was to bring freedom to the people and help them rebuild their country, but she and her engineering unit were given nothing whatsoever to do. For weeks they sat about at Camp Victory, a major deployment base in Northern Kuwait, while the hours ticked emptily by. Occasionally an advance party was sent out to scout for a mission, but not Abbie. Her days were spent waiting in lines at the chow hall, trying to sleep in the huge tent she shared with sixty-five other soldiers—almost all of them men—and sitting around, as Jen had, tense, bored, hot and lonely. She had rarely felt so useless in her life.

In the meantime, Paul Bremer, the newly appointed administrator of the Coalition Provisional Authority (CPA)—the American wartime government—had just thrown half a million Iraqis out of work. Determined to flush all members of Saddam's ruling Baath Party from power, Bremer disbanded the Iraqi military, the national police, the civil services, and several ministries, thus firing the very people who had skills the country badly needed and destroying the only organizations holding the country together. Many of these fired workers were not even anti-

American; under Saddam, Iraqis who wanted to keep their jobs often had to join his party whether they liked it or not, and others were not even Baathists. But these mass layoffs, along with the thousands of businesses closed because of fear of violence and a lack of customers, left 65 percent of Iraqis and their many dependents bereft of income. They also left some 125,000 soldiers and 50,000 policemen jobless, humiliated, and angry, and thus dangerously vulnerable to recruitment by rebel forces. Bremer's move, reportedly encouraged by Ahmad al-Chalabi, the notoriously corrupt and unscrupulous Iraqi businessman who manipulated Bremer and the White House early in the war, took even Rumsfeld by surprise and undercut military plans for the reconstruction of Iraq. As one member of the U.S. Central Command put it, Bremer had "snatched defeat from the jaws of victory and created an insurgency."[1]

Partly as a result of this, the lootings and violence in Baghdad reached a new crisis just as Abbie arrived in Kuwait. Newly unemployed and resentful young men, career criminals, and the long-oppressed poor from the Shia suburbs stormed museums, libraries, and businesses, lugging home everything from priceless ancient artifacts to theater curtains. The looting went virtually unchecked because American soldiers were too few to cope, Rumsfeld having moved all military divisions but one out of Baghdad. The sight of these soldiers standing idle while thieves plundered and thugs attacked civilians caused one of the first great waves of disillusionment among Iraqis toward Americans, leading many to conclude that the United States didn't care about them at all. As one remarked at the time, "If they had shot a few of [the looters] at the beginning it would have stopped. Instead, I saw American soldiers standing by, taking photographs, cheering them on."[2] Meanwhile, the troops who might have helped restore order were stuck a few miles away in Kuwait with nothing to do but yawn and slap at flies, Abbie among them.

While she and her company were waiting in Kuwait (the soldiers making many a joke of that rhyme), Abbie had plenty of time to question her purpose. Still torn between her college and military selves, she awoke in her crowded tent every morning full of doubts. What were she and all the other soldiers doing there? Were they really going to help Iraq, or destroy it?

Meanwhile, the politics of war churned on. On May 29, President

Bush told a public television station in Poland, "We found the weapons of mass destruction. We found biological laboratories . . . "[3] The very next day, the CIA announced its creation of the Iraq Survey Group, composed of more than one thousand international experts, to conduct a methodical search for those very weapons Bush had just claimed were found. And a week later, on June 5, UN weapons inspector Hans Blix announced the UN's failure to find any such weapons at all.

Abbie heard none of this, but the news wouldn't have surprised her. She was already skeptical about whether those notorious WMDs even existed.

On June 21, Abbie turned twenty-one, still stuck in Kuwait and wondering what the war was all about. And on July 2, Bush made his now notorious "Bring 'em on" speech: "There are some who feel like the conditions are such that they can attack us there. My answer is, bring 'em on." This infuriated many soldiers in Iraq, who were already outnumbered and in constant danger. They felt the president's statement revealed only too clearly how little he knew of what was going on.[4]

A week later, Abbie finally received the news she was waiting for. She and her 229th Engineering Company were to join a convoy on an even longer drive than Jen's and head for Tikrit, Saddam's hometown on the Tigris River, about eighty-seven miles northwest of Baghdad.

She was headed for Iraq at last.

PUMPING GAS

Abbie's company was to be based at Camp Speicher (pronounced *Spiker*), which was about fifteen miles outside of Tikrit. The camp had once been a training base for the Iraqi Air Force, but had been badly bombed in the first Gulf War and left to crumble ever since, so the first sight that greeted her was a vast boneyard of smashed yellow-brick buildings and abandoned military equipment. Broken airplanes and rusting vehicles lay half buried in the sand. Gas masks, pieces of tanks, and bricks were scattered over the ground. And heaps of rubble filled the rows of short, flat-topped buildings that had once been barracks. But most striking were the images of Saddam—huge pictures of him painted on walls almost everywhere she looked. "It was spooky," she said. "Soldiers would pose for pictures next to them. His presence was everywhere."

The company's initial job was to fix up the buildings to make them habitable, a nasty task because they were filled with excrement, rotting animal carcasses, and unidentifiable reeking muck. But in a few days, the soldiers had cleared out the mess, laid plywood floors, and even added a recreation center, where they mostly played cards. The quarters were far from luxurious, like a bombed-out college dorm, but they were an improvement on the tents the soldiers had been forced to sleep in up till then, and it felt pleasantly secure to have walls and a roof for a change. The soldiers then moved on to fixing and building runways, even smoothing out a basketball court. "Still," Abbie said, "we were doing nothing to help the Iraqi people."

Abbie was housed in a small room she shared with another woman. "We had two cots, but we were missing a wall, so we built one of plywood." Yet they managed to make it quite comfortable. The interior walls might have been bare concrete with patches of plaster peeling off them, but Abbie was able to prop up a second mattress behind her bed and cover it with a cloth to make it look like a sofa. She blocked the smashed window with plywood to keep out the sand, put up little candle holders on the wall, and made a photograph holder out of an empty bottle and a piece of wire; like prisoners, soldiers surround themselves with souvenirs from home, along with, in the case of many men, pinups and pornography.

Her days began at about five each morning, when she would step outside to look at the landscape. Around her, in the rusty haze of dawn, stretched a flat expanse of gravel-covered desert and dust, interrupted by the rows of squat buildings her company had just finished fixing. Except for the eternally blue sky (the first time Abbie saw a cloud, she took a picture of it), the view was dispiriting. "You don't even realize how much your life lacks color till later. Everything was tan, black, or army green."

She would then gather with three friends, two women and a man, to go for a run, and even though the morning air had the same fetid stink from the "burn shitters" Jen described, it was her favorite part of the day. "You didn't have to listen to anybody's crap, you didn't have to follow orders. You could just be in the silent hours of the day when the sun is coming up. I really enjoyed that."

After the run, she would take a cold shower—the camp had no heaters yet—try to rinse the dust out of her curly blond hair, eat her prepackaged tubes of egg, and get to work. By then the silence was over, replaced by the interminable racket of war: the thudding of chopper blades, the screaming of fighter jets, the growling and clanging of military trucks rattling over the stony ground, and, once in a while, the shriek of sirens and bone-chilling whistle of incoming mortars.

Abbie's engineering company's main job in Iraq was to build and fix bridges, roads, and military bases, but the company also contained soldiers trained to fix and fuel vehicles. Abbie was one of these; her title was petroleum supply specialist, military jargon for gas pump attendant. Why she ended up with this job is a mystery, for when the recruiter read her ASVAB test scores, he virtually begged her to be anything but a mechanic.

Her first duty each day was to take out her fuel truck, make sure it was in working order, and drive it around the base to fill generators and trucks with gas. She would then have a two-hour lull, after which she would go on a second round for the same purpose. Like most soldiers, she worked twelve- to fourteen-hour shifts, and like most soldiers, she was bored out of her skull. "When it was busy it was really busy, and when it was slow there was absolutely nothing to do. So I wrote a lot of letters, took pictures, threw rocks into a box. I became an expert marksman with my slingshot."

Her skin—already pale and delicate—grew dry and sore from being out in the sun all day, and her light green eyes became irritated from the dust that hung in the air like a fog. Her period virtually stopped as well, which is common among women soldiers in Iraq, either because of drastic weight loss, stress, or the Depo-Provera shots. Mickiela, who had the same problem, told me she didn't know any women who were menstruating while they were deployed, and studies have shown that the stress of war does indeed have this effect.[5]

For the first few weeks, Abbie only had the prepackaged MREs to eat, like Jen, which at times were rationed to two a day because KBR was failing to deliver them, causing soldiers all over Iraq to lose an alarming amount of weight. But Abbie said once the contractor did arrive and set up its dining services, the choice of food was impressive. The problem was, she had to wait for an hour and a half to get it.

The waiting in long lines for food was a source of bitter complaint among soldiers in Iraq, especially early in the war on bases where no other food shops had yet been built. KBR ran all the U.S. military dining halls and had a policy of saving money by only opening at fixed hours. This forced already overworked soldiers to stand for ages in the blistering sun or sandstorms, caused those on night shifts to miss meals altogether, and, most gravely of all, turned soldiers into sitting targets because of their predictable schedules. In one of several such attacks, twenty-two people were killed and sixty-nine wounded on a base in Mosul in 2004 when a suicide bomber entered the chow hall at mealtime and detonated the explosives strapped to his body.[6]

KBR was intensely resented by soldiers for this and many other reasons. During the first three years of the war, soldiers wanted to know why civilian contractors were paid more and treated better than they were for doing half the work. "Some of the KBR drivers were making eighty thousand a year, and here I was, an E-5 with eight years in, and I was making frickin' thirty-three thousand a year with danger pay!" as Miriam Barton said. They also wanted to know why KBR overcharged all the time—$45 for a six-pack of Coke, $100 to wash laundry that would cost only $3 in a Laundromat—and why it was buying the most expensive trucks and cars available, only to douse them with gas and set them on fire the minute they ran out of oil or got a flat tire—and this in front of Iraqis desperate for fuel.[7]

The answer to these questions is that KBR had struck a devil's deal with the Bush government: it was reimbursed for every cost, with virtually no oversight, and then given a bonus as well. This led to massive fraud, for KBR could inflate its prices at will and make more money by destroying its property than preserving it. For example, if KBR bought an old $100,000 truck from Kuwait for half the price and then torched it, the company could bill the government for the full cost of a new one, plus some extra. This deal was also why it removed the tools and spare tires from soldiers' trucks, forcing them to abandon and destroy any vehicle that broke down so it wouldn't fall into Iraqi hands; KBR could then bill the government for the cost of a new one, plus the bonus. This "cost plus" deal, as it was known, gave KBR no incentive to keep account of its spending or to be efficient, which put it at direct loggerheads with the needs of the soldiers. Where they required efficiency and speed, KBR preferred waste and sloth.

In 2005, Democrats reported to the House of Representatives that Halliburton had run up more than $1.4 billion in questionable charges. That same year, the Pentagon found that KBR had failed to account for $1.8 billion in charges for feeding and housing troops, including $212 million for meals never served.[8] Yet in December 2007, despite these and many other scandals about Halliburton/KBR employees putting soldiers at risk, as well committing fraud, theft, and even rape, the army awarded it a new ten-year, $150 billion contract to support U.S. troops around the world. The move was quickly criticized and followed by several governmental hearings about contractor abuses. But as this book went to press, KBR still held the contract and was profiting mightily in Iraq.[9]

During Abbie's tour, most soldiers had no idea why their services were so shabby; they only knew that something was wrong with a war in which civilians were paid huge salaries for inefficient work while they had to suffer shortages. Abbie felt this too. But she had another problem to deal with, because whether she was waiting in the food lines at Camp Speicher or trying to fix the army's broken-down trucks, she tended to be the only woman in sight, and the harassment was relentless.

Abbie had deployed with 19 women and 141 men, and the women were usually split up among different convoys, leaving most of them on their own. The men took advantage of this to persecute them. They were always calling out remarks like, "Hey, Pickett, I like your tits in that army shirt." They had cases of pornographic magazines, which they would look at out in the open. And far from discouraging this behavior, some of the leaders were engaging in it themselves. Like Jen, however, Abbie tried not to mind.

"It happens so much you get numb. I don't know if it'd be any different if they put three girls in a frat house. I developed these stupid one-liners to fend it off. Still, it wears away at you without you being aware of it because it's so constant."

She was also disgusted by the members of her command who were still carrying on the way they had at Fort McCoy: getting drunk, stealing property from the army and now from Iraqi civilians, too, and neglecting the safety of their soldiers. Between that, the harassment, and feeling that she was contributing nothing to the Iraqi people, Abbie soon grew alienated and depressed. She found some comfort in the military church, which was set up in a white tent, where she frequently went to pray for her family and fellow soldiers. But she desperately wanted a change.

Finally, after a couple of months, she found one.

OPERATION PENCIL

The chance came through a physician's assistant who was connected to her unit but under a different chain of command. Regarding him as a mentor, Abbie had told him that she wished she could do something more worthwhile, so one day he suggested she join his team's effort to rebuild schools in Tikrit. She jumped at the offer.

The schools of Iraq were in bad shape, half destroyed by the 1991 Gulf War and sanctions. Before then, virtually all Iraqi children had gone to grammar school, girls and boys alike. Afterward, enrollment had plummeted and the literacy rate with it. Now, this new war had made conditions worse. By Abbie's time it was not unusual to find children huddled in schools with smashed windows and no electricity, sharing only a few books and a handful of teachers—half the teachers in Iraq had been fired by Paul Bremer for belonging to the Baath Party. The U.S. military was supposed to help rebuild and reequip the schools, but instead KBR contractors usually got the job, and at much higher salaries than the soldiers were paid, while the soldiers were relegated merely to guarding them—this is what happened to Abbie, in fact. Moreover, most of the fortune earmarked for improving schools—$1 million in Fallujah alone—disappeared into various individuals' pockets, and schools were lucky to get any more than a new blackboard and a lick of paint.[10]

But Abbie was thrilled to be doing something for the Iraqis at last, and she loved the idea of spending her days with children. The downside was that going out on the roads was dangerous, for by this time in the war, the summer of 2003, the U.S. occupation had turned a nation eager to be liberated from Saddam into one ready to kill Americans. Only the Kurds, who had suffered so brutally under the dictator, still had faith in the United States.[11] What had soured Iraqis most was the gratuitous American violence against civilians. Angry and fearful soldiers were indiscriminately shooting and running over people, raiding and looting their houses, crushing cars and homes with tanks and bulldozers, arresting the innocent, and running civilians off the road. And they were showing an indifference to Iraqi customs and etiquette that only added offense to injury. The standard $2,500 offered by the United States to the families of civilians its soldiers had killed was understandably taken as an insult.[12]

But Iraqis had also lost faith in America because of its failure to restore normal life after the invasion. Even by 2006, three years after the war began, they were getting less electricity and clean water than they had under Saddam, and raw sewage was running through the streets— not because Iraqis are dirty, as many Americans thought, but because the United States had bombed the sewage systems and never repaired them. (In July 2008 the water and sewage systems were still not fixed; the water in Baghdad was so polluted by sewage that children were flooding the hospitals with dysentery, typhoid, and hepatitis.)[13] The jobs that might have gone to Iraqis who knew how to fix these things and desperately needed the work were going to American contractors who did not. Millions of dollars that were supposed to be used to rebuild Iraq were disappearing with no return. And everyday life was more danger-ous for more people than it had been even under Saddam.[14]

So as Abbie prepared to drive the roads of Iraq every day, angry Iraqis were ready to strike back. And because weapons and explosives were easily found, left over from the earlier wars and looted from Saddam's stashes, anyone who wanted to make a powerful roadside bomb or shoot a soldier could.

Abbie's routine now changed. She continued to get up early and take her morning run, but after that she had to prepare to leave the base by strapping on her battle gear: her helmet and goggles; her flak jacket; her utility vest, covered in pouches and loops for carrying tools and am-munition; a knife; seven magazines of bullets; and her rifle, all of which added up to more than sixty pounds, nearly half her weight.

The flak jackets she and her fellow soldiers had to wear were the source of many a bitter joke. They were supposed to contain two bul-letproof ceramic plates, one in the front and one in the back, but there weren't enough to go around. "So you only got one plate, and you had to decide where to put it," Abbie said. "The thing is, if you put it on your back, they said a bullet can go through you, hit the plate and bounce back, so you get shot twice." The ceramic plates were also use-less against the bullets of the AK-47s most Iraqi fighters used, and left the soldiers' arms, legs, necks, and sides exposed.

Abbie and her comrades fashioned what armor they could for them-selves and their vehicles out of metal they stripped off abandoned tanks at Camp Speicher. Miriam Barton said her company did the same thing. "Our armor was plywood that we put on the sides of our trucks. We didn't even see metal armor until we found a junkyard up in Mosul, after we'd already lost a few people. Then we went out there with a cutting torch and cut as much metal off old cars as we could and put it on the outsides of our vehicles."

Soldiers protested their lack of armor in vain. When an army specialist named Thomas Wilson confronted Rumsfeld about the lack of armor in December 2004, the defense secretary notoriously answered, "As you know, you go to war with the army you have, not the army you might want or wish to have at a later time." He then added a statement that offended so many soldiers it might well have triggered their first wave of serious disillusionment about the war: "If you think about it, you can have all the armor in the world on a tank and a tank can be blown up. And you can have an up-armored Humvee and it can be blown up."[15]

To soldiers, this sounded like, "You're going to die anyway, so why should we bother to protect you?"

Once Abbie donned all her gear, she and her team would climb into their trucks, form a small convoy with fifteen people from other units, and be on the road between ten and noon. They left at a different time each day because, unlike KBR and its policy toward dining hall hours, they knew a predictable schedule would make them a target for ambush.

The convoy would drive for about a half hour to get to a school, each soldier on the alert for bombs and snipers. "When you go in a town you're always looking at faces, looking at hands, trying to guess their mood," Abbie said. "If you're driving through the town and people are staring at you, not in fear but because they hate you, and the only thing you can hear is your truck or some kids crying, you know you're not wanted. My buddy Rob Acosta, who lost an arm from a grenade, told me he'd just been saying 'the people don't want us here' when he was hit. He could sense something was wrong."

Several soldiers told me they had to rely on body language and instinct to warn them of danger. Unlike in traditional wars, when soldiers would approach one another on battlefields with their weapons ready and visible, the Iraq War is one of sneak attacks. Bombs are hidden in cars and people, logs and plastic bags, donkey carts or dead dogs—anyplace it is possible to hide a small explosive. Bullets, mortars, and grenades can fly out of anywhere: marketplaces, houses, schoolyards, or crowds of shoppers.

But Abbie was also aware of how threatening she looked, sitting there in a military truck decked out in sunglasses and battle fatigues with a rifle in her hand. Indeed, American soldiers do look like an alien species in Iraq, their bulky uniforms and helmets in stark contrast to the simple robes and loose clothing of the people in the street. Even more sinister are the tanks and gun-mounted Humvees rumbling down sandy roads, past what is left of humble market carts, beautiful mosaic buildings, and the graceful domes and minarets of Iraq's mosques.

For Abbie, one of the worst aspects of the increasing hostility toward Americans was the way it affected her view of children. Iraqi kids would run up to soldiers all the time begging for food or candy or just to wave and stare. She loved children and wanted to reach out to them, but in the back of her mind were all the warnings she'd heard: They might be used as decoys, running in front of trucks to make them stop. Or they might be carrying a bomb strapped to their bodies. For this reason, soldiers are ordered never to stop a convoy, even if a child runs out in front of it. And children are killed by American convoys all the time.[16]

As Abbie spoke to me about this in London, her narrow face grew strained and her soft voice dropped. "I was a daycare teacher for six months before I went to college, and one day in Iraq, one of the guys who knew this about me said, 'Ed and I have been talking. If a kid came in front of our convoy, we don't know if you'd be able to run him over; we don't know if you'd be able to kill a kid, if it came to it.'"

"I don't know if I could either," she replied frankly.

She was put to the test the very first day her convoy went out to a school. Children were all over the road, which made her and the other soldiers nervous enough. But then a boy threw a rock against their tank, which made a loud crack like a bullet, sending a flash of terror through Abbie. "And I knew then that if I had to hit a kid and kill him, I would. Not to save my life but to save all the soldiers who might die." She looked up at me as she said that, her pale green eyes watering. "That was really hard to come to terms with," she whispered. "You feel so dirty."

Virtually all the soldiers I talked to said they had heard children could be decoys, yet not one knew of an actual attack in which a child was used.

These hazards aside, Abbie's most positive experience in Iraq was the work she did at schools, especially when she and her team distributed supplies that American children had gathered under a program called Operation Pencil. It was the only time she felt she was giving rather than destroying.

HIGHWAYS OF DEATH

Abbie's work at the schools came to an end in late August 2003 (just as Jen was leaving Iraq) when her company was finally given its real mission: to drive all over the country building bases, laying concertina wire, fueling convoys, installing checkpoints, and fixing roads.

At this point in the war, American soldiers had killed Saddam's notoriously cruel sons, Uday and Qusay Hussein (July 22), and a suicide bomber had destroyed the UN headquarters in Baghdad, killing twenty-two people and wounding hundreds more (August 19). This latter act sent a signal to the world that the Iraqi resistance forces were learning how to attack where it hurt. On August 26, just as Abbie started going out on convoys, Bush played tough once again, making his vow that there would be "no retreat." Once word of this filtered down to the soldiers, they knew that none of them would be going home soon.

Abbie's convoy was now on the road all the time. Her job was to drive a 2,300-gallon diesel truck, and because she was taking occasional gunfire, she knew it could ignite and explode at any second. "It was a bomb on wheels," she said. Miriam Barton put it another way: "Those things were ungodly, uncomfortable, fire-breathing bastards."

Abbie drove to Baghdad, Baquba, Tahji, Samarra, and many other destinations all over Iraq. Often she didn't even know the names of the places she went, only of the bases where she stayed. All along the way there were ambushes and firefights to worry about, but most frightening were the IEDs—roadside bombs made of bundles of heavy artillery shells, wired together and set off by a trip wire or remote control. They cause half the deaths of U.S. soldiers in Iraq and most of the mutilations that have so tragically marked this war.[17]

Sometimes, just as had happened to Jen, Abbie's convoy got lost. Once her leaders led her into a prime ambush area because they didn't have a map. Another time, they took the convoy off course on purpose to sightsee, leading it through narrow streets bordered by two-story, flat-roofed buildings full of windows that could have hidden snipers. They also had a tendency to issue orders worthy of a *M*A*S*H* episode. Abbie's chief warrant officer once told her to drive from Kuwait to Iraq in a truck with no reverse and its transmission falling out—the kind of truck KBR was delivering to the army all the time. But when she questioned these orders, he told her to obey and shut up.

For a long time, Abbie's convoy was supporting the army's 4th Infantry Division, an example of the way in which the line between support and combat soldiers disappears in Iraq. As a woman, she was officially banned from ground combat units like the infantry, but not from driving right beside infantry guys taking fire, nor from firing back if she was fired upon. At times she would have to stand on top of a dump truck with a semiautomatic gun, guarding soldiers as they worked on a highway or checkpoint. This was the same work the infantry was doing.[18]

Laura Naylor, the military police specialist who had found the limbless baby in an orphanage, also worked jobs indistinguishable from those of an all-male combat unit. Her company's mission was to rebuild and guard police stations in Baghdad, but she also traveled in convoys around the city. "One time we came upon a convoy that had got hit with an IED, and while we were trying to help the soldiers out we started getting shot at. We had to search this house nearby, thinking they were the ones doing the shooting, and I was the lead person the whole way. I had a flashlight in one hand, a pistol in the other, and I'd kick the door open with my foot, look both ways, give the all clear, go to the next room, do the same thing. We were interchangeable with the infantry. They came to our police stations and helped pull security, and we helped them search houses and people."

Her unit's soldiers were also getting killed, just like those in the infantry. One of her closest friends, a twenty-year-old specialist named Michelle Witmer, was shot in an ambush, becoming the first National Guardswoman ever killed in action. Another friend, Specialist Caryle Garcia, was wounded when a roadside bomb went off beside her Humvee. Garcia was her team's gunner, so half her body was sticking up from the Humvee's roof with nothing but a helmet and flak jacket to protect her.

"Caryle was a Humvee behind us and the bomb totally destroyed her weapon," Naylor said. "The shrapnel just sawed off its tip. She was pushed inside by the explosion, and the shrapnel cut up her face and arm. She was knocked unconscious. We thought we'd lost her."

Garcia told me what she remembers about the attack. "My ears were ringing, my whole body hurt really bad, and then I must have passed out, 'cause when I woke up I was in the truck by myself. I got shrapnel in my arm and my face, and I was deaf for a month 'cause my eardrums were ruptured. You can see scars now, but it's not hideous. My hearing's not as good as it was, but it's still okay, and I have constant tinnitus—

it's annoying.[19] But it didn't faze me much. I just thought, okay, I'm alive. I hated it over there, so I was kind of pissed that I didn't get hurt worse so I could go home." She hated it because the two men on her team sexually harassed her so relentlessly that she spent every day hiding up in her gun turret to avoid them.

The 32nd Military Police Company that Naylor and Garcia belonged to worked in the most dangerous areas in and around Baghdad, earning thirty-five Purple Hearts for casualties and deaths. Their compound was constantly mortared and their vehicles regularly blown up by roadside bombs. So, as Naylor said, "For anyone to say women aren't allowed on the frontline is absurd. Women are there now. And I would have killed someone as easily as the guys, if it came to that. I'm glad I didn't because now I don't have someone's body on my conscience. But I firmly believe that women can just as easily adapt to war as guys can."

CAMP MORTARHORSE

On October 2, 2003, during Abbie's fifth month of war, the Iraq Survey Group searching for Saddam's WMDs declared that none were to be found, effectively pulling the carpet out from under President Bush's justification for the war. Meanwhile, daily life for Iraqis had become more perilous than ever. Ordinary people were being kidnapped, tortured, and held for ransom by criminal gangs taking advantage of the war to run amok. Children and college students were staying at home, afraid to go to school. Many Iraqis were starving, both in the cities and the countryside. Citizens were furious because American soldiers were taking the guns and cash they kept in their homes for security. U.S. and British soldiers were killing and imprisoning enormous numbers of innocents. People were fleeing if they could, and the lack of electricity and security was making those who stayed behind desperate.[20]

All this was feeding the insurgency. Sunni Arabs who had not fought against the United States in March were now attacking Americans. And in the south a powerful resistance movement was growing under the young Shia cleric Moqtada al-Sadr, who was coupling the outraged nationalism of Iraqis with religious fundamentalism to recruit young men by the hundreds.

In the midst of all this, Abbie was sent to Baquba, capital of the Diyala Province northeast of Baghdad, the site of some of the worst fighting in Iraq. There, she was assigned to help work the checkpoint and fix vehicles on the base.

"In Baquba I stayed at Camp Warhorse, which everybody calls Camp Mortarhorse because it gets mortared so frequently. In fact, when you hear the thuds, you don't know if it's us firing out into the desert or us getting attacked. You can't tell, it happens so much. Do we dive for the bunker or stay here and play cards?" (The bunkers were nothing more than holes in the ground, which the soldiers had to dig for themselves and cover with wooden planks.)

Some of these confusing explosions were the sounds of U.S. soldiers torching abandoned vehicles or detonating unexploded bombs. On certain bases, soldiers learn to look at their watches because their side only sets off explosives at certain hours, but often they have to scramble for their helmets and hit the ground before they have time to figure out where the explosions are coming from. Sometimes a siren or a call of "incoming, incoming" will warn of an attack, sometimes not. And if the mortar is set off close enough, soldiers can hear the ignition being fired—a hard *thoo*—then a horrible high-pitched shriek as it comes flying in, followed by a deathly silence and the weird sucking sensation of the air pressure increasing just before the hit.

"Once a mortar came in only thirty feet or so away from us," Abbie said. "It should have killed us, but we hit the ground and it went above our heads. It made this high-pitched squealing sound. We saw lights, heard nothing for a minute, and then another one came over. When that happens you try to hide, but there's nothing you can do. That's the hardest part. There's no place to go, you're trapped. You're just lying there waiting to see who's going to die."

One night, Abbie went to the recreation building at Camp Warhorse to read her e-mail. The building, which had the Orwellian name of MWR (Morale, Welfare, and Recreation) and looked like a big barn, was where soldiers went to relax, write home, or work out on the gym machines. She was just sitting down at a computer when there was a huge flash and an earsplitting boom. The building shook violently and the lights went out. For an agonizing second she stared into the eyes of the soldier next to her, then dropped to the ground, squeezing her eyes shut and holding her breath.

A mortar had hit the building.

Twenty seconds later a second mortar flew in with a ghastly scream and hit them as well, making another shattering explosion. Not knowing her way around the base, Abbie grabbed somebody's shirt in the dark. "Take me to the bunker!" she yelled.

They ran outside, but there was no bunker to be seen. Then a third mortar dropped fifty meters away with another shriek and blast. Shrapnel whistled over their heads, and the air was so thick with smoke and dust that Abbie could hardly breathe.

"There was a girl lying on the ground outside screaming over and over, 'My bone's popping out of my arm!' And someone inside the building was calling, 'Medic! Medic!'" Abbie had once taken a combat lifesaver training course, which had given her a rudimentary knowledge of emergency first aid, so she ran back in to help. "There were four bodies on the ground, two Iraqi workers and two American soldiers. I started working on them. All I had was this tiny blue flashlight the size of my thumb that we keep on our lapels, and it was black in there, so I had to shine this tiny flashlight around to assess the damage. Blood was all over the place. This female was lying on the ground covered in it and a guy called Sergeant Hill was helping her. I said, 'Is this blood all hers, is an artery hit?' and he said, 'No, I think some of it's mine. I got hit too, but she's worse.'"

A lull followed, so more people ran inside with flashlights, one with a medic bag. The air was still so full of smoke and dust that everyone was gasping for breath. Abbie found someone to help the woman and lifted up Hill's arm—it was streaming blood. "His arm was a mess and he had shrapnel in his back. He was much worse than her, but he didn't realize it cause he was in shock."

She and some others loaded the wounded onto the tailgate of a Humvee and drove through the dark to the base hospital without putting on any lights for fear of becoming a target. "I was just holding back this man's blood with my hand; I didn't have anything else." As soon as they reached the hospital, she and another soldier carried Hill inside. "This is Sergeant Hill, he's thirty-two, he's O positive, and he needs blood now!" she yelled at the first nurse she saw.

The nurse sneered. "How do you know?"

"I know because I'm covered in blood and none of it's mine!"

And she was. All the way from her shoulders to her boots, Abbie was drenched in blood.

A few minutes later, yet another mortar came screaming in, aimed right at the hospital. "We had no flak jackets, Kevlars, nothing, so we threw our bodies on top of the patients." Luckily, the mortar hit a wing of the hospital that was empty just then. All in all, nine mortars were lobbed at the base that night.

When it was all over, after Abbie had made sure the wounded were being taken care of, she returned to her tent. During the attack, she had been reacting so fast she'd lost all consciousness of herself. But once it was over she felt shattered.

In the ensuing days, she was haunted by Sergeant Hill, unable to rid herself of the fear that he had lost his arm. But she also felt irrationally guilty for not doing more to help him. "I cried a lot about that. And I also worried about what I would do if it happened again. Would I be able to run into a building under mortar fire when I knew what it would be like? When you don't know, it's easier. The second time you do know, and that's much worse."

Abbie felt profoundly changed by that mortar attack. Before, her first thought upon waking was, "Oh, fuck, another day. Bring on the mortars, I don't even care." Now it was just the opposite. "I don't know if there's this thing you go through when you have a near-death experience, but every day I'd wake up and everything looked brighter, smelled better, tasted better, and I just wanted to embrace it. My attitude was, 'Okay Abbie, you're going to go out on this convoy, 'cause if you don't, one of your buddies will.' It was like living every day as if it's your last. You make sure you tell people that you really love them, and you take care of the people who take care of you. I just told myself, whatever God has intended for you, you're going to take it."

The attack hadn't softened Abbie toward everything, however, especially not the crooks among her leadership, who had even stolen a generator from some Iraqis, by then a particularly cruel crime as household generators were the main source of electricity for civilians and families often had to use up all their savings to buy one. But now that she had proved herself courageous under fire, Abbie felt more able to challenge this corruption. "Before the bombing, these guys thought I would buckle under pressure. They always told me, 'We don't even know if we can trust you out there.' But when the shit hit the fan, I did the right thing, and I'd seen more action than any of them. That was ammunition for me. I was like, 'You're sending us out every day putting our lives on the line, but when was the last time you were in an attack?'

It probably came off as arrogant, but it was the only thing I had. So I got mouthier."

The attack also changed her attitude toward Iraqis.

"I was always a person who believed in everyone's rights, and for a long time I complained that our treatment of Iraqis was unethical." She had been particularly appalled by the insults soldiers used toward them: bin Ladens, ragheads, sand niggers, camel jockeys, diaperheads, and hajis, the latter of which is a term of respect for a Muslim man who has been to Mecca that has been turned into a pejorative by soldiers. "But after the bombing, I wanted to go out there and hurt somebody as bad as they'd hurt the people that night. I'd never seen that revengefulness in myself before." Like Jen, though, she felt guilty about it. "It took me a long time to shut off my feelings for the Iraqis, because people are people to me."

FRONTING

The person who most helped Abbie cope with the shock of the attack was her boyfriend in Iraq, a soldier I will call David. They had come together because they were both unusually liberal in their highly conservative unit and lonely, but she knew the relationship wouldn't last because he had a girlfriend at home (which is why I cannot use his real name).

After the bombing, though, Abbie didn't feel like being in a dead-end relationship anymore—she didn't feel like doing anything that wasn't essential and honest. So she broke up with David, although they stayed friends. "We realized we needed each other to get by while we were there. And for me it was something that I could write home about that everyone could understand. They can't understand how the dirt builds up in your M-16, and your hand feels hot because the barrel is scorching from the 115-degree heat. And I couldn't write about the mortar attack and what I was seeing every day—they wouldn't understand that either. But they can understand having boyfriend problems, so that gave me something to say."

Besides David, though, Abbie was isolated during most of her time at war. She didn't get along with the female sergeant just above her, nor with most of the few other women in her platoon, for they were less educated than she and had different interests. She missed having women friends to talk to every day and, like Jen, felt that a close friend would have allowed her to deal better with the sexual assault in Nicaragua and the war. This led her to explain another way in which the loneliness of women soldiers undermines them.

"Men get to be with each other twenty-four hours a day, reinforcing their male psyche. Women don't get that at all. But female bonds are really important because sometimes you need to let your guard down and be yourself, instead of having to put on a mask for everyone. Soldiers are always fronting. When women talk about sexual assault only happening to the women who aren't tough enough—well, those 'tough' women are fronting all the time, twenty-four hours, seven days a week. And that sucks because someday it's all going to crash."

When Abbie talked about fronting, she was reflecting a point that I heard many women make about the price of being female in the military: the unnatural act they have to put on, day in and day out, not only to protect themselves from sexual assault but also to live up to the role of soldier. Everyone puts on some kind of front in life, of course, but for soldiers the front is extreme. They must act fearless, aggressive, comradely, macho, crude, and gung ho all at once. But as much as soldiers may have to believe in this act to get through war, inside they feel deeply divided, their private selves torn from their soldierly selves. This is true for almost all soldiers to some extent; many men also tire of the tough act they must maintain in front of their comrades. But for women it is harder because the soldierly identity they have to assume is an antifemale, male-defined identity. When Abbie talked about fronting, she was talking about being divided from herself as a female. She was talking about having to wear a personality that was antagonistic to her real self.

Mickiela made the same point when she said she had to change the way she walked and talked, as did Marti Ribeiro, the air force sergeant who was raped in Afghanistan. "You become very cold and don't show your emotions," Ribeiro said. "You don't let anyone in, 'cause if you do, they walk all over you."

The Demi Moore film *G.I. Jane* is all about this front. To prove herself capable of being the first woman to integrate the Navy SEAL (Sea Air Land) special force, which in fact remains all male to this day, the Moore character must turn herself into a man. She shaves her head and works out to the point where she can do one-arm pushups, and her moment of triumph comes when she shouts at her bullying drill sergeant, "Suck my dick!"—a male statement if there ever was one.

A lot of women are rejecting this front now, saying that one doesn't have to be a pretend man to be a soldier, and that women who force themselves to do so pay a price when they reenter civilian life and find their identities shattered. Abbie believes this too. But while she was at war, she had to struggle against so much suspicion and disrespect that she hardly had the luxury of championing her femininity. Instead, she felt much as Miriam Barton did: that she had to be twice as bad as the boys to prove herself.

ALL GONE

By the end of the month of Abbie's attack, Iraqi resistance forces had gathered more power than ever. On October 27, Sunni rebels coordinated their biggest attack yet, hitting four police stations, the Palestine Hotel, and the International Red Cross all in one day, killing over 35 people and injuring more than 120, most of them Iraqi civilians. After that, Iraqis became so afraid of being killed for collaborating with Americans that many policemen and military interpreters stopped coming to work.

One of those attacks was on the very police station that Laura Naylor had been renovating for three months. She told me about it when I visited her in 2007. "It was a car bomb," she said, and brought out photographs she had taken of the devastation. One showed a crater in the ground so huge that the soldier standing beside it looked like a three-inch doll. Around it were the remains of buildings, flattened and shredded. It was hard to imagine anyone surviving a blast that big. Naylor had spent twelve hours a day for three months at that police station, rebuilding it and training Iraqi police, and had come to know them and the neighborhood children well.

"This is the building where I saw the little girls I knew getting dragged out completely charred and burned and dead," she said, pointing to a picture of a heap of black bricks. "I saw three dead bodies. I saw a hand sitting in front of the police station. Just a hand. About two thousand people were gathered around, staring. When we drove through them, it was like parting the sea, and all of a sudden you're like, 'Holy shit.' Two and a half walls of the police station were all that was left. We would get chai—tea—from there every day—that place was gone. I would watch the kids play—gone. The people who would sleep outside every night to stay cool—all gone."

Like Abbie, Naylor was in such shock that for a few days she was numb.

"Then on the third day I couldn't stop crying. It was my way of finally letting it out. Because you're in such a robotic mode, it doesn't sink in. And that's when I stepped back and said, what are we doing here? Is this even worth it?"

A month later, President Bush flew into Baghdad for a surprise Thanksgiving visit to the troops. He posed with a fake turkey, hoping to boost morale. Abbie's comment: "Morale? There was no morale."

Two weeks after that, on December 13, 2003, U.S. soldiers captured Saddam Hussein hiding in his coffin-size underground hole on a farm near Tikrit, right beside Abbie's base at Camp Speicher. She and the other soldiers in her unit visited the hideout, which they called Saddam's spider hole, and took pictures of one another standing inside it. Several soldiers said this made them feel the war was worthwhile, but Abbie was less sure. She was glad to see Saddam caught, but she still felt a yearning to morally justify her presence in Iraq. After a bleak Christmas on base, she had her chance. She was given permission to take a six-week medical training course in January 2004 at Saddam's former palace in Baghdad. "It was a good break from my leadership and a chance to see how the good side of the army worked. It restored my faith in the military."

After the training, Abbie carried a medical bag wherever she went, which contained an IV and various first-aid items, but she also made sure to have condoms to give out to soldiers, because the army no longer distributes them as they used to in earlier wars. (Some medical facilities will provide them, but only on request.) The only explanation I can find for why the military offers birth control shots, diaphragms, and the pill to women but not condoms to men, despite the threats of AIDS, is that birth control keeps women from getting pregnant and leaving, while condoms are seen as encouraging sexual activity—and perhaps homosexuality—which the Bush administration cannot appear to condone.

Abbie never needed to save anyone's life again after the mortar attack, but she did find herself becoming a sort of medicine woman for the other soldiers, who would come to her for help with anything from wounds to marital problems. "I liked that a lot better; it gave me a sense of belonging. And this is just generalizing, but I think women often take on this role of caretaking over there. You'd be surprised what guys tell you while you're pulling surveillance together for twelve hours straight. One guy told me about when insurgents had fired an RPG at him from the back of their truck, but it bounced off and killed an innocent civilian instead, while his wife was standing right next to him. For days later this soldier couldn't stop hearing her screaming and crying in Arabic. He's like, 'I close my eyes and that's all I hear.'"

Most often, the soldiers confided in Abbie about their wives and girlfriends at home. "I think it's 'cause you have nothing to do over there but think about everything you're missing out on." The worrying about whether your partner is being faithful or how your children are doing is something all soldiers abhor. Many say they prefer action and danger to inaction and brooding.

While Abbie was training inside Saddam's palace in the highly protected Green Zone, only a few meters away the Iraqi Governing Council, a circuslike arrangement of twenty-five rotating Iraqi leaders appointed by the Americans, was infuriating civilians. Already widely despised and distrusted as a puppet government, it further besmirched its image by moving to reverse women's rights for the first time in decades. President Bush had made a big deal of telling America that boosting women's rights was essential to creating a new democratic Iraq, leading many Americans, soldiers included, to believe their invasion would help Iraqi women. The truth was quite the reverse.

In 1959 a family civil code had passed in Iraq that was the most progressive in the Middle East. It prohibited marriage below age eighteen, arbitrary divorce, and male favoritism in disputes over child custody and property rights, and discouraged polygamy. As bad as Saddam was, he never touched this code, and women enjoyed more equality under his reign than anywhere else in the Islamic world aside from Turkey. Iraqi women made up 40 percent of the work force and half the students, dressed in Western clothes if they chose, and participated in politics. During the last years of Saddam's rule, he made a show of embracing Islam to consolidate his power, so he put more restrictions on women—those under forty-five were no longer allowed to travel abroad without a male relative, for example—but women could still have careers and relatively independent lives.

In December 2003, however, just before Abbie took her medical course, the Governing Council tried to concede to the fundamentalist clerics who were rapidly gaining control of Iraq by agreeing to wipe out the old code and introduce the strict Islamic legal doctrine called Sharia. Iraqi women marched in protest. "This new law will send Iraqi families back to the middle ages," said one. "It will allow men to have four or five or six wives. It will take children away from their mothers. It will allow anyone who calls himself a cleric to open an Islamic court in his house and decide about who can marry and divorce and have rights."[21]

The proposal was withdrawn at the time, but in August 2005 the new Iraqi constitution, negotiated by American and British ambassadors and ratified by a referendum on October 15, succumbed to the clerics and stripped women of most of their rights, despite protests by human rights groups within and without Iraq.[22] As a result, Iraqi women were driven under the veil and into their homes as never before, where they remain to this day. By 2008, 76 percent of Iraqi girls were no longer allowed to go to school.[23]

TROUBLE

Once Abbie had finished her medical training, she had to return to Camp Speicher and the disheartening corruption and incompetence that characterized her company. One officer in particular had it in for her, knowing she was aware of his illegal activities and liable to report him. This came to a head when he found out she was being recommended for a Bronze Star with Valor, one of the highest honors in the military, to recognize her bravery at Camp Warhorse. He put a stop to it instantly, saying within hearing of other soldiers, "There is no way in hell that she is going to get a Bronze Star while I am the commander." And she never did.

Abbie reported the corruption she witnessed but nothing changed, except that her leadership began watching her even more closely, just as Jen's leaders had watched her. "Once you get on the shit list, it's everybody's eyes on you no matter where you go," Abbie said, echoing Jen's words. "And there's no break from it.'"

Soon her leaders were constantly accusing her of doing things wrong. "It was partly the fact that I was an outspoken female—I was definitely seen as a threat. But it got so bad that every day I just didn't want to wake up. I even started thinking about suicide." This frightened her so much she went to the camp's medic for help. He put her on antidepressants and sent her back to work.

As the end of Abbie's deployment grew near, her leaders stepped up their efforts to silence her by slapping her with an Article 15 for failure to PMCS her truck, which means checking the oil and gas before turning it on. An Article 15 is a serious matter, punishable by up to two months in prison and demotion by two ranks. "It was bullshit," she said. "I'd never heard of an Article 15 for something like this." What's more, the accusation was untrue.

She was given a choice: accept the punishment, or choose a court-martial trial. She chose the latter, figuring that the criminal actions of her leadership would come to light in a trial, whereas at worst she might be convicted of an infraction so minuscule she would receive only the lightest of reprimands.

Abbie declared her choice and was sent to a military lawyer, who told her she had to sign an affidavit in front of her commander, which she did. Although the rules state that a court-martial must follow within forty-eight hours of the accused soldier signing for it, her commander immediately left for Kuwait and stayed there for ten days.

While he was gone, people kept pulling Abbie aside to tell her she was making a mistake. The news went all the way up to the battalion commander, who summoned her into his office. "Soldier, this is going to look bad for your career," he said. "You know that you can get a felony if you're convicted?"

"A felony for not checking my oil? While these guys are stealing?" Abbie thought incredulously. So she told him about all the illegal activities that would come out in her trial, and revealed that she had tape recordings as proof.

The commander countered with an ultimatum: If she would drop her request for a trial and keep quiet, she would be given a letter of reprimand, a mere slap on the wrist. But if she insisted on going to trial, she would risk her career and have to stay longer in Iraq. What's worse, any soldiers she subpoenaed as witnesses would have to stay behind, too, while the rest of the unit went home.

Abbie could not bear to be the cause of keeping her fellow soldiers in Iraq, so she agreed to keep quiet—for the time being.

In early April 2004, her unit was sent back to Kuwait while she was kept in Iraq over the Article 15 mess. But before the unit left, several of its members put together a detailed list of sixty-seven infractions they had witnessed (which Abbie showed me) and sent it to Brigadier General Kerry G. Denson, commander of the Wisconsin National Guard.

As soon as Abbie was finally allowed to leave Iraq for Kuwait, she went to the investigating general and once again reported all she knew.

"And they gave me the runaround yet again." But she persisted, and at last the investigation went all the way up to the lieutenant governor of Wisconsin. She was never privy to the final outcome, but she does know that three of the offending officers in her unit suffered repercussions. One was forced to retire, and the other two were positioned so they would always be under supervision.

Abbie had at last finished her tour of active duty. Eleven months had passed since she had arrived in Iraq, and it felt like eleven years. Now it was time to face going home.

TEN

You Become Hollow, Like a Robot

Eli PaintedCrow, 2004

Eli flew into Kuwait just as Abbie was flying out of it, in early April 2004. She was forty-three by then and a grandmother of seven, so going to war at all seemed absurd. And she was surer than ever that the American occupation was a disaster.

Her opinion was being bolstered daily by events in Iraq. On April 5, marines launched a major attack on the entire city of Fallujah, killing hundreds of civilians, most of them children and teenagers, in retaliation for the murder of four American Blackwater contractors.[1] And later that same month, the media released the now infamous photographs of Americans humiliating and torturing prisoners in Abu Ghraib.

So Eli decided to allay her conscience by counter-recruiting from the inside, the way antiwar soldiers had done in Vietnam. "My idea was to talk to the soldiers, especially the young soldiers of color, and get them to not sign up for another tour," she told me in her house in California. "They're so young they don't think; they just do what they're told. So my secret mission was to get them to think and resist."

After a two-week holdover in Kuwait, she and her unit, the army's 736th Transportation Company, were sent to Camp Cedar II, a convoy pit stop about 185 miles southeast of Baghdad near Nasiriyah, the city where Jen had been at the start of the war. Once Eli arrived at the base, which resembled all the others—desert, tents, wire fences—she was put to work with a lieutenant in charge of organizing the movement and repairs of all the vehicles. It was a huge job, given to Eli because of her experience and rank as a sergeant first class, but when she started she was overwhelmed. "They were so messed up, they didn't even know how many soldiers they had. You could be missing for a week and nobody would know. They couldn't keep track of anything. They would tell you to go pick up water, and there would be no water there. So this poor lieutenant I worked for—he was an Irish guy—he was getting in trouble every single day.

"I sat there for a couple of days to watch them, and I thought, 'Oh, okay, they don't know what they're doing any better than I do.' So I started organizing the whole thing myself."

She was helped by another sergeant who was particularly skilled at arranging transportation, and between them they managed to save the lieutenant's skin. "So he loved me to death," she said with a chuckle. But although she got on with him, her commander was still the white female major who had been so hostile to women and soldiers of color back at Fort Bliss. It wasn't long before this woman was causing trouble again.

"One of the first things she did when we got to Iraq was make me and the other female noncommissioned officers move into the same tents as the privates. We literally had that much space between our bunks." Eli spread her hands two feet apart. "You do not move a higher-ranking soldier in with a lower-ranking soldier—it makes you lose your power because it's their territory. The major knew this. That's why she did it."

Sure enough, the privates were soon refusing to obey orders from Eli and the other officers who shared their tent. One in particular was insubordinate, a young woman I'll name Green. "She had a canopy over her bed and pink blankets, and I thought, 'What the fuck?' But when I tell her to move her bed over a foot to make room for me, she goes, 'I don't care what you say, I'm not moving, Sergeant PaintedCrow.' And then she stopped talking to me. I had to get the first sergeant to come in and yell at the privates to move their beds, so I became a witch again to these people. And they're having sex with their boyfriends in there, everybody knows it, but now that I'm there they can't, so they're really pissed off about that too. What could I do?"

When she wasn't dealing with these troublesome young soldiers, Eli worked in the office all day, so she remained on base rather than driving out on the roads as Abbie had done. I asked her if this made her feel relatively safe compared to the soldiers in convoys. "If you don't know what's going on, yes, you can feel safe. But if you work nights and hear the radio, like I did, then you hear about the firefights and the IEDs and you know you're not safe."

She felt even less secure once she'd taken a good look around and realized how vulnerable the base was. The soldiers were sleeping in rows of colored tents—orange and yellow and pink—right next to the highway. "Talk about a target! There were even flags waving! Fuck! We were *asking* to be targets, and we were. We got closed down several times because they found IEDs near us. They would catch people left and right out there about to bomb us." What's more, there was only a single bunker to shelter all four hundred or so soldiers in her area.

Eli was so disturbed by this lack of protection (after all, even in World War I soldiers slept in trenches) that she went to her first sergeant to ask him what the plan was in case of attack. "Well, guess what? They didn't have a plan. They didn't even have a working siren. And that battalion had already been there four months."

She was also concerned about the trauma her soldiers were undergoing. One was a young female sergeant who had trained as a driver but had been made into a gunner because there was a shortage of military police to do the job, another example of the many ways women are being turned into combat soldiers in this war. "She came in really skinny and left with the biggest arms I've ever seen because she was holding an M-60 in the back of a truck all the time." An M-60 is a twenty-three-pound machine gun.

One day, this young sergeant and her team were out on the road when they were attacked with mortars and grenades. The sergeant fired back with her machine gun, killing several civilians. Her action was nothing unusual, for although the U.S. military has a policy of no shooting until shot at, once soldiers are attacked, they tend to fire back with such power that they mow down fighters and civilians alike, who are often mixed together and indistinguishable.

The sergeant returned to the base wrought-up and shouting about what had happened. "Calm down," Eli told her. "Right now your adrenaline's up. Tomorrow's going to be a different story. I know, I've been a social worker, I've dealt with trauma." Then she realized the combat stress team hadn't shown up. Soldiers who've been in battle are supposed to be debriefed by a group of trauma experts on their return, with the idea of staving off psychic distress. But nobody had bothered to come.

"'Go to bed," she told the young sergeant gently, "it'll be fine." But she knew it wouldn't.

Sure enough, the next morning the sergeant and two other young women on her team were a mess. One was lying on her bunk in a fetal position, the others were sobbing. "They were crying because they'd killed all those people. And they wanted to beat up the squad leader who'd got them into the situation because they thought he'd made a bad decision." Eli rushed out to look for the trauma experts to help avert the crisis, but once again they were nowhere to be found.

Another incident like this happened to Green, the private with the pink blankets, when she was driving a large truck in a convoy. "Over there you drive on the opposite side of the road a lot to avoid IEDs, and you drive fast," Eli explained. "Well, this car was coming toward her, but nobody had time to move out of the way. The car ended up driving right underneath her truck. It killed four children and both their parents. There was blood all over the place."

When Green came back to the camp, she was in shock. "I guess she thought I was still mad at her because she just stood there and didn't say anything. So I hugged her, and she started crying. How was I going to stay mad at her over not moving her bed when this horrible thing had happened that she was going to have to live with for the rest of her life? She was twenty years old. She was the kind of girl that said 'Sergeant PaintedCrow' in this itty-bitty voice, like a baby.

"They should have debriefed these girls; they should have had a combat stress person there in case somebody breaks down. But they didn't. Nobody was taking care of those kids, so you can imagine the condition they were in when they went back home. And I'm sure it's not getting any better."

Research has proven Eli right. The military provides every division of three thousand or so soldiers with nine combat stress experts. But the stigma is so strong against admitting to being traumatized that most soldiers either refuse to seek help, or cannot get the time or permission to receive it.[2]

THIS IS NOT PUNITIVE
It wasn't long before the white female major was stirring up trouble yet again, this time by turning on one of Eli's friends, a young African American sergeant I'll call Wilson. (Eli gave me his real name, as she

did Green's, but to protect their military careers I have changed them.)
Two ranks below Eli and considerably younger, Wilson often turned to
her for advice, and she felt responsible for him.

Sergeant Wilson was an upstanding soldier who knew his job perfectly, according to Eli. Nevertheless, while he was away on a four-day
leave, the major replaced him with a white sergeant who had no clue
how to do his work. When Wilson returned, she told him his new job
was to train his replacement. If Wilson did that well enough, she said,
he could stay on as the white man's assistant. "This is what she did to
every soldier of color," Eli told me with a grimace.

Insulted, Wilson refused to comply, at which point the major threatened to send him to Camp Scania to be on a shooter mission. Scania is
known as a base where soldiers are sent as punishment because, being
a U.S. military refueling point on one of Iraq's major highways, it is
mortared all the time. Furthermore, being a shooter is one of the most
lethal jobs in the war, for it means guarding convoys by riding in the
passenger seat of a vehicle in front or behind them with a weapon, as
the first line of defense. "Shooters don't live very long," Eli remarked.
"IEDs get them. And if they live, they live without a body part."

Eli was so outraged by the major's actions that she went to the equal
opportunity officer, another major, to complain. "I think that's a problem
we can handle," he told her.

"Major, if you don't handle it, *I'm* going to handle it, and you're not
going to like that."

"What's that mean?"

"I'll get rid of her myself."

"Well, that's all it took—I'm threatening an officer. The next morning
they call me in, take my weapon away, and this male battalion commander tells me, 'I don't know why you have a problem with the major.
She can do anything she wants. She's the commander.'" Then came
the bad news. "We're going to transfer you to Scania too. You will leave
tomorrow morning on convoy at 0500. This is not punitive."

"What will my job be there, sir?"

"You're going to be on a shooter mission." She was being punished
in the same way as Wilson.

"Sir, that sounds punitive to me," she said.

"It's not punitive. You just need to understand rank and position, and
follow rules when they tell you to follow them. So be on that convoy."

"Yes, sir."

But Eli was thinking, "Screw you, I'm not going. I'm going to JAG."
JAG stands for Judge Advocate General, and it is every soldier's right to
seek justice there if she feels unfairly treated.

Eli persuaded Wilson to go to JAG with her to plead his case, but
then the commander denied them permission. Newly infuriated at this
violation of their rights, Eli then told Wilson that the two of them were
going to refuse to get on the next morning's convoy. "We are going to
disobey an order. And I am going to be right here with you."

Word flew around the base. These two sergeants were going to disobey an order! That could get them both court-martialed and thrown
in the brig.

Eli's first sergeant, who had always liked her, pleaded with her not to
do this, but he had no idea how tough she was. She hadn't gone through
a youth filled with violence and twenty-one years of being a soldier to
be that easily defeated.

"I'm sorry, First Sergeant, but I requested to go to JAG and that is
my right," she told him. "I'm not going to be on that truck. And you tell
that bitch that I'd better not see her because I'm going to shoot her or
beat the shit out of her. She doesn't know who she's messing with. I'm
a quiet person, but I can't deal with it no more. So you'd better tell her
not to show her face to me."

The first sergeant slunk away.

When the Irish lieutenant heard what Eli was doing, he also begged
her to change her mind, but her reply was equally firm. "Sir, I have to
do what's right in my heart. I have to take care of my soldiers, just like
you're trying to take care of me."

The next morning, a few minutes after the convoy had left without
them, Eli and Wilson were dragged by their collars out of their tents and
over to the commander's office. They were under arrest.

They arrived to find the despised female major waiting for them,
who immediately started yelling about how much trouble they were in.
Eli waited for her to quiet down, then turned to Wilson and said, "Here's
the number to JAG. Call them now. It's our right." He did, and the JAG
officer promised to see them at Camp Scania.

Appeased, the two disgraced sergeants finally agreed to co-
operate. They were shoved onto a truck like prisoners and driven
away.

MOTEL 6

Once the truck arrived at Camp Scania, Eli and Wilson were dumped onto the desert floor in the middle of the motor pool—a vast parking lot—and left without a word of instruction. They wandered across the dusty base until they found the headquarters of the Motor Transport Company, where they were to work. When they walked in, the first person Eli saw was a captain she recognized from her old unit back in California.

She introduced herself and Wilson. "We were told to report to you, sir, because we're supposed to be shooters for your mission."

"I remember you," the captain said. "Well, today is your lucky day."

"Why is that, sir?"

"Because the shooter mission just ended."

"Oh, my creator is so great!" Eli exclaimed. She and Wilson were then assigned to new jobs, neither of them as shooters.

Eli's job now was to work for a Major Smith, who was in charge of all the trucks and tents in the camp and of transporting supplies and hazardous materials. When Eli first reported for duty, Smith squinted at her with suspicion, clearly thinking, "Oh my god, they've sent me another one in trouble." But once he looked at her papers, which listed her qualifications and cleared her to take on important work, he gave her the task of reading all the intelligence information that came through the office and reporting it to the commander. "You have to read about all the injuries and bombings in surrounding areas," he told her. "You need to know what's important and what the commander needs to know. Got it, Sergeant PaintedCrow?"

"Yikes," Eli thought.

But she soon mastered the job, although often found it grueling because she had to read accounts and examine photographs of the deaths and wounds caused by grenades, mortars, and improvised bombs. She saw amputated body parts, torn-off faces, burnt flesh, smashed-in heads. "Who knows what that's done to me, seeing those pictures?"

For relief she liked to spend time in the mess hall tent meeting the many people who passed through the camp. Scania is halfway between Kuwait and Baghdad, and Eli described it as a sort of Motel 6, where traveling soldiers stay overnight to refuel their trucks, eat, and sleep before moving on. "I made it a point to go to chow hall when I knew there would be an influx of marines, or British or Korean people, and

I'd talk to them. A lot of the marines were eighteen, nineteen, and they had pictures of their girlfriends they wanted to show me. So I'd chat with them and send my prayers, tell them what to watch out for. Then they'd be gone."

This influx of soldiers also gave her the opportunity to hear news of the war, and what she heard was dismaying.

During Eli's first three months in Iraq, April through June 2004, the balance of power between the United States and the resistance had shifted dramatically, with the United States losing. By the end of April, the United States had lost Fallujah to Moqtada al-Sadr's Mahdi Army of Shia rebels, and on June 6 it also lost Najaf, one of the holiest cities of Shia Islam, after a two-month standoff. These rebel victories made it possible for Sadr and other resistance leaders to recruit more fighters than ever. Between them and the Sunni fighters, who had been attacking Americans for some time, only three of Iraq's eighteen provinces were even near secure, all of them Kurdish.[3]

In reaction to its weakening position, the United States had hastily disbanded the despised Iraqi Governing Council on June 28 to make way for Ilyad Allawi as interim prime minister. In spite a lot of trumpeting about this as a transfer of sovereignty to the Iraqis, which Paul Bremer hoped might appease the resistance and lessen the violence, only thirty people turned out to watch the ceremony.[4] Then, on July 9, 2004, the very week Eli was kicked over to Camp Scania, the Senate Intelligence Committee released a report that confirmed many of her suspicions. It criticized the Bush administration and the CIA's justifications for the war and questioned their assertion that Iraq had nuclear, chemical, or biological weapons. It also stated unequivocally that there was no relationship between Saddam Hussein and al-Qaeda.[5]

Those soldiers who hadn't already been disillusioned by America's lack of success in finding those WMDs were sorely put to the test now, at least those who heard the news and could bear to think about it. Eli was only more disgusted with the war than ever.

MORNING SONGS

As tough as she was acting through all these troubles—"fronting," as Abbie would say—the strain pressed hard on Eli. The only way she could cope was by cutting off her feelings, and even her thoughts of home.

"I hardly ever wrote home. I called home, but I didn't think about home. I would think about writing letters, but I would never write them, even to my sons. It's because you become hollow, like a robot. You get up, you do your job, you hear people complain, you talk about this, you talk about that. But you don't look inside."

She did find some small comforts, however. "My sister sent me a medicine box with my prayer stuff in it. I'd sit at night and smoke a cigarette and offer my prayers—that's what smoking is for me, an offering of prayer—and I'd watch the moon. That brought me some peace."

She also took solace from the songs she heard as the sun rose each morning, when the local Iraqis who worked at Camp Scania would spread out their carpets to pray. "The songs would echo, and, oh my god, it was so beautiful, like angels. I'd wake up peaceful because of those songs. I think they saved me from myself. Because there were times when I thought I was going insane. 'What the fuck am I doing here? Why am I not just getting on a plane and going home? What am I doing on this base? It's a concentration camp.'"

Camp Scania did somewhat resemble a prison camp. Bleak, dirty, and fenced in by razor wire, it was filled day and night with smoke-belching trucks, the stink of motor oil, and the noise of large machinery groaning and banging over the stony ground. Soldiers slept in narrow rows of dust-covered tents, with sandbags piled around the entrances and sides to protect them from mortars, and everything was gray and gloomy. The one exception was the forest of bright green palm trees surrounding the camp. But that lay outside the wire, like a promise of peace that always lies just beyond reach.

As upset as Eli was during her time at Scania, she still carried out her secret mission to make the soldiers question the war. "I would look for soldiers who were really disgusted with the whole thing we were doing over there, smart college kids, and make friends with them. I had some philosophy books, and they would ask to read them. Then we would talk about why they enlisted, and I would go into this whole spiel about how we were being used as people of color, how we were doing the same things to Iraqis that had been done to us as black people and Native people. The white boys didn't want to hear this, but the ones of color did, and because they were really young I felt I could tell them to consider their options before they reenlisted. I'd say, 'That might be the easy way, but will you lose your soul in the process?'"

I asked Eli if this subversive talk got her into trouble.

"No. It could have, but no one told on me."

Whenever she could, Eli also tried to befriend any Iraqis she could meet. One of her duties was to escort civilian workers on and off the camp, so she would talk to those who knew some English. These workers had a small building on base where they were allowed to sell velvet paintings like those on Eli's wall and to draw touristy portraits for the soldiers who brought in photographs. And directly beyond the wire borders on one side of the camp, nestled under the palm trees, was a row of colorful market stalls, their tin roofs propped up by spindly poles, their counters made of roughly painted plywood. There, the villagers sold fake Rolex watches, water pipes, bootlegged DVDs, Korans, worry beads, and a mass of other trinkets and souvenirs, like the colorful blankets Eli bought for her house back home. (Many of the goods were in fact made in China.)

"I started going out there and talking to them, and the young ones would say, 'You're Indian, from India.' I would say no. Then they'd say, 'Take off your sunglasses, let me see your eyes.' I would say no. So finally one of the kids comes back after seeing the movie *Dances With Wolves,* and he goes, 'You're Indian! Red Indian!' And I said, 'Yes. I'm a Red Indian.' And he said, 'Native American.' And I'm like, 'Yes!'

"So I was invited to have a meal at the market. They cooked the same kind of rice my people cook, and the same kind of bread and chicken, and I'd tell them, 'Oh, we make this kind of bread. Tell me about your people. I want to know about your religion. I want to know about your women. I want to know what you think about this war.'"

Eli took to going to the market whenever she could. She learned some Arabic and became fascinated by the similarities between Iraqi culture and her own: traditional significances of the moon, tobacco ceremonies, the use of sage as a medicine. "And their clans: how people marry into and out of clans, their rules about paying things back, reciprocity. Some of it's not exactly the same, but I found it so close that I thought, 'What the *hell* am I doing here? Why am I doing this to these people?' I started to see how we were changing their clan system, their council system that's been there for thousands of years. I started to see how imposing democracy means it's not a democracy anymore. And I'm thinking, 'How can I do this to another people? How can I participate?'" Eli paused to catch her breath while she was telling me this, for she was speaking in a low, intense voice, her passion rising. "And I began to think this war is a genocide. If it wasn't, we'd have things in place to help the women, to help the children, to help the civilians. But we don't care about them. We'd rather they die."

She fell silent a moment, the emotion visible in her black eyes, and leaned forward in her living room armchair, which by then was swallowed in afternoon shadows. "My tour in Iraq was a real eye opener for me because my biggest enemy there was my own company," she said with quiet intensity. "Officers would brief us by saying, 'It's Indian country out there, go get 'em!' I found that very shocking. It would make me wonder: 'If this is Indian country, perhaps I'm on the wrong side.'"

THE ARMY DOESN'T CARE ABOUT YOU

The entire time Eli was in Iraq, her health, like Jen's, was failing. The trouble had begun back at Fort Bliss, Texas, when she had developed painful endometriosis, a condition in which the uterine lining grows over other organs, causing severe cramps and bleeding. This brought her smack up against the inadequacy of the military when it comes to women's health.

Her uterus began to bleed uncontrollably toward the end of March, a month before she was to deploy, so she went to the doctor at Fort Bliss for treatment, knowing it would be hard to find in Iraq. The doctor did a series of tests, but they were so badly recorded that the hospital staff couldn't make head or tail of them. "There's nothing wrong with you," they said. "You can deploy. Just take birth control pills." Eli explained that she had tried that before and it hadn't worked, but nobody would listen.

"They decided I was faking it to get out of going to war. But if something was wrong with a man like that, I know he wouldn't have to deploy. There was a first sergeant in my unit who didn't have to go because he had surgery for prostate cancer. But when it's a woman's uterus, they don't care."

Once she arrived in Iraq, there were no doctors who could help her, as she had predicted, so she was sent to the only U.S. military gynecologist the army could find, who was in Tallil, forty-five minutes away. Once she moved to Camp Scania, though, Tallil was no longer so close. To get there, she would have had to drive for four and a half hours along bomb-laden roads. "You were hearing about IEDs all the time—one of our jeeps got blown up, and one of our soldiers got hurt. I wasn't going to risk my life because they couldn't get a GYN doctor to me. It's their job to take care of me. So I opted not to go. I was being arrogant, maybe, I don't know."

Then her health grew rapidly worse. Her period would last for fourteen days, stop for seven, and then come back for another fourteen. She was losing so much blood it exhausted her, and she was in so much pain she needed shots to help her sleep. Soon she was on bed rest three days a week and could barely stand up. Finally, a female sergeant said to her, "I'm going to give you a piece of advice, and I hope you take it. The army does not care about you and your uterus. You're going home on leave. And when you go home, get a hysterectomy. Because even if they give you medication for it over there and you come back, they're not going to help you if something else goes wrong."

"But I don't want a hysterectomy!" Eli objected. "I just want something to ease my pain."

"Well, you choose," the sergeant replied. "But I know how it works because I've been through it too."

"I didn't want to do this, but the pain was so bad I couldn't even walk or do my work. So they sent me home for fifteen days of leave."

Eli left Iraq in September 2004, just as the death toll of U.S. soldiers reached one thousand and the number of attacks on American troops had climbed to a new high, averaging eighty-seven a day.[6] That same month, UN Secretary General Kofi Annan declared the war illegal.[7] Two months later, Bush was reelected president of the United States.

The trip home took three days of Eli's leave, and as she was going to lose three more getting back, she only had nine days to take care of her problem. But when she arrived at the VA hospital, the doctors told her that the treatment she needed would take weeks. "I can't do that!" she said. "I have to go back to Iraq."

In that case, they replied, the only thing to do is to have a hysterectomy after all. Feeling cornered, Eli agreed, but the decision upset her so much she still can't talk about it without her voice shaking. "I'm really angry because my uterus didn't have to leave my body. For Native people, that's a very important thing. My uterus is where my children were made, my uterus going into menopause is a ceremony that puts me into grandmother lodge. I don't get to have that ceremony now. There's a lot of things that were taken behind my uterus. It wasn't just some part that didn't work anymore."

After she had spent her entire leave in the hospital, the doctors sprung more bad news on her: she would need another six to eight weeks to recuperate. She called her commander, the same white major who had it in for her, and sent e-mails and text messages asking permission, but the only response she got was a threat. "You will be AWOL if you don't come back now." (AWOL means absent without leave, and is a court-martial offense.)

"How can I be AWOL when I'm on medical leave?" Eli countered, but to no avail. She tried every channel she could to solve this mess, finally succeeding with the help of a female friend who was a twenty-year navy veteran and knew how to pull strings. The woman managed to have Eli's leave cleared.

But her problems weren't over yet. She went back to Fort Bliss on medical hold, only to find out she had a fallen fallopian tube that also had to be removed by surgery. It took so many weeks to work through all the mistaken reports, lost files, and muddled bureaucracy of the VA that it was February 2005 by the time she had the second surgery, five months after she had been sent home for a fifteen-day leave from Iraq.

"In the meantime, I'm working for the Medical Holding Company, and it's a bigger mess than the place I left in Scania. They had soldiers they'd lost for over a year. They didn't know who was missing. They didn't know who was in the hospital system. They didn't even have a working database—I had to create one. Only one soldier, a staff sergeant, was overseeing all of this, and he was working from six in the morning until eleven at night and not making any headway."

Two years later, in February 2007, the *Washington Post* published an investigation into the Walter Reed Army Medical Center that echoed Eli's findings.[8] Records of soldiers were constantly being lost and confused with one another. One amputee received orders to report to duty at a base in Germany while he was still heavily medicated and in a wheelchair. Another wounded soldier had to bring in photographs and letters to prove she had served in Iraq. And the Medical Holding Company in charge (the military creates a company even for those who are ill and wounded) was in such shambles that soldiers were languishing at Walter Reed for months or even years in a bureaucratic vacuum, some of them sleeping in outbuildings so run-down they had black mold on the walls, holes in the ceiling, and were infested with mice and cockroaches. After the *Washington Post*'s exposé, President Bush professed to be shocked, as if all this was news to him, even though other news out-lets had been exposing the terrible conditions of military hospitals and the failures of the VA for years.[9] He fired the general in charge, and the Pentagon was soon boasting of improvements. But seven months later, the Government Accounting Office (GAO) followed up and found that little had changed at all, and on January 2008 a military nurse at Walter Reed went public to say the hospital was still riddled with life-threaten-ing problems, such as unsanitary conditions in surgical units, spreading bacterial infections, and lack of necessary lifesaving equipment.[10] The following February the GAO found improvements in general medical care for veterans, but by May 2008 there was still a drastic shortage of staff trained to care for post-traumatic stress disorder or traumatic brain injury—two of the most common wounds of this war—and a critical lack of facilities to handle the growing number of wounded soldiers.[11]

When Eli had finally recovered and was preparing to redeploy to Iraq, the major who commanded the Medical Holding Company called her in. "Sergeant PaintedCrow, I have some news," he said. "You're not going back."

"Why not, sir?" Eli replied in surprise.

"Because your commander has been relieved of duty, and she's here." He was talking about the dreaded female major.

"She is? Sir, I'm telling you right now, I'd better not run into her."

"I don't think you will. She doesn't want to see you either. But I don't want you to go back. I want to offer you a permanent job here."

"Well, sir, if I can get a civilian job here, I'll stay. But I'm not staying in the military anymore."

He did offer Eli the job, but then there was a hiring freeze. "By the time I came home, I was just too broken to even follow up on it."

The female major was never reprimanded for the many offenses Eli said she committed, and to this day Eli is indignant about it. "She destroyed the careers of many soldiers of color, but nobody stopped it, nobody could say anything. If you said anything, you'd be punished."

Eli stayed at Fort Bliss until June 2005, when she had finally finished out her military contract. After twenty-two years, her life in the army was over.

ELEVEN

I Wasn't Carrying the Knife for the Enemy, I Was Carrying It for the Guys on My Own Side

Mickiela Montoya, 2005

At the same time Eli was battling the VA over her health—January 2005—Mickiela was leaving the hospital devastated over the loss of her baby. She longed to tell her boyfriend Joseph what had happened, but he was far away in Iraq, so she could only wait until he had the chance to call her. The very next day he did, just as she was boarding the plane back to Fort Dix. When she told him she'd lost the baby, he fell silent. She assumed he was as devastated as she was.

As soon as she arrived back at the New Jersey base, the command informed her she had one month to recuperate before she had to go to war. She was shocked. "That was just ridiculous!" she said to me, her brown eyes widening in outrage. "It takes months for your body to get over losing a baby!"

She asked to see a therapist, whom she knew had the authority to grant her more time, and was immediately summoned by her unit's commander. He made it clear that he thought she had gotten pregnant on purpose to get out of going to war and was now only trying a new way of malingering by claiming she'd had a miscarriage. To qualify to see a therapist, he told her, she had to prove that she was no longer pregnant. To do that, she would have to take a blood test.

"But sir, the blood test won't work!" Mickiela answered, confused by the illogic of this argument. Ignoring her, the commander summoned her squad leader and ordered him to take Mickiela to the lab then and there. She resisted, for she still had a terror of needles, but the squad leader seized her by the arm anyway, marched her across the base like a prisoner, and stood over her threateningly while her blood was drawn. "They forced me! I was crying and flipping out because I wasn't in charge of my own body anymore."

Sure enough, her blood did still contain the pregnancy hormone. But she also had an ultrasound, and only that proved to the army's satisfaction that her womb was empty.

Mickiela went to her therapist appointment miserable and furious at the way she had been treated. "I don't feel like a person," she told the woman. "I don't care if I die because my heart is in Iraq with my boyfriend and my soul is with the baby."

The therapist was unsympathetic, clearly assuming, like everyone else, that Mickiela was trying to get out of the war. "Iraq will be good for you; it's just what you need," she said, and handed Mickiela a standard pamphlet on grieving. Outraged, Mickiela demanded a civilian therapist instead.

"I think you're fine," the woman replied coldly. "I don't think it would be healthy for you to see another doctor at this point."

"That made me hate the army even more! They all work together against you. I don't think the military has any respect for us. It's just them needing bodies. I told them I don't mind going to Iraq, I just can't go right now. All I wanted was more time." She tried to get help from the priest and the chaplain but neither would listen. Eventually, she gave up. "It was miserable in the medical hold anyway. You're there with broken-down soldiers and people who think you're trying to get out of the war. It wasn't even tolerable. So I figured I might as well just go to Iraq. It sucked."

Mickiela spent February finishing the training she missed while pregnant. Then, still feeling hollow and sad, she boarded a plane to Kuwait, where she stopped for only an hour, just long enough to buy two paperback books: a Penguin edition of the Bible and a matching copy of the Koran in English. "I really wanted to understand where the Iraqis were coming from. I knew they were fighting for God, and just as much as we think we're right, they think they're right. I was reading it the way I read the Bible, like a story, for my own understanding." With the Koran in hand and her heart still troubled, she got back onto the plane and flew to Iraq.

Mickiela entered the war in March 2005, the second anniversary of the U.S. invasion, when Iraq was more violent than even in Eli's time. The announcement of the January 30 election for a National Assembly, the first general election in Iraq in fifty years, had led to a sharp increase in Sunni attacks on Americans and their collaborators, because the Sunnis feared the election would take away the power they had held for decades. And the number of Iraqi civilians killed by the war had reached at least eight times the number of people who had died on 9/11.[1]

Mickiela was to join her company, the 642nd DASB (Division Aviation Support Battalion) at Camp Speicher near Tikrit, the same place where Abbie had been based two years earlier. The first thing she noticed when she walked off the airplane was the quality of the silence. "It's a different type of silence than at home. Here you have silent silence. But there, the silence is loud because you hear the wind, you hear trucks crunching over the rocks, you hear planes."

FOB Speicher, as it was known by then, had changed quite a bit since Abbie's day. Most of the buildings had been fixed up into tidy yellow-brick boxes, and the camp now offered fast-food stands, a gym, a movie theater, laundry facilities, shops, and even a massage service with Filipina masseuses. (KBR and other private contractors have been importing Filipino and South Asian women to work as laundresses, cooks, and masseuses on military bases all over Iraq. Some of these women have been illegally trafficked through Kuwait, and the question of whether they are being prostituted has been raised but not fully answered. In 2004 the Philippines banned its citizens from working in Iraq after a Filipino truck driver was kidnapped, but many soldiers told me they found them there anyway.)[2]

Speicher had also been expanded to accommodate many more battalions since Abbie had been there. But the lack of color and monotony were the same. "All you see is brown, brown, brown, and the blue sky," Mickiela said. "The rocks—everything is brown. Joseph always hated that. I was a redhead, so that was color!"

There was another difference as well: instead of living inside the old barracks, as Abbie had, the soldiers were housed in little white trailers made of tin, which they called a "hooch" or (backward) "choo." Shaped like a shoebox, each choo was protected by sandbags stacked four feet high against its outside walls, the idea being that soldiers could drop to the ground when under attack to avoid being impaled by shrapnel—at least if a mortar didn't come through the flimsy roof. The tiny trailers were built for only two people, but the soldiers had to share them between three.

"The night I moved in, it was so tight in there I had to squeeze my way into it!" Mickiela said. "I didn't end up getting along with the girl to my right, but the girl to my left was my friend from before. She was so excited to see me! No one even knew I was coming, 'cause the last everybody heard, I was pregnant."

Mickiela wasted no time in seeking out Joseph, for she hadn't seen him in four months. "He knew I was coming, but he didn't know when. So I went to his little choo and knocked on his door, but his roomie didn't know where he was. Then I remembered the time difference— how when it was midnight for him, it was three o'clock for me, and I'd always be online with him at that time, every day. So I'm like, 'I know, he's on the computer!'"

She dashed back to her choo, put on her favorite perfume, and ran over to the recreation hall. And there he was, sitting at a corner computer with his back to her. Instead of going right up to him, she quietly waited for a turn on the computer behind him. When it was free, she sat down with her back to his and logged online. Sure enough, he was writing to her.

"I'm stuck in Kuwait, but it's cool being on your time zone," she wrote back.

"Hey," he typed in reply. "I don't know why—it's weird, I smell you. I must really miss you 'cause I smell your perfume."

"Turn around," she wrote.

"And he turned around and just started laughing. It was so cute!" Mickiela grinned at the memory, her freckled cheeks bunching up in delight.

BATTLE BUDDY BULLSHIT

The next afternoon, Specialist Montoya, as Mickiela was now known, reported for her first day of work. Her title was automated logistical specialist, military gobbledygook for supply clerk, a job both dull and riddled with chickenshit. "We'd get a shipment, and you'd have to scan everything, and then manually put the digital number into the computer for the inventory, then track it from there to the storage area.... I hated it. We had to deal with a lot of aviation people who were spoiled and a lot of high-ranking people who wouldn't go through the proper procedure. And we worked the longest hours and days, with no days off because we were always short of people. It sucked!"

But more difficult was the harassment from the men, which she found even worse than it had been during training. As one of only five women among twenty-four men in her platoon, and an even smaller ratio in the company at large, she felt as if she were always on stage. "You know how I told you there are only three kinds of female you're allowed to be in the military—a bitch, a ho, or a dyke? Well, in the beginning I was considered a ho cause I was nice to people. Then, I realized what they were saying about me, so I became a bitch. I wasn't mean, but I had to change so nobody would think I was flirty." Then she echoed the words I'd heard from Abbie and Marti Ribeiro: "The people over there didn't even know who I was, 'cause I always had to put on an act. And a lot of the men didn't want us there. One guy told me he thinks the military sends women over to give the guys eye candy to keep them sane. He told me in Vietnam they had prostitutes, but they don't have those in Iraq, so they have women soldiers instead."

Both male and female soldiers commonly blame the prevalence of rape and sexual assault by soldiers in Iraq on the lack of prostitutes, an idea not exactly discouraged by the command. Even after forty years of research debunking the notion that rape is caused by pent-up lust, the military still promotes it, for to do so is useful: It keeps women fearful and blames them for provoking rape, thus letting men off the hook.

Part of keeping women fearful is the idea of the battle buddy. As at Camp Arifjan, the women at Speicher were told never to go anywhere at night without a battle buddy for protection. Ironically, because there were so few women, that buddy often had to be a man. ("Battle buddy bullshit," as military policewoman Caryle Garcia said about this arrangement. Chantelle Henneberry, the army specialist who served alone with fifty men, said, "My battle buddy was my gun and the knife in my pocket.") At the end of Mickiela's shift one night, she was walking back to her trailer with one of these so-called buddies, when he turned to her and said, "You know, if I was to rape you right now, nobody could hear you scream. Nobody would see you. What would you do?"

"I'd stab you," she shot back.

"You don't have a knife," he jeered.

"Oh yes I do."

"Actually, I didn't have one," Mickiela told me a year later, "but after that, I always carried one. I practiced how to take it out of my pocket and swing it out fast. But I wasn't carrying the knife for the enemy, I was carrying it for the guys on my own side."

So many women soldiers told me they carried knives for the same reason that I began to ask them, "If the men are threatening, harassing, and even attacking you like this, where does that leave you in the middle of a battle?"

Almost all of them gave me the same answer: Alone.

PROBLEM WOMEN

The loneliness of women soldiers might, one would think, be ameliorated by the companionship of other women, at least if there are some, and this is sometimes the case. But just because women are thrown together doesn't mean they are willing to help one another. Like the major who so enraged Eli, some people, women and men, react to oppression by competing rather than joining in solidarity. Several soldiers talked to me about this, including Miriam Barton, the blunt army sergeant from Oregon.

"Most people don't realize that females are not very friendly toward each other in the military. In fact, most of the hostile treatment I ever received was from other females. And every time a female runs into another female, it's like, 'Oh, are you one of those that brings us all down?'"

I heard many stories about those women who "bring us all down" by being sexually promiscuous, but the stories are hard to verify. Most of them are an obvious manifestation of the age-old double standard that admires sexually active men and considers such women sluts or "walking mattresses," as some soldiers like to say. Rumors of promiscuity are also a way of blaming the victims of rape and denigrating women in general. Specialist Chantelle Henneberry found out in Iraq that someone had written on the camp's latrine wall that she had slept with dozens of men. In fact, already traumatized by several assaults and constant harassment, she spent every moment she wasn't working at prayer in the military chapel or asleep, but there was nothing she could do to counteract the smear, which only made her feel more persecuted than ever. Mickiela too was the subject of a demeaning rumor: "I found out that because I had long hair, everybody was saying I'd been a stripper before I was in the military."

Still, it is true that women in the military are in high sexual demand, and a few do appear to take advantage of this. As Eli said, "Those kinds of women make it very hard for the rest of us to do our jobs. But sex has a lot of power out there. You can get promoted, and you can get a lot of freebies."

Mickiela had trouble with the women in her unit, too, but for a different reason, the same one she'd had at Fort Leonard Wood. "I was the only Mexican girl from California with a Brooklyn unit, and they didn't accept me. People stuck with their own kind, like in high school. There's a lot of racism in the army, and prejudice. I felt bad for the gay soldiers and the lesbians, too, 'cause of that."

The baiting of lesbians is indeed commonplace and cruel in the military. This is not only because of homophobia among the troops but because of the Pentagon's fifteen-year-old "don't ask, don't tell" policy of banning gays and lesbians from the military unless they keep their sexual orientation a secret, which essentially hands a weapon of persecution to anyone who wishes to wield it. Charges of lesbianism have been used to silence gay and straight women who report sexual abuse or other misdoings, to punish those who rebuff sexual advances or excel in their jobs, and to drum such women out of the military altogether.[3]

Gay men too are persecuted because of this policy, but in recent years more women than men have suffered from it. In 2007, 627 lesbians and gay men were discharged from the military, a rise from 612 in 2006, and a disproportionate number of those were women: 46 percent in the army and 49 percent in the air force.[4] As 14 percent of the armed forces are women, the fact that they represent nearly 50 percent of those discharged for being gay indicates an alarming prejudice against lesbians.

As for the racism, Mickiela said this was not only evident in whom the soldiers chose as friends. "We were the only company who was all black or Spanish, but all our officers were white. And we always got the shitty details, like guarding the checkpoint."

Her boyfriend Joseph concurred. "We didn't have the numbers we needed to deploy, so they took soldiers from all over the place, and at first there was some favoritism and yeah, racism," he told me. But then, he said, matters improved. "In Iraq, everybody merged together after a while and we became like brothers. It was a beautiful thing."

Mickiela's experience of being sent to war with strangers is common in Iraq, especially in the National Guard and reserves. Ideally, the military prefers to deploy people who have trained together because it builds loyalty, but with a war in which less than 1 percent of the country is taking part, this is often no longer possible.[5] Like Mickiela, both Eli and Terris were deployed with strangers, and, unlike Joseph, all three said it exacerbated their isolation.

HEALTH PROBLEMS

Before long, Mickiela's health began to deteriorate in Iraq, as it does for so many soldiers. "You get no days off for the first two weeks, then only one day off every six days. You wake up at seven and work twelve hours. It's a hundred and thirty-five to a hundred and forty degrees. You're tired all the time. And I lost so much weight! I was slim to begin with, but there I was bones. We all were. We couldn't eat in that heat, and the food was so nasty," she said.

Her period stopped and her hair began falling out by the handful, she thought because of stress. And she had constant bladder infections. "You can't take enough showers. The sand, it's like dust there and it gets into everything, even inside you." But she said the bladder infections were also caused by the same problem Jen and many other soldiers mentioned: the lack of clean and safe toilets. "All our trailers and tents were together, men and women, and there were only two Porta Potties for your whole unit [120 or so people]. They're really far away, and they're only cleaned once a day. So you can't go in the day because it's too disgusting. And you can't go at night because you can get raped.

"Everybody's bladder got screwed up. I came back and I couldn't hold my pee. I'm twenty-one and I have an old lady's bladder. I don't know a single girl from the military who doesn't."

Chantelle Henneberry said the same thing. She was based first in Mosul and then Rawah, near the Syrian border. "Rawah was nothing more than a tent camp covered in sand that reminded me of powdered sugar but tasted of salt." The latrines were so far away that she stopped drinking water every afternoon to avoid having to take the dangerous walk to them at night. "I'd go for sixteen hours eating nothing but Skittles and not drinking, and I collapsed so often from dehydration that I had IV tracks on my arms from medics reviving me."

Another reason Mickiela lost weight was because the chow hall was so far away from her trailer that she either had to catch a trolley to reach it or walk half an hour each way. Given her long work hours, this was often more trouble than she could face. Moreover, as explained earlier, the KBR dining hall was only open at certain hours. "If your work conflicted with meal hours, you were screwed. They'd bring you food at night, but it was only leftovers of the nasty mealtime food. And there were rats everywhere, so I didn't want to eat it."

As soldiers and Iraqis went hungry, KBR was leaving food supplies to rot, rather than bothering to deliver them; throwing them away and billing the government for the losses; and driving them all over Iraq on open flatbed trucks, which were easily and frequently looted.[6] Because of this, to Mickiela's incredulity, Camp Speicher actually ran out of bottled water one day.

I'M A SOLDIER, NOT A GENDER

Mickiela was so unhappy the first two months of her deployment that when the command asked for volunteers to work nights at the check-point, she jumped at the chance. She knew the mission was dangerous, but she badly wanted to get away from her boring job and unfriendly colleagues. Anyway, it would mean she could work next to Joseph.

Now her whole world switched upside down. She would sleep through the heat of the day, then dress in her battle gear and drive a tank or a truck the forty-five minutes it took to get to Speicher's entrance. She sent me a photograph Joseph took of her at this time, squinting down the sights of a machine gun. Between her heavy helmet and the formidable gun barrel, which was pointed right at the camera, I could see a plucked ginger eyebrow, a patch of smooth freckled cheek, and one brown eye readying her aim. Mickiela had changed from supply clerk to combat soldier.

It was May 2005 by this time, and the war was quite different than it had been when Abbie was at Speicher. Instead of an uprising against a foreign occupation, it had become both that and a civil war. The January election had given the Shia most of the important positions in government for the first time in history, with the Kurds coming in second, knocking the previously powerful Sunnis aside. In reaction, Sunni militias were attacking the Shia, whom they now saw as American collaborators and traitors, while the Shia fought back with a new weapon they had gained through the election: control over the Ministry of Defense and its twelve thousand police commandos, whom they quickly formed into highly visible and organized death squads. So on one side, Sunni suicide bombers were attacking both Shia and Americans, and on the other, uniformed Shia death squads were slaughtering Sunnis.

All this turned civilian life more terrifying than ever. Nowhere was safe from suicide bombers or gangsters, and kidnappings, murders, and mass attacks were a constant. Women who had once been free to dress as they wished were now afraid to go out without a headscarf, for fear of being chased down and beaten by fundamentalists, and they were being kidnapped, raped, and murdered in frightening numbers.[7] People were being shot dead for something as simple as having a cell phone. And shops and restaurants were being looted and destroyed.[8]

To make matters worse, back at home, President Bush and British Prime Minister Tony Blair were looking like liars. The so-called Downing Street Memo had just been leaked to the press, revealing that British officials had always known the case for war was thin, and that the Bush administration had pushed for the war to be "justified by the conjunction of terrorism and WMD," despite clear evidence that Iraq had neither. It was now obvious that Bush and his cohorts had planned to invade Iraq long before 9/11.[9]

Mickiela heard little of all this, of course, but she did know the war was more dangerous than ever and that she was about to enter its fray. Her new job was to protect Camp Speicher from attack by guarding its entrance and searching incoming convoys and cars. Sometimes she sat in a tank just outside the camp, either as its gunner or driver. Other times she walked the guard tower, a high platform mounted with a powerful machine gun, from which she was supposed to radio in to headquarters whenever she saw signs of danger or attacks. "I was in a daze the whole time, 'cause I worked nights and we were shot at all the time. When they say only men are allowed on the frontlines, that's the biggest crock of shit!"

Often she witnessed incoming convoys being blown up or mortared because Highway One, the main artery through northern Iraq, passed right by the camp's entrance; a road so dangerous it was known as the Highway of Death.

"Once this convoy got hit—it looked like a huge flash in the night— and it drove in to us with the wounded. This civilian got out of his car throwing up 'cause his brother right beside him had been shot in the throat. I was on the tank out on the road, right there looking at him—the guy throwing up was shot in the leg." She watched anxiously while her comrades radioed for an ambulance, but it took forever to come because the system of radio contacts and permissions was so inefficient. "By the time it finally came, it was too late. The guy who'd been shot in the neck had died, and his brother looked like he was losing his leg."

Mickiela saw several American soldiers wounded in attacks like this, but never any who died. "I only saw dead hajis. But ever since Nana died, death doesn't affect me in the same way. It just makes me sad."

While Mickiela was talking about her time at the checkpoint, some self-protective lore came out in her words. "I don't know if it's true, but I heard that Iraqis shoot with their eyes closed and they pray, so when they shoot the bullets go up and don't hit anyone. So I was never too worried. It's only when they were down in the road and they'd shoot straight when you'd be worried. Or when the mortars came in, which was about twice a month. The mortars is death! I couldn't think about that."

Not infrequently, Mickiela's team had to fire back, either at the invisible fighters shooting at them out of the night, or because a vehicle wouldn't slow down as it approached the base. They shot at a civilian once because they mistakenly thought he was a suicide bomber. "Thank God he had bulletproof windows, or he would've been dead."

I asked Mickiela if she was frightened when she had to shoot back. "No, but sometimes I'd be scared when we were getting attacked. I would envision these crazy Iraqi guys coming like an Indian or something. But mostly, I didn't let myself think about it. I've always lived like everything happens for a reason and I'm gonna die anyway. So I was never afraid of dying. I was afraid of losing limbs or scarring my face. Or of tripping because walking is hard. You're hot, you've got all this heavy equipment, and if you make one mistake you can end up injuring yourself really bad. Same with the vehicles; a lot of people get sent home from falling off the vehicles 'cause they're so high off the ground."

Her sense of danger was fed by her unit's creaky equipment, for even though Mickiela was in Iraq two years after Jen and Abbie, she had the same Vietnam War–era armor and broken radios. "And the ambulances rattled and shook—I can't imagine riding in one of those if you're wounded."

As nerve-racking as her checkpoint work was, she still preferred it to her previous job. The sunsets and sunrises were beautiful, and she liked her team of five guys, even though they gave her trouble over being female. "When we were being attacked, they tried to make me stay in the back. They'd say, 'It's because you're like our little sister. We don't want something to happen to you.' I said, 'Don't look at me like I'm your little sister, 'cause I'm not. I'm a soldier, not a gender. I'm a soldier just like you.' So then they took it to the next level. We had to go out on the road, and no one likes to be on the road. They consider the soldiers who go out on the road sacrifice soldiers, 'cause they take the first hit if anything happens. So for a while, they put me on the road every night!"

LOVE AND THE WOLVES

Mickiela worked at the checkpoint for six months, and the entire time she and Joseph spent every moment they could together. "His roommates were cool; they got along with me. We put a sheet up for privacy. But if he hadn't been there in Iraq, it would have been terrible. We kept each other sane."

Being with Joseph also gave her protection from the other men, especially as he was the team's sergeant and well liked. But as soon he left for a two-week vacation, this changed. "The other guys hit on me as soon as he was gone. And when he got back they all told him bad stories about me. They wanted us to break up so they could have a chance with me."

It has long been the practice for military women to choose a boyfriend or a husband to protect themselves from their predatory colleagues. Colonel Karpinski lamented this in her memoir: "Many of the women felt besieged. They couldn't take a step without the wolves closing in. All too typically, a young woman would settle on one guy as a way to deflect all the others." The tragedy, she wrote, was that a young woman who had joined the army to seek an education and build a career would instead end up married and pregnant at nineteen.[10]

Another reason why so many women cling to a boyfriend during their time at war may be because he is her substitute for what every soldier should have but so many women don't: a cadre of trustworthy comrades.

All together, Mickiela spent eight months in Iraq, but even though she was longing to go home, she would never let herself count down the days as other soldiers did. "You never know if you might be extended and that's too disappointing. You can go nuts like that." She was right to worry. Recruiting for the army and National Guard had dropped so drastically by 2005 that soldiers were having their tours extended all the time, often by more than a year.[11] Many were also being sent back to Iraq involuntarily after coming home, even though they had finished out their contracts, under the stop-loss provision, which allows the armed forces to keep soldiers on active duty until six months after a war ends. Stop-loss has been a major cause of distress among soldiers in this war, for it has sent back thousands of troops traumatized by earlier tours who had counted on being able to stay home and recover. Some even question its legality, calling stop-loss a backdoor draft. Nonetheless, by early 2006, over 50,000 troops had been redeployed under stop-loss measures, and 12,500 more were in the pipeline.[12]

By the time Mickiela was in her last month, November 2005, over two thousand soldiers had died and the war was looking like a disaster even to Americans. Rep. John Murtha (D-PA) reflected this when he called for the United States to withdraw its troops with these words: "The war in Iraq is not going as advertised. It is a flawed policy wrapped in illusion." He then cited a leaked opinion poll from the British Ministry of Defense showing that 80 percent of Iraqis now opposed the presence of foreign troops in their country.[13]

Had Mickiela heard this, she would have agreed. "We dug ourselves into a big hole and it's never-ending. We never gave the Iraqis full power to protect themselves. Everyone felt it was wrong to be there. Everyone I knew wanted to get out."

On November 15, 2005, her unit's service in Iraq was finally over. Tired and thin, she flew back to the States with Joseph sitting beside her on the plane. They held hands and slept, leaning against one another. But as for what would happen to their future together once they got home, she had no idea.

TWELVE

Mommy, Love You.
Hope You Don't
Get Killed in Iraq

Terris Dewalt-Johnson, 2005–2006

Terris arrived in Iraq a month after Mickiela, on April 12, 2005, with the same company of teenaged soldiers and incompetent leaders she'd had at Fort Bragg. As the plane rose up and away from North Carolina, she thought about the family she'd left behind: Terrence, who was being so supportive, and her four children. So when the young soldiers around her started cracking jokes about going to Iraq, she gave them a piece of her mind.

"I don't know what this means to you, but to me it isn't a game," she told them fiercely, glaring at them with her striking hazel eyes. "I have four kids who will have no understanding if I'm killed. Nobody, the president or anybody, can make a child understand 'your mother died for your country, she was a good soldier, she fought well.' All they'll know is they no longer have a mother. If I'm killed, they're gonna hate their president and the U.S. government for the rest of their lives.'"

Terris never forgot this thought throughout the whole time she was at war. She had to stay alive for the sake of her family.

Her unit only lingered for nineteen days in Kuwait before it was sent into Iraq on a convoy, and she was as shocked as Jen had been at the country's poverty. "We saw kids on the sides of roads using hand signals to beg for food and water, kids no more than two or three years old, barefoot and dirty." She raised a cupped hand to her mouth over and over to demonstrate. "We saw how they live in makeshift mud houses put together with pieces of clothing or plastic. It makes you realize how easy you have it in the U.S., how we are blessed."

The poverty Terris saw was no longer only that caused by the earlier wars and sanctions, but also the result of three years of the new war, with all its corruption and incompetence. Under Saddam, the poor had at least received food rations. But rations were no longer distributed, food markets were regularly bombed, truck drivers bringing food were being kidnapped and killed, aid was being stolen, and work was scarce and dangerous because anyone seen cooperating with Americans could be murdered. And there was still so little power that farmers could not grow their crops and families could not preserve their food. The sight of this poverty sowed the first doubts in Terris's mind about whether she and her fellow soldiers belonged in Iraq at all.

The unit was based at Camp Adder in the south, another bleak pit stop of run-down buildings and gravelly sand. About twelve miles southwest of Nasiriyah, Adder was close to where Jen had been stationed, but unlike Camp Bucca it had a few luxuries: fast-food joints, air conditioning, a gym, an Internet room, the same kind of tin-box trailers Mickiela had lived in, and what soldiers liked to call their outdoor movie theater—a patch of painted brick wall. Nothing looked chic—the Internet room was made of bare plywood and many of the buildings were wrecked, with shot-out windows and empty gray rooms—but it was more comfortable than the bases that Jen, Abbie, and Eli had stayed in. The oddest sights were the Iraqi-built cement bunkers, which looked like giant gray molehills dotted over the landscape.

What impressed Terris most about Camp Adder, though, was that it was only a few miles from the ancient Sumerian city of Ur, which is mentioned several times in the Bible as the birthplace of the prophet Abraham. Ur was settled in about 900 BC, became the capital of the Sumerian civilization, and is one of the world's most ancient and famous structures, a huge fortress of yellow clay brick that resembles the peak of a pyramid topped by a giant pair of shoulders. "I had the privilege of taking a tour there, and the person that gives the tours said he's a descendent of Abraham himself. But then, aren't we all?" Terris said. Being a religious Christian, she was thrilled to be so near Ur; yet that very month, other American soldiers were defacing it with graffiti and stealing its bricks.[1]

Because Terris arrived in Iraq already in trouble with her first sergeant and commander, she was initially put in a backroom as a pencil pusher. "These people were convinced I was cuckoo," she said with a grin. However, when the company's colonel found out that its convoys were under the command of a lowly E-4 specialist, which was against the rules, he ordered the command to find a noncommissioned officer to take over instead. The only candidate was Terris, an E-5 sergeant and experienced driver with fourteen years of military service under her belt. Yet instead of putting her in charge, her leaders made her assistant to the specialist, even though his rank was below hers. She was outraged, and in her indomitable way, she let them know it.

"I'm going to suck this one up," she told them crisply, "but the next go-round, it won't happen again."

Soon Terris was going out on convoys almost every day. Sometimes she drove the new five-ton, which resembled a Humvee but was bigger and better armored, and sometimes she was its gunner, handling the machine gun on the roof. (She showed me a photograph of herself at this time, sitting behind the gun in the uniform, helmet, goggles, and mouth cover that make American soldiers look like space warriors.) Then, for a reason she had never fathomed, a month after her unit had arrived, her leaders ordered her convoy to drive up to Camp Anaconda, near Balad, fifty miles north of Baghdad. Anaconda was so dangerous that soldiers called it Mortaritaville, yet her convoy's trucks had no armor and were not even authorized to be out on the road. Nevertheless, out they were sent—at night.

Like most convoys, Terris's was made up of three gun trucks, one in the front, one in the middle, and one at the rear, with a row of tractor-trailers between each one (often driven by civilians hired by KBR and other private contractors). Terris was driving the middle gun truck when, not far from Anaconda, a roadside bomb exploded beside one of the trucks in front of her.

"It was so loud it scared the living shit out of me! My heart was pumping so fast and hard it felt like it was going to jump out of my chest. I felt lightheaded, as though I was dreaming, and I was confused and shaking. I remember saying something like, 'Oh shit, what the fuck was that?' It was dark and I couldn't see 'cause of the smoke from the blast, so that made matters worse."

The drivers at the front drove out of the "kill zone"—the immediate area of the bomb—but the rest, including Terris, had to sit and wait in their trucks for the bomb squad to come and destroy another bomb that had been spotted in the same area—they couldn't move for fear of triggering it. "The worst part was sitting out there in the pitch black for an hour and half, waiting for them to get there. I was expecting to get attacked at any minute and my head was racing with thoughts. But I showed none of what I was feeling to my soldiers.

"Finally they came and blew it up. That was probably one of the brightest lights I've ever seen in my life! Thanks to the grace of God nobody got killed, but we had no business being on the road with those vehicles! It was a suicide mission."

When the higher commanders found out what had happened, they ordered the crew to leave their trucks at Anaconda and take an airplane back to Camp Adder, making it clear to everyone how reckless the excursion had been.

Two days later, the unit's leaders ordered the soldiers into formation, the military version of an assembly. Terris expected an apology, or at least a mention of this colossal error, but her leaders said not a word about it.

"They were blabbering on about nothing—setting up the Internet, this kind of stuff. Then they asked, 'Anybody got anything to say?' Nobody said anything—but the soldiers were young and trained not to question their seniors. So I raised my hand. 'First Sergeant, did y'all forget about the incident two days ago? We were attacked up at Anaconda, and from what I hear we had no business being up there? Somebody needs to apologize to us. Do you realize your soldiers have no confidence in the leadership now? Don't you give a damn about us?'"

The first sergeant, the same man Terris had clashed with at Fort Bragg, looked daggers at her but declined to answer.

"When you have a female with that type of attitude in the military, it does not go over well with a lot of men," Terris said with a chuckle. "I was a little too boisterous for them."

MAYHEM

Not long after the attack, Terris was promoted to convoy commander. She deserved the honor, but it meant she now had one of the most dangerous jobs of the war. She was in charge of three gun trucks and fifteen to twenty huge white tractor-trailers called reefers, and she usually had to drive in the front, which put her in the position most likely to trigger a roadside bomb or receive the first fire of an ambush. Her task was to get these monster convoys to one base or another, deliver the goods they carried, and bring everybody back safely.

Almost all her missions were at night, so she would leave the camp at eleven at night and be out on the road until seven the next morning, which could hardly have been a riskier shift. "For a long time I was the only one in the whole company who escorted convoys out on the roads," she said. She was also usually the only woman. "We only had two females, but I did more missions and the most dangerous ones." One of her regular runs was north to Baghdad International Airport, but she also went to Mosul, Balad, and Tikrit, all of which took her along the Highway of Death, a fact she chose not to tell her family.

Ironically, while Terris was risking her life every day in these convoys, she usually didn't know whether they were carrying something as harmless as toilet paper or as dangerous as fuel or ammunition. Sometimes the KBR trucks she was escorting had nothing in them at all because KBR likes to charge the government for as many convoy runs as possible, whether they deliver anything or not.[2]

As convoy commander, Terris had to enforce the rules governing the way convoys are supposed to work: trucks must always stay in their place in line, must never allow outside vehicles to squeeze between them, and must never stop on the highways because that leaves them vulnerable to attack. But road conditions in wartime Iraq are much too chaotic for rules. Convoys up to a mile long barrel down the sand-covered highways, swinging into oncoming traffic lanes to avoid bombs or broken-down cars. Traffic lights don't work because of the dearth of electricity. Civilian drivers become inadvertently trapped between convoy trucks. And because soldiers are afraid of being attacked, their reactions are often barely under control. All this leads to constant lethal accidents; it is how Private Green, the rebellious young soldier in Eli's charge, killed a family of six.

The mayhem is worsened by the lack of cultural training that so worried Jen and Abbie. Soldiers commonly point a clenched fist at cars to make them stop, whereas the Iraqi stop signal is to form an oval with your finger and thumb and move your arm up and down. And then the sight of an armed soldier shouting in an incomprehensible language, red-faced and angry, is so terrifying it often makes people freeze or panic. Freezing can be misinterpreted as a refusal to obey orders. Running or driving away in a panic can get you shot.

Terris described this chaos as she saw it. "When we're coming, civilians need to get out of the way, so we're flashing them off, giving them warning shots. But when your vehicle is moving and jumping around, if you fire a shot, it's not going to be as accurate as it would if you were stationary. So sometimes a round goes where you don't really aim it to go, and an innocent Iraqi or a child or a woman winds up dead. You feel for them, but the military has been in Iraq for so long that all Iraqis have got to know the routine. You've got to know the law, what's allowed and what's not allowed. You know you're not supposed to be on that road."

She paused, as if questioning what she had just said, and then went on to argue with herself. "I mean, I know this person may be trying to get their kids somewhere in a hurry, and you're telling them to sit on the side of the road and wait until the convoy passes. And then a few feet behind, maybe another convoy's coming. It could be hours. But we don't know when a car might be a VBED [Vehicle-Borne Explosive Device, i.e., a car bomb]. So you don't take a chance. Because if you do, you're gambling with your life."

Terris warmed to her theme, trying to get across the sense of danger every soldier feels on Iraqi roads. "You can't let your guard down, especially when you go through cities. They got their fruit stands out, there's congestion. You're going through beeping the horn and waving or firing in the air to get these guys out of the way. But sometimes they crash into each other in their hurry to move, and roll over on their sides—they already drive crazy, no speed limit. Sometimes they get so scared that instead of hitting the brakes, they hit the gas and crash into people. So yeah, innocent people die."

Terris told the story of a young gunner who panicked in these circumstances. He had been working in the base office, which had earned him the nickname Professor Stapler, much to his chagrin, and had felt left out when other soldiers came back with battle stories. He wanted to tell stories, too, so he asked to go on a mission and was assigned to Terris's convoy.

"We're in the lead gun truck going through a crowded street. I was in the passenger seat and he's up in the gunner's chute. We've got traffic coming at us, civilians all over the place. And this car comes toward us, closer and closer. It could be a bomb in a vehicle, or it could cause an accident. Now, we're told the procedure to follow on the road. You have an escalation of force, EOF, from warning to fatal. The first step is you wave at the vehicle or people and tell them to get out of your way. If that doesn't work, you shoot a flare, although in the daylight people might not see it. The third step is you show your weapon. If that doesn't work, the fourth step is you give them a warning shot in the air. And the last step is you fire that .50-cal [belt-fed machine gun] to kill. But soldiers think they have to go through all those steps before they can shoot to kill, so they get confused. And they've got to account for every bullet they shoot, and that makes them not want to fire too.

"So being that this is my gunner's first time, he doesn't really know what to do. This vehicle is coming too close for comfort, but when I tell him to fire a warning shot, he doesn't shoot. So I tap him. 'Hey, man, don't be afraid to fucking shoot that weapon. You do know how to shoot, right?'

"'Uh, okay, Sarge.'

"This vehicle is getting closer and closer, but he still doesn't shoot. Most of the time the Iraqis know the rules, yet they will test your convoy to see how close they can get. It's like playing chicken. But we don't have time to play chicken with these idiots. So I hit him hard, and I say, 'I tell you to fucking fire, man, you fucking fire, okay? Don't never let a vehicle get that close to my fucking convoy.' He knows I'm not playing now.

"So the car is coming, he fires at it, and he makes the hood fly up. The metal just peels right up, and the whole car just goes *whomp, whomp, whomp*—rolls over on its side and tumbles over this bank. My gunner panics. He's only nineteen. He grabs his head. 'Oh my God, I think I killed somebody!'

"I shake him. 'Look, it wasn't your fault. I don't think you shot nobody. He's all right. He knows damn well he didn't have no business coming that close to our convoy. Now we've still got shit coming at us, you hear me? So I need you to focus right now and pay attention.'

"But his face is red, and he's like, 'Oh my God, my God!'"

The young gunner was not only panicking but reacting to his first "kill" with horror and remorse, which military psychologists say is typical of most soldiers, despite all their training. It is only after they have killed a few times that they become inured or even addicted to it.[3]

Terris never did find out what happened to the driver of the car because convoys aren't allowed to stop and check on injured civilians. But after that, she said, the gunner changed from a quiet, shy country boy to a gung ho, raging soldier. I asked her if she thought this was an improvement.

"In a sense, no. But after he had a story to tell the guys, it made him feel like he'd matured from a boy to a man. A lot of young soldiers feel that way. They see themselves as men 'cause they fought for their country. Women too. They think, 'I'm not some wimpy female because of the job I did in Iraq.'"

Many of the accidents she witnessed were caused not only by the chaos on the roads but also by the civilian truck drivers with whom the military had to work, who had never been trained to drive in convoys or how to avoid bombs and deal with attacks. What's more, these men, who were from poor countries such as Nepal, the Philippines, and Pakistan, as well as Iraq, were so desperate for jobs that they would claim they could drive stick-shift trucks and tractor-trailers when they couldn't. KBR would hire them anyway, paying them a fraction of what they had previously paid American drivers, who by this time in the war were too afraid to do the work.[4]

One accident that haunts Terris was with an Iraqi driver like this in her convoy. They were returning from a mission at five in the morning when he lost control of his tractor-trailer, which slid down a sand embankment and rolled over, twisting with a terrible shriek of metal. The front cab snapped right off the trailer, flipped over, and landed on top of it. Terris was sure he was dead.

She stopped the convoy in horror and ran over with some other soldiers. To her astonishment, the driver climbed out of his smashed cab. "These were strong little people, I'll tell you!" She hurried to help him. "He's got blood running down, he's trying to speak, but I don't speak Arabic so I don't know what he's saying. We're telling him to calm down, we're putting an IV in him, and he's still trying to say something and pulling out his papers to show us. And when he leans over, his head is open, and we can see all this white liquidy stuff. He's more worried about losing his job and not being able to feed his family than about his head being split open to the brain."

Most of Terris's missions were harrowing like this, but when it was time for debriefing back on base, all her leaders would talk about was chickenshit. "They're telling us soldiers are violating dress codes by wearing the wrong T-shirts for PT. Dude, I been fired at! I don't wanna hear about no damn T-shirt!"

CHILDREN AND TROUBLE

Like Abbie, Terris took solace from meeting the children of Iraq, who would surround the convoys whenever they stopped, begging for food and drink. The command had forbidden the soldiers to give them anything, but many found this so heartless that they disobeyed, Terris among them. "It made me mad! We have more water and MREs than we can use, and we can't give them any? These kids are hungry and thirsty! You tell us we're over here to help them, but I can't even give them water?"

The sight of these children made her yearn even more for her own kids. She wrote e-mails to them and called home every other day, but the knowledge that she was missing landmarks in their lives ate at her painfully. She knew they were missing her, too, especially when Ronald, her youngest, wrote her a Mother's Day e-mail:

"Mommy, love you. Happy Mother's Day. Wish you were here. Hope you don't get killed in Iraq. Okay, bye."

"My youngest don't beat around the bush," Terris said, smiling sadly. "But oh my goodness, that got to me."

She knew the family was suffering from her absence in other ways, as well. Terrence was doing his best, but it was hard to work full time and look after four children, even though the occasional friend would help. He didn't have time to take the kids to the library or sit and help them through their homework, as she had done, and their grades were suffering as a result.

The difficulties of being a parent and a soldier have become a pressing issue in the Iraq War, exacerbated by the length and repetition of deployments and the high numbers of reservists and National Guard members with families: over 760,000 parents were deployed in 2008.[5] Terris and several other soldier parents told me how much it hurt to call home and hear a little voice say, "Mommy, please come back." And they agonized over what would happen to their children if they were killed. This is especially hard for the single parents in this war, who make up some 74,000 of regular troops and at least 68,000 of the National Guard and reserves. Because the military demands that parent soldiers deploy as long as they have anyone at all to care for their children, parents must sometimes leave their kids in fraught and uncertain circumstances. This makes them worry constantly while they are away, and they are right to worry. The rates of child neglect and maltreatment more than double while parents are on active duty.[6]

Terris was at least able to keep up with her family through the Internet, but that had a downside, too, for it meant she had to keep parenting as well as being a soldier, which only added to her anxieties. (Many soldiers say the easy access to their loved ones through Web-cams, e-mail, and cell phones is so wrenching that it makes being at war harder, not easier.) This came to a head on June 2, 2005, two months after she arrived in Iraq. It was the day of her daughter Shawntia's high-school graduation, which upset Terris deeply to miss. It was also the anniversary of her brother Ronald's murder.

She was sitting in her trailer talking to a friend about this when there was a knock on the door. She opened it to find the company commander standing there holding a piece of paper and flanked by two big sergeants with rifles. The commander ordered her friend out of the trailer and stepped inside.

Terris's feelings about her commanding officers had not improved over her first two months in Iraq. She had continued to question them when she felt their orders made no sense, and they had continued to dislike it. But because she was particularly upset that day, the commander's presence was even less welcome than usual.

She asked him why he had done her the honor of visiting her trailer.

He told her to sit down. She did. "Remember the, uh, issue we had in Bragg?" he stammered, clearly afraid of her. "They said you need to go see the medic people?'"

"Yes, sir, I remember that."

"Well, it's come back up. They say..."

"Sir, hold on. Who is 'they,' sir, and what's come back up? Is it on the paper there? Can I see the paper, sir?"

He handed over the paper. It was the same order for a mental evaluation that she had been threatened with back at Fort Bragg when she had refused to shoot on the firing range. The paper called her a "loner," which she found pretty laughable, as she had plenty of friends, and it said she was "acting out of character."

"Sir, didn't we go through this once before? Who are these people saying this?"

The commander looked over at Terris's rifle leaning up against the wall, then turned to the two sergeants. "Is that her weapon?" he said.

Terris was sitting right there. "Sir, yes, that is my weapon," she replied, trying to keep her temper. "Do you want to check it to see if it's clean?"

"We're going to have to remove the weapon."

Having a weapon removed is a serious disgrace, for it means the soldier will have to be escorted everywhere, even to the bathroom, and will no longer be able to defend herself. This was what had been done to Eli, another outspoken woman of color, and like her, Terris was convinced that both racism and sexism were at play in this incident. "A week or two before, we'd had a little white boy that locked and loaded his weapon at another soldier in the trailer behind me because they'd had a disagreement. But this little white boy was able to walk around with his weapon. I hadn't threatened anybody and they wanted to take my weapon from me—and I'm in a war zone?"

Terris was still outwardly calm, but inside she was furious. "Remove my weapon? I don't quite understand you, sir," she said between her teeth. "You're taking my weapon because I don't want to have a mental eval? That doesn't make sense, sir. Is this a direct order?"

"Yes, this is a direct order."

"Well, sir, I'm bucking your direct order. You know I haven't threatened anybody."

"We're taking the weapon."

"Sir, let me explain something to you," Terris said, her voice rising. "I didn't have a problem with you before. But if you remove that weapon, sir, I am going to have a *major* fucking problem with you, sir."

He looked at her to see if she was serious. She was. "Get the weapon," he said to the sergeants, and handed her a memo stating she would now have to be escorted wherever she went. She jumped to her feet, balled up the memo and threw it at his head.

"Sir, let me tell you something. You fucking started this, sir, okay? You want a fucking war? I will give you a war! You fucking pussy, all of you! Get the fuck out of my trailer!"

The three men scuttled out, leaving Terris's rifle behind.

Terris slammed her door and began throwing care packages and cans of food around her trailer in a rage. She opened the door and screamed, "You fucking idiot!" slammed the door shut again, and continued her rampage.

The next thing she knew, three military police officers (MPs) banged on her door—she could see them through the window. She ignored them for fifteen minutes. They cleared the whole area, afraid she would start shooting at random, as soldiers sometimes do when they crack up at war: the source of some of that "friendly fire" we hear about. They kept knocking. Finally, she yelled through the door, "I'm not coming out there, okay? Where the hell is that pussy commander of mine?"

"Your commander isn't out here," they called back. Friends told her later he was peeking around a corner.

By now the MPs had surrounded her trailer; Terris could see their shadows through the window. She still wouldn't open the door, but they had a master key, so they tried to unlock it themselves. She stuck her own key in from the inside, jamming the lock. But when she heard the hinges of the flimsy door straining as they pushed against it, she realized she couldn't keep this up. So she pulled out the knives she always carried on her, and stood facing them.

"I always had knives strapped to my chest and my waist and my boots because I was a pretty rough individual in my day, you know, fighting and all," she explained to me. "I was a hooah [gung ho] kind of soldier, a type A personality."

The MPs burst through the door to a frightening sight: Terris in full battle gear, standing in fighting position, a knife in each hand and an expression ready to kill.

"Whoa," said the lead MP, backing up, his two subordinates stumbling behind him. "Calm down. We just wanted to make sure you was okay."

"I'm okay. You can leave now. Did my commander send you in here after me?"

"No, no. Someone heard some commotion and called us about it."

The MP ran his eyes over the mess she'd made until he spotted the family pictures on her wall. Among them was a photograph of her three murdered brothers. And when she saw him look at it, she seemed to hear one of her brothers say, "Are you crazy? They're going to slam your little butt down."

She turned toward the picture and said, "Be quiet."

When she turned back, she could see that the MP thought her pretty loony by then, but he stayed calm. "That your family?" he asked. "Your family would like to see you get back safe, you know." And with more talk like this, he finally calmed her down enough to persuade her to leave without her knives and with no more resistance.

Her punishment was that she had to undergo the despised mental evaluation. Her triumph was—to do that—she had to go home.

MARY POPPINS

Terris was flown back to Fort Bragg at the end of June 2005. There, she had her requisite interview with two psychologists, who decided there was nothing wrong with her and declared her fit for duty. She figured the real problem was that the commander was scared of her as a woman with a big mouth, and this was confirmed when he later did something he never would have done to a man: he tried to call Terrence to ask why his wife was so rough.

She got wind of this and stopped it, knowing if Terrence got a call from the military he would assume she was wounded or dead. "So the commander went behind my back and called my momma!" Her mother told her the conversation had gone like this:

"She's so stern at times," the commander said. "Is she always like that?"

"Well, she has a way about her. If she feels things ain't right, yeah, she will question it."

"She's got a classic G.I. Jane personality."

"Well, she is at war," her mother snapped back. "What kind of personality do you expect her to have, a damn Mary Poppins?"

"They called the wrong person," Terris told me, laughing. "They should have known I got my mouth from somewhere."

Terris returned to Iraq at the end of August 2005, and during that fall and winter she continued to run her convoys through attacks and accidents and continued to criticize her command. One of her pet peeves was the lack of Arabic taught to soldiers; something that often caused lethal misunderstandings out on the roads. "I told our colonel one time, 'Sir, I'm going to have to get a translator or something because I almost killed me a couple of Iraqis today, I really did.'"

What had happened was this: Terris was leading a convoy of three gun trucks and twenty-five tractor-trailers one night just after Ramadan, the Muslim holy holiday—a time when violence in Iraq had peaked every year of the war—when the convoy ahead of them was hit with a roadside bomb, injuring its commander. This brought her own convoy to a standstill. The drivers were told to turn off their lights and wait until the bomb squad swept the area and gave the all clear to move again. After the usual nerve-jangling wait, the clear came, and they moved a mile or two down the road only to be attacked again with small arms fire. "You could hear it. *Ping! Ping!* You could see the rounds flying." Terris whistled loudly. "You could hear the pinging hitting the vehicles."

As soon as the civilian truck drivers heard the guns they panicked, pulled out of line, and tried to drive away. This tangled up the convoy like a ball of knotted string, blocking in Terris's lead gun truck and bringing the entire row of twenty-eight trucks to a halt.

Just as they were trapped like this, a firefight burst around them: smoke, screaming bullets, jacked-up soldiers, terrified drivers.

The soldiers fired back, and when at last the fight died down, Terris managed to untangle her convoy and get it moving again. "We go about three hundred meters out of the kill zone and I have to stop and get out to assess the damage, make sure I got all my vehicles and that everybody is still alive and kicking. But when I get out, the hajis want to jump out of their vehicles too. And I'm thinking, somebody who looks like you has just got finished firing at me, okay? I don't know who you are, so I don't want you out on the road near me."

She yelled and gestured at them to get back in their trucks, but they wouldn't move. "They think I'm telling them they got a lovely paint job on their cab or something. So finally, I'm like, *Pow!* I fire a warning shot. And it's as though the muzzle is speaking itself. They get in."

"So, sir," she said to the colonel after it was all over. "The only thing they seem to understand is this weapon. That's why I need a translator."

CHRISTMAS TROUBLES

By the time Terris had been in Iraq for nine months, she and the children were missing each other badly. "Mommy?" read one plaintive e-mail from her youngest daughter Martrese. "Are you coming home for my birthday?" Martrese is a spry little girl, all skin and bones, who loves to read and ask questions. Her birthday is on Christmas Eve.

"Well, sweetie," Terris wrote back with regret, "Mommy can't say, 'cause I don't know."

But then, with surprising luck, she was given leave to go home after all, which meant she could be there for Christmas and the holiday birthdays of both Martrese and her oldest son, Alexander.

Terris had spent every Christmas of her life with her mother and siblings, and this holiday of 2005 was going to be no different, so once she was back from Iraq, she and Terrence packed up the kids and drove up to Washington, D.C. But the family was still burdened with trouble. Her mother had never really recovered from the murders of her three sons. Her sisters were both still addicts, and one had also been diagnosed with bipolar disorder. Her violent stepfather Frank was still on the scene. And, to make matters worse, a deep resentment had arisen between two of her sisters because of a horrible tragedy: one sister had taken the baby of the other home to baby-sit him, had fallen asleep with him on the couch because she was drunk, and he had slipped between some pillows and suffocated to death.

Both these sisters were to be at the Christmas dinner, so the atmosphere was already explosive. Then, one of the sisters arrived drunk, saw their grandfather sitting at the table, and said, "What the hell you doing here?"

"Hey, don't talk to Granddad like that," Terris snapped in her sergeant voice. "Tone it down or leave."

Her sister sneered and retorted, "I hope when you go back to Iraq you fucking die."

At that, Terris lost it. She grabbed her sister's head and was about to flip her onto the ground, using a hold she'd learned in training, when her children and nieces came running in. That stopped her. It was one of those painful moments common to soldiers when they realize how brutalized they've been by war.

She let her sister go. "You know what?" she said, "I need to leave."

Terris returned to Iraq in January 2006 to find discipline at her base falling apart: four rapes had been uncovered, two of which were being prosecuted; several "peeping Toms" had been caught in the women's bathrooms; and the soldiers were openly fed up with what they had come to see as a nightmare of meaningless fighting. "We saw what was going on and we didn't see any improvement, so we're thinking, we're putting our lives on the line for what? If you asked the majority of soldiers, 'Do you know what our purpose is in Iraq?' they couldn't tell you. Some of them would give you some political bull-crap to justify it, or say because we wear the uniform we're supposed to not speak bad about it. But most soldiers would say they don't see the point." According to a poll taken at the time, Terris was right: 72 percent of the soldiers in Iraq believed America should end the war within a year.[7]

"See the circle where this table is?" she continued, leaning over the frame of the coffee table she had broken in a rage. "Say right in that circle is where the military has built a place for us soldiers. You've got running water. You've got showers. You've got a toilet in there you can flush. You've got trailers with beds and mattresses and air conditioning. You have washers and dryers. You've got big generators running all night. And we're not paying the Iraqis anything for this. No property taxes, nothing. You've got Taco Bells, Subways, PXs, good food. I mean, some nights you have lobster, shrimp, steak. They provide all of that for you here in this little circle." She moved her finger over. "But here, right on the outskirts, you've got Iraqi families living in huts with no running water, who are starving."

She looked up at me and shook her head. "We're just bullies."

Given how critical she was of the war, I later asked her the question all soldiers hate the most to be asked. I put it in an e-mail, knowing she always answers immediately. This is a difficult question to answer, I wrote, but had she killed any Iraqis? And if so, how did she feel about it?

After a longer pause than usual, she wrote back.

"You're right, that is a difficult question to answer, but I will answer it to the best of my ability. Yes, I manned and fired the .50-cal, but I was never on it during a big attack. I did fire my M-4 [assault rifle] at Iraqis, and honestly I can't say whether I hit one or not because I never stopped to check. I always kept my convoy moving.

"The battalion I was under did call all the convoy commanders in and inform us that we were shooting and killing innocent civilians. They called us in because the civilians were complaining about soldiers. So they wanted us to be aware of what was going on and to make sure there was a threat before firing our weapons. That only happened once. I hope I answered your question."

Terris may be no Mary Poppins, but she is honest. And soldiers are not often willing to be honest about what they do in war.

A LAST ATTACK

In March 2006, just a month before her tour was up, Terris found herself in another situation where speaking a little Arabic might have saved lives. She was driving in a convoy when its lead truck swerved to avoid an oncoming car, causing the trucks behind it to crash into each other, hard. Terris's truck slammed to a stop so violently it propelled her forward, cracking her head against the windshield and her knees against the front of the cab. When she'd recovered enough to look around, she saw the steering wheel had snapped. She and her team were marooned.

Shakily, they climbed out of the truck and took up guard positions in case of attack, but immediately were mobbed by Iraqi children. Two hours passed like this, the crowd of civilians around them growing. Terris knew this was dangerous; she thought she and her team should get into a working truck and drive out of there, but her command thought otherwise.

Finally, some Iraqi police arrived, but just as they were dispersing the crowd a car came hurtling toward them. The soldiers and police waved at it to slow down, but it didn't. This is often the sign of a suicide bomber. "So we fired at it. *Pow!*" Terris said.

The driver hit the brakes, jumped out, and ran to the passenger side. He looked inside and started screaming. The front passenger had been hit.

"I'm like, 'Oh, shit!' Next thing you know, the kids were yelling at us, 'You bad, bad, bad!'"

Then the Iraqi police disappeared, the children vanished, and the street was suddenly empty and still. The soldiers stood there, looking around uncertainly.

"Then something went boom!" Rocks and gravel rained down on the soldiers—a building right beside them had been mortared. "Then there were rockets, and the ground shook. *Boom! Boom!* Then small arms fire, *Ping!* It's like, 'Fuck, let's go!' So everybody runs toward the vehicles. We left our broken-down truck and got out of there."

If Terris or any of the other soldiers had spoken Arabic, she realized, they would have understood that the people around them were talking about an attack coming, and the man they'd shot was simply trying to get out of the way.

Terris was left with a knot on her forehead and injuries to her knees and back. They were still hurting when she flew home a month later. It was April 13, 2006, by then, and she had just spent an entire year as a combat soldier.

Now she had to put all that behind her and be a wife and mother again.

PART THREE

After

q

THIRTEEN

Coming Home

MICKIELA MONTOYA

On the long flight back to Fort Dix from Iraq, Mickiela drifted in and out of uneasy sleep, her head on Joseph's shoulder. Every so often she would awake with a start, not knowing where she was, what awaited her, or even quite who she was anymore. Then she would doze off again, trying to push away her qualms.

Normally soldiers go through one to six days of demobilization (known as "demob") when they return, which includes having a medical exam, listening to lectures about how to cope with being home, and answering a questionnaire designed to reveal whether they are traumatized, the latter of which most see as a joke. But the minute Mickiela landed in New Jersey, she was given bad news. One of her great-grandmothers had died that very day, and Mickiela was needed at home immediately. So she skipped the demob, except for the physical, said a rushed goodbye to Joseph, and, heavy with unknowns, caught a commercial plane to Los Angeles.

For the entire flight Mickiela felt out of place, sitting in her uniform amidst all those civilians, sure that most of them had no idea where she had just been, let alone what she had experienced. "I was so nervous. I didn't know how my family was going to act with me, and I didn't know how I was going to act. I didn't know how I was going to fit back into being a civilian."

When the plane landed, she stumbled into the airport in a daze. The blaring colors made her dizzy, everybody looked sloppy and fat, and she felt self-conscious about the clumping way of walking she had developed to deflect the attention of men. "And nobody said welcome back or nothing. I was disappointed because you see on the news when people get home they get like fireworks and all this, but it was just me by myself. I just walked off the plane carrying my bags. And I still didn't believe I was out of Iraq until I seen my grandpa and my aunt, and my aunt gave me a hug."

The lack of reaction in the airport might have been caused by people's obliviousness to the fact that women were going to war, but it might also have reflected growing national doubts about the American presence in Iraq. It was November 2005 by then, and the fact that over 2,100 soldiers were dead and some 16,000 wounded while no visible progress had been made had caused support for the war to plummet to 37 percent, the lowest it had been since the invasion.[1]

When Mickiela found herself in the arms of her young aunt, she began to cry. "I never cry, ever. Only when Nana died. Then, 'cause we made a scene, someone finally said 'welcome back.' And that was the first time I believed I was out of Iraq."

For the next few weeks, she struggled to fit back into her previous life. She couldn't sleep for more than five hours at a time, having grown used to that schedule in Iraq; loud noises terrified her because they sounded like mortars; and she was constantly angry without knowing why. But hardest was feeling so out of sync with everyone else. "It's like you're a ghost, like you died and you're coming back to life and you've got to weasel your way back in because everybody had to adjust without you."

She also felt as if no one knew her anymore. "I came back a totally different person. I'm not as easygoing, I can't stand noise, I don't like being around a lot of people. And I lost how to dance! It's because I'm so in tune with marching. Now I have to be drunk to dance."

By a few weeks after her return, Mickiela was slipping into depression. "I've never been that way before, I've always been able to deal with things. But Iraq and the army and losing the baby and my grandma—it was really too much." She was also angered by the reactions she was getting as a woman. "We don't get the same respect, we have to fight for it. I don't even tell people about seeing death and being shot at anymore, 'cause they don't believe me. They assume all I did was office work."

It is not easy to change from a soldier back into a civilian. You can't drive through traffic lights or bully people out of your way anymore, you can't extract obedience at the point of a gun, and you have to try to care again about things like shopping and the problems of family and friends, even though these matters now seem maddeningly trivial. One of the main reasons soldiers reenlist is because they feel so alienated from their previous lives and families. Training and war have taught them to see their fellow soldiers as their families instead, and they feel unbearably guilty about being safe at home while their "brothers and sisters" are still at war, especially if they found real camaraderie there. As one male veteran told me, "I was in a medical unit in Iraq; I saw people killed every day. But for me that wasn't as hard as readjusting to the real world when I came back. I'm not the same person. My temper's changed. I've forgotten how to be a father. And my wife, she doesn't understand." Within a few months, he had filed for divorce and reenlisted.

Many returning soldiers are so shattered they can barely function. Their sleep is intermittent and plagued by nightmares. They are haunted by memories of the horrors they saw: mutilated bodies, children screaming in pain, dogs and cats eating human remains. Loud noises and traffic make them jumpy and aggressive, sick or paralyzed. Many cannot stop searching for or hallucinating bombs on the road and so are afraid to leave home. And any reminder of war, no matter how slight, can make them vomit, shake, or explode with anger.

War veterans also often feel worthless, numb, and withdrawn, unable to love or even care about anything, which can propel them into suicidal depressions. Some are so distraught they find themselves back from war only to be locked up in psychiatric wards for weeks. And then no one at home really knows what they've been through, and it seems impossible to explain.

"To this day I've never spoken about Iraq to my family," Mickiela said. "When they ask me how it was, I'm like, 'It was hot.' I don't want them to know anything, 'cause I don't want to feel sorry for myself. And the people you're close to won't understand anyhow. You can't hate them for not understanding, but a lot of times you do."

All the soldiers I talked to described feelings like these, feelings once known as soldier's heart, shell shock, or battle fatigue but now unfortunately labeled PTSD: post-traumatic stress disorder. (As one soldier put it, "What part of being emotionally and spiritually affected by gross violence is a *disorder?*")[2] This bland term is flung around constantly but is rarely described in any more detail than "nightmares, flashbacks, and irritability." Miriam Barton, the army sergeant from Oregon, described it more colorfully: "After I beaned this broad with a can of peas and tried to run somebody off the road, I was diagnosed with severe PTSD. It feels like God is pissing on your Cheerios."

The Pentagon estimates that 18–20.5 percent of troops come back from Iraq with PTSD or depression, but the true rate is likely much higher because this war is characterized by the four most potent triggers of trauma: killing close-up and the remorse and horror that accompanies it (as early as July 2004, 48 percent of soldiers and 65 percent of marines had already killed, and 95 percent of both had seen bodies and human remains);[3] seeing death and mutilation, often of one's friends; the terrifying unpredictability of guerilla warfare, when you cannot tell who or where the enemy is; and sexual violence by fellow soldiers, which all by itself is four times more likely to cause PTSD than combat.[4]

For these reasons, Iraq War veterans are suffering higher rates of war trauma than the veterans of Afghanistan or the first Gulf wars, and some think than of the Vietnam War as well. The rate of PTSD is also rising as more soldiers are kept at war longer and redeployed, despite having been diagnosed with trauma from earlier tours. By 2008, one-third of all the soldiers in Iraq had served there more than once.[5]

The Pentagon's count also fails to include the 50–60 percent of traumatized soldiers who are too ashamed or discouraged to seek help.[6] The military attitude is to "suck it up" when it comes to pain and trauma, so soldiers who break down while at war tend to be ridiculed as cowards or punished for "malingering"—that is, faking an illness, a legal offense that can result in jail time, demotion, and dishonorable discharge. Soldiers are also wary of admitting to trauma for fear they will be kept from going home or that their medical records will harm their military careers.[7] And many who do seek help are either ignored by military therapists who are dismissive of PTSD and sexual assault, or find VA treatment inadequate or harmful: overlarge therapy groups that retraumatize rather than comfort, insensitive counselors, and delays of many months for any treatment whatsoever.[8]

All this adds up to a cruel trap. If soldiers admit to being traumatized, they are seen as weaklings and cowards. If they don't admit it, they have to deal with it on their own. But when left untreated, war trauma is dangerous to soldiers and those around them. Iraq War veterans already have alarming rates of homicide, domestic violence, divorce, alcohol and drug abuse, and mental breakdowns; suicide rates are the highest they have ever been in the army; and the number of attempted suicides and self-inflicted injuries among soldiers has jumped six-fold since the war began.[9]

Mickiela dealt with her own reactions to war by leaving home. Having deleted her former friends from her cell phone in an effort to avoid falling back into her old lifestyle, and found her family in its usual disarray, she just couldn't bear to stay in Rosemead. Anyway, Joseph was in New York. So she decided to move East and see what would happen.

Her first year was difficult. She was still struggling to find the personality war had taken from her; she was working and going to school at the same time; and she was living with the roommate who was acting out her own war trauma by getting into fights. And although she was still hoping things would work out with Joseph, their relationship was rocky. She tried to explain why.

"The thing every girl hates in the army is that you meet a guy and you get close, but you never know what type of person he'll be on the outside because people can present themselves as whatever they want over there. Joseph's different than before. I know he's a sweet guy, but he's from the hood and has whoever he had before he met me. I don't know if he has them now, but he has to go back into his life, and I have to go back into mine."

She also spent a lot of time thinking about what she had learned from the army and war. "Some things were good. I got direction, like now I think about retirement and buying a house, and I'm able push for higher positions at work." But mostly she just felt angry.

At the end of Mickiela's first year home, a friend told her about Iraq Veterans Against the War, an organization that was speaking out on behalf of soldiers as well as criticizing the government's case for war. Mickiela decided to go to a meeting the group was holding in New York to see if she could find an outlet for her frustrations. This is where I first met her and arranged to talk.

By the time I visited her in Jersey City a couple weeks later, she'd discovered she was pregnant for the second time by Joseph. "He said he wants me to have an abortion," she told me. "That's why he keeps texting me. He says I'm manipulating him." She paused and added, "Some girls have to wait till the baby's born to know that the guy doesn't want to be there. So, whatever." Then, in classic Mickiela fashion, she laughed.

The next time I saw her, she told me her father, who had the habit of popping into her life every so often, had offered to take her into his home in California and support her and the baby. "Me and Joseph are on good terms now. We were on bad terms, but he apologized for everything and said he was just scared. He was like, 'I can't be mad at you, we've been through too much.' I think everything he said before was really messed up, but I want to give him the benefit of the doubt, 'cause we're not together and he's only just turned twenty-five. But he said he really cares about me and wants to be there for the baby, for sure."

I asked what her plans were now.

"My plan is to move in with my dad. If Joseph asks me to move back here for the baby's sake, I will, even though I don't want to. And if I can convince him to move to California, I will. And if I don't ever hear from him again, and it's just a child-support check—whatever. I'm planning to take care of the baby for about a year and then join the police academy. My cousins and aunts will look after the baby while I'm at work." She chose the police not because she liked the idea, but because her military experience would allow her to start at an advanced salary, and she needed the income and benefits as soon as possible.

When I next talked to her two weeks later, her father had forgotten all his promises and vanished, as he had done so often before. She relayed this new disaster to me with her usual cheer, then flew back to California anyway, first staying with a cousin, then with her sister in San Diego, then with the grandmother I met in Rosemead.

By the time I went to see her in California in 2007, she was three months from her due date, wrestling to get her discharge from the army as a single mother and applying for food stamps. "The welfare people are treating me like I'm a bum," she said bitterly. "I'm just trying to get benefits. The army's giving me nothing."

That a soldier who served her country in a war should end up on state assistance within eighteen months of returning is a sad but typical example of the way this nation treats its veterans. VA benefits may sound good to recruits, but in reality veterans face such a tangled bureaucracy to get them that many stop even trying. As of 2007, all soldiers who served in Iraq and received honorable discharges are given five years of free medical care at VA hospitals (before 2007, it was two years).

But getting medical compensation and disability checks is much more difficult. Once a soldier is discharged from the army, she must wait to be transferred to the VA system to receive any benefits, during which time she will get no money at all, even if she's in a hospital with both her legs missing. Moreover, just to apply for her benefits, she must fill out twenty-two paper documents to be processed by sixteen different information systems that don't even communicate with one another; a procedure so complicated it defeats many uninjured veterans, let alone those disoriented by PTSD or traumatic brain injury, two of the most common wounds of this war. And even if veterans do manage to fill out all these forms, they usually have to wait for their benefits for between six months and two years because of horrendous backlogs and delays— six hundred thousand claims were pending as of early 2008.[10] But what particularly infuriates veterans is that the VA runs on the assumption that every veteran is trying to cheat, so to qualify for any medical compensation whatsoever, a soldier must prove that her injuries, physical or mental, occurred while she was at war.

The Bush administration's ill-timed cutbacks to the VA in 2005 only made these problems worse. Since then, Congress has put more money into the system and implemented more rules to try to improve matters, but the VA is still woefully underfunded and unprepared: in 2009 over three hundred thousand troops will return from Iraq, three times more than the VA is equipped to help.[11]

The situation is particularly dire for women. So far, at least 191,500 women have served in the Middle East, and half that number will be returning soon, adding to the 1.7 million female veterans already here. Yet the VA has only six inpatient PTSD programs for women; most VA hospitals were built with large open wards intended only for men, and although all 153 VA hospitals treat women, there are a mere twenty-two stand-alone women's health clinics that offer a full range of services. And many clinics are miles from where veterans live, are open only a couple hours a week, and have no staff trained to deal with the combined effects of combat trauma and sexual violence.[12]

This lack of services is disastrous. Women make up the fastest-growing group of veterans today, have different needs than men, and do not necessarily feel safe in a male therapy group or with a male doctor or counselor; it is too reminiscent of being outnumbered by men at war. They also have different PTSD symptoms and need different treatment—they are more likely to turn their anger and blame in on themselves rather than becoming violent toward others, especially if they have been sexually assaulted, are more prone to anxiety and depression, and take considerably longer to recover.[13] Women also have different medical needs than men, among them the fact that most returning female soldiers are of childbearing age yet are contaminated by the anthrax vaccine and depleted uranium.

In 2008 the VA announced plans to open more PTSD clinics in the future, although how many will be just for women remained undecided. Meanwhile, the shortage of services for women is leaving many with no VA health coverage at all, a serious hardship considering that 1.8 million veterans lack health insurance.[14] An added shame is that women are getting much lower quality treatment at VA outpatient clinics than men.[15]

"I look around at all the broken soldiers and it makes me so mad," Mickiela said. "Where are we supposed to get the money for what we need? Like, they pay for the expenses of my pregnancy, but they won't pay for the baby because the baby isn't a veteran. So if the baby's born with something wrong, everything comes out of my pocket."

During the last few months of her pregnancy, Mickiela moved several more times, ending up back with her grandpa, where she stayed until the baby was born on May 15, 2007. She named her Nyla Amor Joseph. "Nyla stands for New York and L.A., cause that's where me and Joseph are from, and Amor means love." Joseph visited a few times, but when I asked where things stood with him, Mickiela was as unsure as ever.

"I don't know. He's not with me and he's not with anyone else, far as I know. We're just friends. We have to be friends forever now."

In September 2007, Mickiela took Nyla with her to New York for a two-month visit with a friend and to see Joseph. But the minute she arrived, Joseph was ordered to leave for a training camp upstate, where he had to stay for most of her visit. The reason: he was to be redeployed to Iraq.

"He's devastated," she told me. "We both are. We've got to find a way to get him out."

Whether they would was dubious, for Joseph had become part of the Bush administration's so-called surge: the thirty thousand extra troops sent to Iraq in 2007. From Mickiela's point of view, it was just another kick in the guts from the army.

A few days later I talked to her on the phone. She sounded exhausted—the baby had woken up twice in the night—and I could hear the loneliness in her voice. Joseph, she'd found out, did have another girlfriend after all, and didn't seem interested in seeing Mickiela or the baby.

"I'm going to see his mother today," she told me. "I'm hoping she'll help. I don't have any money."

TERRIS DEWALT-JOHNSON

Terris returned from Iraq five months after Mickiela, in April 2006. She was hugely relieved to see her children and husband again, but right away something felt wrong. "You would think because you're home you should be comfortable and fit right in, but it wasn't like that. My mind was in Iraq. I kept thinking about things that had happened there, and thanking God I'd come back in one piece." She too felt like a ghost, though it took her a while to recognize this.

"I couldn't tolerate being startled. And it just seemed to burn me up when my husband complained about stuff. It seemed so small compared to Iraq. I'd want to say, 'You have no idea how good we have it here!' But I didn't see it as shell shock or anything. I thought I was normal."

What she knew wasn't normal, though, was that she seemed to have disappeared as a mother. "The kids kept asking their dad for stuff instead of me. I had to tell them, 'Hey, it's okay to ask me too, you know.'"

Soldier parents often feel pushed aside like this when they come home. Their children are hurt and distrustful after their absence, and the family has learned to function without them, so the soldiers must win everyone back with patience, love, and gentleness, the very attributes that have been beaten out of them by training and war. Women in particular struggle with this because mothers are expected to be so close to their children. Hard as it is to leave your children behind, coming back too numbed by war to feel part of the family, or even to love your children as you once did, is unbearable.

Terris didn't realize how much she had changed until she read a blog Terrence wrote for a television program that was doing a story on returning soldiers. The first part touched her: "When my wife got her orders to leave I felt like a part of my life just dropped. . . . The main thing I missed was not having my wife next to me in bed. I also missed the little things like her eating off of my plate, turning the light on early in the morning getting ready for work, kissing her off to work, hearing her slippers flip flop around the house."

But then she read what he had to say about her return: "It was like the military had done something to her mentally.... She wasn't the same person she was when she left, she seemed to be stressed and moody like she had a lot on her mind and she didn't want to be bothered."

Terris was shocked. "'Whoa, I'm like that?' I said. And he said, 'Yeah.'"

It was true. As much as she tried to be her old self, she couldn't shake her tough military persona or her thoughts of Iraq. And how could she forget the war when she had to don her uniform and go to drill once a month? Nor did it help that she had to make an agonizing decision: whether to reenlist right away and serve out her full twenty-year contract, reenlist later, or leave the army altogether.

As she was driving me to the Atlanta airport after we'd spent a long day together at her house, she explained her dilemma. (It was dark, but she was driving like a bat out of hell anyway, a habit soldiers pick up in Iraq.) If she left the army, the option she most wanted, she would receive no benefits and her sixteen-year career would add up to nothing. If she postponed reentering in the hope of avoiding war, the uncertainty of her fate would hang over her head for years. But if she did reenlist to get her last four years over with, she risked being redeployed.

In light of this, I asked her if she had any regrets about having signed up in the first place.

"No," she answered firmly. "My kids have what they have because of my job in the military."

"But if we'd been at war in Iraq, would you have joined then?"

She paused a second, then shook her head. "Hell, no!"

Terris did reenlist, though, driven by economic necessity. She switched from her old company to the 2125th Garrison Support Unit because she had been assured that it was unlikely to go to Iraq. "I'll be sent to a U.S. base somewhere not too far away, I hope," she told me with cautious optimism. "So, I'll get home sometimes and see the kids."

Nevertheless, the worry that she might be called back to war began to tear at her; she couldn't even glimpse the news without having an anxiety attack. And her body was giving her trouble too. Her head and back wouldn't stop aching from her accident in the convoy, and her knees were in pain from jumping off high vehicles all the time when she was loaded down with heavy guns and armor. For months she resisted taking painkillers because she didn't like the idea of being on medication, but eventually she hurt too much to ignore, so she went to the Atlanta VA for treatment. There, she was diagnosed with the injuries she expected, but also with depression and PTSD. She was sent to group therapy twice a week for three months and put on Prozac, thus joining the legions of Iraq War veterans now getting through life on drugs.

Then, on September 12, 2007, her worst fears came true: her unit was put on alert for deployment to Baghdad. She had been caught up in the surge, just like Joseph.

"This really bothers me," she wrote to me in quiet understatement, adding that her unit was leaving in three waves but she didn't know which, if any, she was on. "My oldest son is a senior this year, and if I'm called to leave, I may miss his graduation and prom like I did with my daughter."

She hadn't been able to make herself tell her family yet; she was waiting until she heard something more concrete and hoping she would somehow escape. "I'm keeping my fingers crossed," she wrote in the e-mail. And at the end of her message, she typed a little face, its mouth turned down in sadness.

ABBIE PICKETT

By the time Abbie returned home to her little town of Darlington, Wisconsin, in April 2004, she was profoundly depressed. Unable to shake her memories of the mortar attack, her outrage over the battle with her command, or her horror over how war had changed her, she kept falling into long bouts of uncontrollable weeping. If anyone came up to her when she was at a computer, she would jump and snap in uncharacteristic anger, not even seeing until later that this was because she'd been at a computer when she was attacked. She couldn't sleep for more than fifty minutes at a stretch, with two hours of miserable wakefulness in between. And when she did sleep, she was plagued with nightmares filled with bloody bodies, the shrieks of mortars, and a crushing foreboding of death.

She also couldn't bear any noise that reminded her of mortars and so had to shut off the steam heaters in her apartment because they whistled. And in a classic symptom of trauma, she was so haunted by

Sergeant Hill, the soldier wounded in the Camp Warhorse attack, that she kept thinking she was seeing armless people all around her.

Like so many veterans of war, Abbie also suffered from flashbacks, those waking nightmares that send soldiers back into a particularly horrible moment of war. The worst happened on the New Year's Eve after her return, in the main square of Madison, Wisconsin. It was triggered by fireworks, which so resemble bomb attacks that they are difficult for all war veterans. "As soon as I heard the booms, I fell to my knees. Every time I opened my eyes, the faces in front of me would fade away and I'd be brought to that night we were attacked. I was crying hysterically. My friends didn't know what to do."

Soon Abbie began to fear for her sanity—terrifying in itself—but she kept quiet, convinced, like Mickiela, that no one would understand, not even her loving family, and too ashamed to make a fuss. After all, she told herself, other soldiers had been through worse. And then she too felt out of sync with everyone around her, as well as out of touch with herself.

"I had nothing to talk about. All my friends' conversations were about movies I hadn't seen or fashion I didn't know about. Anything I talked about turned morbid very quick—little kids in Iraq, death, mortar attacks. Then everyone would get quiet and no one would know what to say." She smiled ruefully. "I remember this girl I grew up with was talking about how she wanted some designer purse, and I said, 'Yeah, I know what you mean. There was one time in Iraq when these kids wanted some food, and I felt really bad because I wanted to give them some but we didn't have enough. I hate it when you can't get what you want.' Everyone just sat there. They felt like assholes, and I felt like an asshole."

Abbie was also in physical pain, like Terris, her back damaged from carrying so much weight in Iraq every day, and from bumping around in her truck, which had such inadequate shock absorbers that it kept catapulting her into the ceiling, crumpling her spine. The VA has since pronounced her 80 percent disabled because of the muscle spasms and sclerosis this caused. She reenrolled in college, but was in too much physical and mental distress to pay attention, so she almost dropped out. And she was so confused by the complicated paperwork veterans have to file to get their tuition benefits that she missed signing an essential piece of paper, which lost her a semester's tuition, forcing her to use most of the earnings she had saved in Iraq. (War veterans are often too shocked to be able to concentrate on things like school or complicated paperwork; ironic in the face of all the forms the VA demands they fill out.)

Throughout the first five years of the Iraq War, about 65 percent of its veterans never got the tuition benefits they were promised because the requirements to qualify for them were so full of catches. A few examples: They had to have won an honorable discharge, which 20 percent of soldiers never get. They had to have fulfilled their contract, which excluded soldiers who are discharged early because of wounds or PTSD, unless they fought back. They had to pay a nonrefundable $100 a month the first year of their enlistment to get their tuition money, which many could not afford. And most military branches only paid up to $4,500 a year anyway, vastly below the average cost of college. This was a sad contrast to World War II, when the G.I. Bill paid enough tuition and fees to allow veterans to attend 90 percent of the nation's colleges and paid for their books and living expenses too.[16] In 2008 the Post-9/11 Veterans Educational Assistance Act of 2007 was signed into law, which should improve the situation.

After months of struggling with all these difficulties, Abbie went to a rally in Madison for Senator John Kerry when he was campaigning for the 2004 presidential election. Another veteran introduced them, and later Kerry talked about Abbie in a debate, which brought her to the attention of the media as an early example of a female veteran with PTSD. Several news outlets then did stories on her, making the point that women veterans of the Iraq War are suffering much higher rates of depression and trauma than men.[17]

The reason for this has not yet been adequately analyzed by social scientists, but it seems obvious that it is due to the compound traumas experienced by women at war. Not only are they in combat like men, but, as said, many more women than men are also sexually abused during their military service.[18] (One study found that women who were sexually assaulted in the military were *nine* times more likely to show symptoms of PTSD than those who weren't.)[19] What's more, this double trauma is often in fact multiple. As mentioned earlier, half the women in the military have been sexually assaulted in their pasts, most often as children, so if you add that to the one-third who are sexually attacked in the service, a high percentage will be experiencing abuse for the second, third, or umpteenth time. Even worse, women who are redeployed with the same units they served with earlier may be going back to war with the same man or men who attacked or harassed them before, which is not unlike sending a rape victim to prison with her rapist.

In other words, there are women soldiers in Iraq who have been abused as children, who are abused again by their fellow soldiers, who are harassed by their comrades, who are serving with the men who attacked them, and who are enduring mortar and fire attacks, seeing the wounded and the dead, fighting in combat, and living in constant fear for their lives. Every one of these experiences is a trigger for PTSD, and many women are enduring them all at once.

Abbie did not have to contend with childhood abuse, but she was exposed to all these other horrors, as were the majority of women I talked to. Unfortunately, for a long time after she came home, she was too isolated to know her reactions were normal.

This changed when her media exposure led her to Paul Rieckhoff, founder of Iraq and Afghanistan Veterans of America, a nonpartisan group that advocates for veterans' rights. With his help, Abbie began to work as an activist for veterans, and the experience was enlightening. "Before, I didn't know people were going through the same thing I was, and I felt alone and crazy. Paul probably saved my life."

Working with other veterans also showed Abbie that soldiers who have tight bonds with one another at war do much better when they get home than those who don't. They call each other, compare nightmares, exchange tips on how to sleep, and help one another realize the misery they feel is a normal reaction to horror and war. Sadly, very few women have this kind of bond. Of all the women I talked to for this book, only a handful had veteran friends to help them readjust.

By the time I met Abbie in London, several months after we had begun talking by phone, she was going to school again, majoring in political science and psychology, and had a good relationship with a boyfriend. But she still felt shattered. "I'm a lot more emotional than I used to be," she said, looking at me from across the kitchen table, her light green eyes sad. "Before I left I could go out and drink and all I'd ever get was super happy and a little bit horny. Now when I drink I end up crying for a very, very long time. And I still have a hard time falling asleep. I take medication for that, and for depression. But even with the medication I'm still too anxious sometimes to sleep. Or I wake up with nightmares."

The military wasn't helping either. She was trying to get a medical discharge for her back injuries so she could qualify for severance pay and benefits, but the army threw so many hurdles in her way that in the end she gave up. She was only six months from fulfilling her eight-year contract anyway, and had mainly been fighting the system to get the college tuition she'd been promised and never paid. But the hurdles defeated her, just as they defeat so many, and the army got to keep its dollars.

While Abbie and I were talking about all this over our mugs of English tea, I asked her what she thought of the war now that she had endured so much. Did she think we should have invaded in the first place?

She answered thoughtfully, her soft voice subdued. "Do I think Saddam was a bad person who needed to be removed from power? Yes. Do I think that was the reason for us going in there? Not really. And it's not the guys sitting in their air-conditioned offices at the White House and the Pentagon who are feeling the aftermath of it, it's the mother and father who are getting their child sent home in a box. It's the people who don't have money or power—the innocent people in Iraq who've been killed and raped and had their villages turned upside down."

She paused and stared down at her mug, her slim fingers grasping it tight. "I really do love some of those people of Iraq, and I don't know how to help them. Some of those children were so beautiful. They only wanted attention and food." She fell silent for a moment, then added quietly, "Still, I knew if I had to kill a kid to save myself or my buddies, I would. How could anybody love anyone who has such horrible thoughts?" Her voice dropped to a whisper as she said this, and when she looked back up, tears were running down her narrow face.

"Why doesn't it ever end?" she said, her voice anguished. "It just never ends."

JENNIFER SPRANGER

Jen was so frail by the time she left Kuwait that she was kept in the Landstuhl Regional Medical Center, a military hospital in Germany, for nearly a month. The doctors gave her tests, put her on medicine to moderate her dangerously high heart rate, and treated her for anemia. They also made her fill out a questionnaire asking if she had been in or near any explosions that might have exposed her to depleted uranium and took several vials of blood, which she assumed were to test for DU, although she was never given any results. But they could find no cause for her drastic weight loss or for her shaking hands. So, at the end of August 2003, they flew her to the Walter Reed Army Medical Center in Washington, D.C. "That was probably the worst place I've ever been in my life. It's so, so sad, all the young guys with no legs. I made a good friend there who was addicted to painkillers; the military gives those out like candy. He'd had his ear blown off, and his buddy had died in the same explosion."

She stayed at Walter Reed for about six weeks, at the end of which the doctors told her they couldn't figure out her problems any better than the doctors in Germany, so they were letting her go. They sent her back to Fort Dix, where she was put on medical hold for several more weeks and given yet more tests. But although the doctors kept telling her she had abnormal symptoms, they still couldn't explain them, even though she was sicker than ever. "As soon as I ate something it would just go right through me, and that hasn't stopped. But eventually they decided I was making everything up. I felt that from everyone. To be told that you're a liar is the worst thing in the world. To sit there and be honest with people about nightmares and sickness and be told there's nothing wrong with you—it hurt me so bad."

Despite her nearly four months in military hospitals, Jen was never diagnosed. She was, however, sent to a psychologist at Fort Dix, which mortified her, for she saw it as proof that the doctors thought her problems were all in her head. She dragged herself to the therapist unwillingly, but there she found a surprise. "I liked her a lot! I talked to her a bit about the prisoners, and she was very understanding." Jen's command had told her by then that she would be sent back to Iraq, so she was relieved to be taken seriously at last. "The therapist offered me a medical discharge with no repercussions—failure to readjust or something. And I was fine with it. I didn't want to go to war anymore."

Jen told her parents about her medical discharge on the phone, and her mother was hugely relieved to have her daughter out of harm's way. But, she added, "Your dad's upset. He's worried about what he'll tell his friends, and he thinks the shame of leaving the army for mental problems will follow you all your life."

"I wish my mom had never told me that," Jen said. "It messed with my head."

Jen's father does not remember the conversation that way at all. "Maybe I didn't put it as clearly as I could've," he said to me, "but I just thought she should think hard about whether she really wanted to leave the army in case she regretted it later. I didn't know half of the things that were wrong with her then."

Either way, Jen took his words as advice not to leave. She refused the medical discharge and went home for Christmas. "I was still nineteen and I really did think my parents knew everything, so I listened to my dad. I wish I hadn't. It's too late now."

Back at home, Jen waited for the rest of her unit to return in January and attended her mandatory drills at a nearby base, feeling as bad as ever. She still couldn't retain her food, she hadn't stopped shaking, she couldn't sleep, and she was having nightmares. The worst was that she kept suffering terrifying spells of being unable to breathe. But she was also fighting again with her parents, frustrated because she felt they couldn't understand what she was going through and upset because they were finally getting divorced.

Soon after her return, Jen applied for a job with a security company in Racine, which raised a problem she'd never expected as a veteran who had guarded a prison camp at war. "They said I didn't have enough experience! I was so mad I wanted to start throwing things at these people. I wonder if it would have been different if I'd been a guy? Maybe they thought I spent the war sitting in a tent typing papers." She sighed, then added a phrase that probably every war veteran has said at one point: "Nothing was like I expected it would be when I came home."

The military promises recruits that they will come out of the service with experience and education that will make them more employable than before, but for Iraq War veterans the case is often quite the reverse. Many are too physically or psychologically injured to work. Others have family troubles that mounted while they were gone and now get in the way. And an alarming number run into employers who either have no respect for their experience or regard them as too risky to hire. By the end of 2007, tens of thousands of National Guard troops and reservists had lost seniority, pay, benefits, or the jobs that were supposed to be held for them while they were serving.[20] As a result of all this—along with ever-mounting rents—Iraq and Afghanistan war veterans are slipping into poverty and homelessness much sooner than did the veterans of previous wars. Eleven percent of these new homeless veterans are women.[21]

Tragically, sexual violence seems to be a major cause of homelessness among female veterans—as said earlier, 40 percent of these homeless women say they were raped or assaulted in the military—and one of the main reasons is lack of familial support.[22] Nothing helps a person recover from rape better than an understanding partner or family, but many women join the military exactly because they have no such thing. When a woman (or a man) is assaulted and has no one to turn to for help, she can spiral into just the sort of depression and self-destruction that makes people lose their jobs and homes.

Jen did find work eventually, as a supervisor in a factory that provided jobs for mentally disabled adults. "I loved the job. It was really rewarding to help those people. It was what I needed at the time." The job, however, led to a new crisis.

"I'd made best friends with this other girl who worked there, and one day she brought in some cocaine. For some reason that just did it for me. I don't know if it's the numb feeling where you can't think—'cause that's my problem, I sit there and feel bad about things—but the cocaine became an everyday thing, to the point where I even did some before I went to drill."

It was at drill that she got caught, in one of the surprise urine tests the military gives its soldiers every six months or so. "They sent me a big packet of legal papers, which my parents opened without me being there, so that's how they found out that I was getting kicked out of the army. That was huge, absolutely huge. They were very, very upset about it."

The papers explained how to get a military lawyer to fight the discharge, but Jen was too depressed to care. "I figured let whatever happens happen; I'm done with it. I'm going to try and make my life better and forget about the army. I knew physically and emotionally I couldn't go back to Iraq. You'd see me in Canada first.

"But my dad pretty much disowned me then. He wanted me to fight to stay in; he thought I was just trying to get out easy. So we had a lot of fights and he kicked me out of the house. There was a little bit more to it, but not really. I wish I could say that I tried harder to stay in. The thought of it makes me sick now. I did so many stupid things and I was just so unhappy. Drugs would make me happy for about an hour, then they would drive me even crazier than I am now. I mean my whole body would shake instead of just my hands and arms. It was terrible."

In the end, Jen was given an honorable discharge, she thinks because her good military record outweighed the urine test.

Jen's cocaine habit continued for six months until her boyfriend at the time shocked her out of it. She'd moved in with him after she left home, and although he liked his drink, he had no tolerance for drugs. "Look at what this is doing to you. Look at yourself!" he yelled at her once. And that, she said, is really all it took.

But even after she gave up cocaine, she was still a wreck. She was on antianxiety medicine that killed her appetite, so she dropped once again to eighty-five pounds, and by the summer of 2006, she was a thin and jangly mess. "I was dying. Without even meaning to, I was killing myself."

Her parents tried to help, but from Jen's point of view neither of them understood. She and her father were going through bouts of not speaking to one another, and her mother seemed too caught up in a new romance to pay attention. "My parents could tell I was sick, but my mother still blamed it on the drugs, even though that was over. I was such a golden child before this happened, a straight A student. I never got in trouble. It makes me wonder why nobody put that together. But they had their own problems at the time with the divorce."

Many soldiers feel this sort of alienation, regardless of what is happening at home. The gulf between somebody who has been at war and somebody who has not can seem insurmountable.

Jen's boyfriend was causing her trouble as well. She had first dated him back in high school, and he'd waited for her all the way through her brief marriage (her father had handled the divorce for her while she was in Iraq), as well as her deployment, writing her letters every week while she was at war, so she couldn't resist getting back together with him when she returned. "But he was kind of a violent person. And he didn't want to hear anything about the military. 'I didn't do it so you didn't either,' was his attitude. One time he made fun of me for the way I was breathing when I was having a panic attack. It's hard for me to admit that I put up with it for so long, but my self-esteem was just so low and he was pretty much all I had, which sounds pathetic."

Jen had broken up with that boyfriend by the time I met her in Racine in February 2007 and was back at her mother's house. But although three and a half years had passed since she'd left Iraq, she was still as traumatized as ever; PTSD sometimes grows worse with time, not better. On the telephone I would often hear her breathing become ragged when we talked about the war, and sometimes she had to end the conversation so she could lie down and catch her breath. "There are times when I'll start thinking about the wrong stuff and my heart will race. I can feel it pounding, just wanting to beat out of my chest." This was sad enough, but when I first met her in person—saw her fresh little face, felt the anxious sweat of her palm, and watched her shake like an old woman with Parkinson's disease—the abstract term *PTSD* became very real.

She explained how easily her panic attacks could be triggered. "My boyfriend and I were at a bar downtown once, and a guy there began saying the things you'd say on a military shooting range. My heart started beating so fast I almost dropped my drink. 'Cause that's something I don't want any part of anymore. I don't want to hear about it, don't want to think about it."

She was working as a checkout clerk in a grocery store by then, the only kind of job she felt she could handle, yet even there little things could trigger her panic. One day she saw the same kind of round box of cheese that used to be given to prisoners at Camp Bucca. Her eyes filled with tears and her whole day was ruined.

"Going into a room full of people never scared me like it does now," she added, echoing Mickiela. "I don't even like going to the bank. I don't like talking to people on the phone. I really don't like people in general anymore."

Miriam Barton, who now lives back at home in Oregon with her three-year-old son and several pet wolves, said much the same thing. "I'm real isolated. I spend most of my time in the house. I'm not really suited to civilian life. I just can't get on with people."

Soldiers commonly react to war like this. They become antisocial, paranoid, and painfully lonely.

Like Abbie, Jen was on medication for depression and anxiety by the time I visited her, but was neither seeing a therapist nor talking to anyone besides me about the war and the sexual persecution she'd experienced. Once in a while, she would travel to meet Vets4Vets, a support group she found useful, although the only other combat veterans there were men. But she knew no other women veterans to help.

"My life has been an absolute wreck since I've been back," she said frankly. "I remember being happy a couple years ago, but I haven't been happy since. It sounds melodramatic, but it's true. I wasn't like that before. Nothing seemed hopeless. I didn't want to just give up like I do now. Now there are days when I can't stand being in my own skin."

As I listened to Jen talk over the months, it became clear that the root of her problems was remorse. Every time she returned to the subject of how much she had hated the prisoners and what she had done to them, her breath grew ragged and her self-loathing spilled out. And when I asked her, as I'd asked the other soldiers, what she thinks of the war in Iraq now, her answer was vehement.

"At the beginning, I wanted to believe that Saddam was the reason we were there, but that was the biggest lie. The civilians didn't want us there—I can't tell you how many Iraqi children were standing by the side of the road pretending to shoot us. Seems to me we're just breeding a new generation that hates us even more. I can't think of the war as anything but a waste now, a waste of money and human lives. It's really, really disgusting. In the end I didn't believe anything I was told. I saw how we weren't helping their lives at all. We were making it worse."

She paused, raising her plastic cup to her lips for a sip of water, then shakily putting it back down. "I was nothing but proud when I first went into the military. I can't tell you how proud it made me to put on that uniform. I still have it . . ." she gestured upstairs to her bedroom. "But I won't even look at it. I thought we were so noble. Now I'm ashamed."

Jen's shame is something I heard expressed by many soldiers, men as well as women, yet the subject is curiously absent from public discussion, and even from studies of PTSD.[23] In general, shame and remorse are taboo subjects in the military, and to some extent, in the press. But when you listen to veterans and look into their stunned eyes, the subject they dwell upon is not always how afraid they were in war, or even how guilty they are about surviving when their comrades didn't, which are two of the standard explanations given for combat-related PTSD. They also talk about how they are haunted by the people they saw killed, tortured, abused, or wounded: the children blown up, the pregnant women shot, the soldiers mutilated, the little girls and boys run over by trucks and tanks. Most of all, they are disturbed by their own complicity in this, their sickening discovery that war has turned them into haters and killers. And when this happens in a war they don't even believe is justified, the shame is devastating.[24]

ELI PAINTEDCROW

When Eli went home to California in June 2005, she expected to pick up her life where she had left it: gathering Native women in her house, conducting healing ceremonies in a teepee in her back yard, and continuing her job as a social worker. But almost immediately her hopes were crushed.

"I couldn't deal with those women anymore. To me, everything they talked about was petty and I didn't want to hear it. They felt very abandoned. I lost connection with my mother, my brothers, my sons, my boyfriend, everybody." She gestured to her ceremonial drum in the corner. "I used to have a drum circle. I don't have that anymore. I can't even remember how the songs go. My world fell apart because I came back so angry and I didn't know why. Nobody could stand me. I couldn't even stand myself. It's really hard to admit that you have PTSD. It feels weak because the military teaches you to suck it up and drive on. I'm sure I had PTSD from the sexual assault back in Honduras, but I wouldn't admit it."

By the time she'd been home for half a year, she realized she needed therapy. "I was such a mess, I wouldn't even dress up. I wouldn't wear makeup. I didn't care. I wanted my life to end." But when she went to her local VA clinic, it only offered male therapists. "No, I need to have a woman," she said. It took the clinic three months to find one.

For the next year, nothing much changed. She was still so angry—at herself for having been part of a war she felt was wrong, and at the racism and injustice she'd encountered—that she couldn't work, couldn't sleep, couldn't concentrate, and she felt empty because nothing that used to give her life meaning mattered anymore. She was also broke, because the meager disability pay she got from the VA for her PTSD—$25 a week—could not even buy enough food. She wrote to California governor Arnold Schwarzenegger to complain, and after that was supposed to receive $750 every two weeks, but there were so many delays between each check that she became desperate. Like Mickiela, she was reduced to living on food stamps and general assistance. And she had to put her home up for sale, which broke her heart.

"I joined the military with the idea that I would never be on welfare again, but now here I am on it again," she said at the time, her voice bitter. "And even then I had to argue with the government for it. I had to prove that I was indigent. So that is what my twenty-two years in the army did for me.

"But I'm not the only soldier going through this. My friend who I served with in Iraq came home a year ago, and they found her dead in her home. She'd been dead for two days. She had PTSD and depression so bad, and she couldn't tell anybody because there was nobody to tell. So she killed herself. She was a lieutenant. The war isn't over when you come home."

Eli's new understanding of what war can to do a person changed her so much that when her brutal former husband, Eddie, died in 2005, she was actually able to feel sympathy for him. "I went to his funeral—maybe just to make sure he was dead. But there was another part of me that cried, not because he was my husband but because he was a Vietnam vet who got lost. He didn't come back from war the same. He always talked about raping girls in Vietnam, so what he did to me wasn't any different than what he was used to. So whose fault is it? I don't know. But the military should have done something for him to make him a better person. I don't think he was born that kind of person, I think the military made him like that. And I forgave him, because, after all, I have a son from him.

"So that part of me cried for him and cries for every soldier who comes back. Even if you come back in one piece, there's something you leave behind. I met a Mexican man who actually went to Iraq, to the spot where his son died, to tell his son's spirit that he had come to take him home. He picked up some of the dirt, and then he punched the commanding officer in the face because he knew why his son died. It was in a firefight, and when they called for the helicopters to come in, the commander ordered that no helicopter could land until the debris was cleaned up, and that took two hours. Who's going to live with wounds for two hours? So the man's son died needlessly."

Like so many veterans, Eli soon found her life consumed by battles with the VA, only in her case she had a double fight. "I had to be my own advocate, then I had to be my son's advocate too, because he's brain-injured. They wouldn't even drive him home from the hospital because he wasn't in a wheelchair, even though he couldn't drive himself. So I made this big stand: 'You're going to have a lot of brain-injured soldiers who might not be able to drive but can still walk. How are you going to deal with them?'

"So I had to go to Angel's appointments, and then to my appointments—I was living at the doctor's just about every day. I did resolve some of the issues, but I spent a lot of time writing letters to my congressman and the VA. And that's what I still do. My desk is a mess right now 'cause I'm trying to organize it and I can't even do that. I used to be really good at papers and developing systems. That's what I did in the military. Now I just can't."

After Eli had been home for a year or so, she began speaking out about veterans' rights and peace, and soon became inundated with requests from women veterans for help. They were calling her, flocking to her house, and telling her they felt suicidal and filled with hatred for the men they had fought with. Some could not even stand the word *veteran* or to hear anything about the military, so they were shunning the VA and veterans groups altogether. But they still needed help. "All the Vets for Peace and other organizations are male-dominated and, like the military, treat women as second-class citizens," Eli said. So she was trying to set up groups to help these women without imitating the military hierarchy. By late 2007, she and some other women had founded such a group called S.W.A.N., described in the Appendix.

Eli was also working with the women's activist group CODEPINK (which she criticizes for being too white) and appearing on television and radio. One fall, she sat in front of the White House for two weeks, drumming for peace. But she is not a pacifist. "I don't have a problem with war if you're defending your family and your land. And I don't have a problem with women being at war. We give life, so we're more apt to protect it. But what I do have a problem with is how we're using our children to fight battles of greed, and misleading them with a language that's false. War has its place—I'm going to defend my house, hell yeah. But I'm not going to try to take yours."

Yet even with all her peace work, Eli still longed to make amends with Iraqis. A modest chance to do this came when CODEPINK brought a delegation of Iraqi women to America and invited her to meet them. "It was hard because they were very afraid of me. I was an army veteran and they didn't know if I had killed somebody they knew. They didn't even want to talk to me. But I really needed to tell them I was sorry, that I was wrong.

"We did a march in front of the White House, and CODEPINK asked me to do a closing ceremony. But before I did that, I looked at these women and said, 'I want to tell you, in front of the White House and all these people, that I'm very, very sorry that I participated in this. We're wrong for being there, and I'm sorry, for myself, and for what my country is doing to yours.' They just looked at me. They probably thought, 'Oh, that's such an insincere thing.'

"That night we were asked to speak at a church to about two hundred and fifty people. CODEPINK asked me to bring my drum because I always drum a prayer song for them. So I brought it, and some sage, and I spoke to these women as my sisters. I sang a Native woman's song—it wasn't in English—and when I was done I turned around and I gave each woman a stick of sage and they started crying. They hugged me and they said, 'You're right. We are the same.' And they became my friends. They said, 'When this war is over, you come to Iraq and you stay with us.' So I feel like, at least with those women, there's a healing."

But Eli is still struggling with her need for forgiveness, for even as she has become increasingly visible as a peace activist, she is far from at peace with herself. She talked about this in her house. The sun was going down by then, the room darkening, and her face kept changing with the light, one minute looking soft and beautiful, the next hard and grim. "You know, the one thing I really can't stand is for people to come and say, 'Thank you for your service.' I hate that. Are you thanking me for participating in a genocide? Is that what you want? Because I'm not protecting anybody's country, I'm taking somebody's. Even though I never pulled the trigger, I feel that I participated in a genocide." She paused and swallowed, "And it hits me close to home because I feel it's my own people. I feel very responsible, and that's a hard thing to live with."

She began to cry when she said this, a wrenching sight in a woman so dignified. Tears ran down her face as she slumped in her armchair. "Everything we've done in Iraq is a lie," she said, her voice shaking, "and I'm very ashamed that I didn't see it sooner and stand up against it. I was torn between that truth and my father's truth of finishing what I started. I was a drill sergeant. My job was to teach other people's children how to kill. People ask me how could I, as a spiritual person, teach people to kill? I ask myself that. I bought into the whole thing. I thought it was the honorable thing to do. But it's not."

She fell silent, staring into space with her dark eyes. Then she whispered, "How could I be a social worker, spending my life helping people, and then send my own sons to war?"

She stood up slowly and went to the open door to light a cigarette, blowing the smoke up toward the moon. "I can only hope my ancestors will forgive me. Or that I will be able to forgive myself."

FOURTEEN

Fixing the Future

As I write these final words, the Iraq War is killing and maiming more citizens and soldiers every day. According to some estimates, it has slain half as many Iraqis in five years as Saddam Hussein managed to kill in thirty-five. The number of dead soldiers has mounted to over 4,170, and more than 30,600 troops have been wounded.[1]

To wage this catastrophic venture, the U.S. military has relied upon women as never before, and for many it has been a devastating experience. Most of these women enlisted in the military to better their opportunities, to serve a nation whose ideals they believed in, and to do something noble. For this they sacrificed their bodies, their personalities, and their peace of mind. They meant well and their hopes were high. But instead, they found themselves abusing and killing innocent Iraqis, denied respect by a military they once believed in, and persecuted and attacked by the men on their own side.

There are those who will take this as proof that women shouldn't be soldiers at all: if the military is so hostile to them, the reasoning goes, then women should leave. But all the female soldiers I know would reject this suggestion with scorn. We have all the qualities a soldier needs, they would argue—loyalty, willingness to sacrifice for the common good, readiness to obey, courage, military skills, fitness, an ability to command, stamina, strength, and intelligence—and it is our right to be soldiers if we choose.

Their argument is sound. In a nation that considers all humans created equal, no one should tell women what jobs they can or can't do. A military career is often the only path out of poverty and broken homes available in this country, and to deny it to women would be a grotesque injustice. And just because some men attack their female comrades doesn't mean that women should give up and go home; after all, women are attacked in civilian society, too, and we don't expect them to spend their lives locked up in fear. Women have always met with hostility when they first tried to enter male domains, whether as voters or police officers, firefighters or politicians, and the answer has never been to give up, but to stay and fight for reform until the culture changes and accepts them.

The reality is that America needs its female soldiers. Women have been in the armed forces for over a hundred years already, and have long since proven themselves excellent at the job, which is why the Pentagon has opened 30,000 more positions to them just since 1991. By March 2008, 11.4 percent of officers serving in the Middle East were women, 1.7 percent above the female ratio at large. And as of 2006, more than 2,000 women who fought in Iraq or Afghanistan had been awarded Bronze Stars, several for bravery and valor in combat, and more than 1,300 had earned the Combat Action Badge.[2]

The question is not whether women should be soldiers. The question is why male soldiers are abusing them and what can be done about it.

Rape and war have accompanied one another since the beginning of time, as Susan Brownmiller famously pointed out in her book *Against Our Will*, but the victims have traditionally been the women of conquered or occupied lands—the mass rapes in the Congo, Sudan, Bosnia, and Vietnam being a few recent examples.[3] But now, with more women becoming soldiers throughout the world, sexual violence is escalating within the military, too, and not only in America: Canada, Britain, and Italy have also reported the problem.[4] It has long been clear that war and military culture encourage rape and assault, but some scholars suggest that in America a disproportionate number of sexually violent men may be volunteering for the military as well.[5] This is probably because such men are attracted to the aggressive role of soldier, but it could also be because half of male recruits, like females, enlist to escape abusive families, and childhood abuse often turns men into abusers.[6]

But there is another factor contributing to violence against women as well, and that is the nature of the war in Iraq. Robert Jay Lifton, a professor of psychiatry who has studied the Nazis and soldiers in Vietnam and at Abu Ghraib, theorizes that in a war of brutal occupation, where the enemy is the civilian resistance, the command sanctions torture, and the war is justified by distorted reasoning and obvious lies, soldiers are particularly prone to commit atrocities.[7] Thus, American troops in Iraq have deliberately shot children, raped civilian women and teenagers, tortured prisoners of war, and abused their own comrades because they have lost sight of their moral bearings and are reduced to nothing but feelings of self-loathing, anger, fear, and hatred.

This combustible mix of senseless war, a misogynist military culture, and rape-prone recruits may well explain why sexual violence continues to be so prevalent in the military and so resistant to reform.

So what can be done? Even if we left Iraq tomorrow, the military will never be able to screen out all potential rapists or remove the violence from war, but it can work on changing its own culture so that sexual violence, whether toward comrades or "enemy" women, is widely recognized as shameful and criminal. Below are some suggestions as to how this change can be wrought, suggestions I have shown to several military personnel who have helped to hone them.

- Promote more women. As the number of women in authority increases, they will be less isolated and threatened, and more able to become positive role models and to prevent abuse. Already plenty of women heroes have come out of the Iraq War: women who have saved lives, like Abbie; who have stood up against injustice, like Eli; and who have led convoys through attacks without losing a single soldier, like Terris. With better recognition and more authority, such women will help to increase respect for female soldiers, and respect is the single most important weapon against harassment and rape.
- End official antipathy toward women. As I have shown, military culture still socializes men to regard women with contempt. The misogynist rhymes, the insults used by drill instructors, the pervasiveness of pornography (most pornographic magazines are not allowed to be sold on military bases, but soldiers can buy them easily by mail or from civilian peddlers), the historical tradition of providing prostitutes to male soldiers, the exclusion of women from combat—all these traditions and more train male soldiers to see women as the

inferior "other," good for nothing but sex and slapping around. As one recent Iraq War veteran wrote about his training, "The Drill Instructor's nightly homiletic speeches, full of an unabashed hatred of women, were part of the second phase of boot camp: the process of rebuilding recruits into Marines."[8] Yet there is no reason why this misogyny needs to persist. The rhymes, sexist insults, and pornography should simply be banned (violent pornography is highly correlated with increased rates of rape),[9] and just as drill instructors are now prohibited from using racist language, so they can be forbidden from using sexist language. Ordinary soldiers will, of course, continue to insult women in their everyday speech, but this will change as more women achieve the respect I discuss above.

- Distribute women more evenly. No women should serve alone with all-male platoons, for it leaves them isolated and vulnerable to assault.

- Strike the "don't ask, don't tell" policy toward homosexuals in the military and accept them equally. Some platoons are already ahead of military policy on this issue: gay soldiers have publicly spoken and written about being openly accepted by their comrades.[10] The current policy only encourages persecution.

- Reverse criminal waivers. Screen out recruits with records of domestic or sexual violence.

- Expel all personnel who have been found guilty of domestic or sexual violence while serving. Too many soldiers convicted of sexual violence have been allowed to stay in the military with only the slightest of punishments, conveying the message that men can do what they want to women with little consequence. Such cases abound, but one example is army sergeant Damon D. Shell, who ran over and killed twenty-year-old Private First Class Hannah Gunterman McKinney of the 44th Corps Support Battalion in her Iraq camp on September 4, 2006. Shell pleaded guilty to drinking in a war zone, drunken driving, and "consensual sodomy" with McKinney, an underage junior soldier to whom he had supplied alcohol until she was incapacitated (having sex with a person incapacitated by alcohol is legally rape). Yet a military judge ruled McKinney's death an accident, sentenced Shell to thirteen months in prison and demotion to private, and declined to even kick him out of the army.[11]

- Advertise loud and clear that *rape is a war crime* and a form of torture and is no more tolerated within the military than it is by international courts. This should be writ large on the DoD Web site and emphasized repeatedly in training.

- Hold commanders accountable for assaults that occur in their units.
- Educate officers properly about sexual violence. Studies have shown that commanders who ban pornography, treat their female soldiers with respect, and insist that other soldiers do likewise significantly reduce sexual persecution.[12] Therefore, all officer training schools, from West Point to the humblest ROTC (Reserve Officers' Training Corps), should teach their candidates to understand that rape is an act of anger, hatred, and power, not of out-of-control lust, and that sexual harassment and assault destroy camaraderie and cohesion. Officers should learn to take pride in ensuring that all their soldiers are safe from disrespect and violence by their comrades.
- Stop the culture of brutal hazing, abuse, and rape that permeates officer academies.[13]
- Improve training in the prevention and understanding of sexual assault for all recruits, enlisted and officer. Too much of the DoD's sexual assault education is riddled with implications that women are inferior, good for little else than sex, and invite assault—implications that promote a culture of rape. The military needs to withdraw all the training films and scripts now in circulation and revise them with the help of trained civilian experts.
- Officially recognize that women are fighting in combat in Iraq, instead of only acknowledging that "women are exposed to combat danger," as the DoD now phrases it.[14] Many women believe such recognition will win them more respect and so reduce sexual violence, and there is logic to the argument, for at the root of every sexual abuse is the assumption that women are inferior or the wish to prove them so.
- Open ground-combat positions to women. For over a decade now, women have argued that excluding them from infantry and armor divisions denies them the chance to rise in the ranks or win full respect as soldiers.[15] Yet, although women have fought in civil and guerilla wars throughout history (in Eritrea, Mexico, Greece, and Russia, for example), were admitted to most armies back in the 1940s, and are drafted by eight nations, only 1 percent of the world's armies of-

ficially allow women in ground combat.[16] Like the United States and Britain, most countries would rather put women in the line of fire under the rubric "combat support."

The Pentagon justifies the U.S. ban by blaming civilian attitudes. American society, it says, believes that femininity is incompatible with combat and will not tolerate the killing and mutilation of its mothers and daughters. Likewise, it argues, soldiers are more troubled by the sight of women being wounded and killed than of men, and so they will put themselves at extra risk trying to protect women in battle. And finally, women in combat would endanger men because of their lesser strength. These arguments have been made for decades by conservatives, too, but ironically a 2005 Gallup Poll, reported by the military itself, belies them: 72 percent of the public favored women serving anywhere in Iraq, and 44 percent (and here I quote the military's own report) "favored having women serve as the ground troops who are doing most of the fighting."[17]

The fact is that not one of these arguments against women in combat has been borne out in Iraq. Any sign of public or media outrage over how many women soldiers are being killed and wounded in Iraq has been conspicuously absent; rather, the press has focused the bulk of its war stories on men, as if female soldiers barely exist, and the same applies to feature films and documentaries. Far from protecting women, many men are attacking them. Studies have long shown that some women's strength matches that of some men, and that women use ingenuity instead of strength where necessary. And there is no evidence that women soldiers add to the danger of men in any way. On the contrary, it is women who are in more danger than before, both from being in battle and from those very men who are supposed to feel so protective of them.[18]

A 2007 study by the nonprofit Research and Development (RAND) Corporation has already called for a reassessment of women's role in combat, but ultimately the decision is up to Congress and the White House. This is a direct challenge to the status of women in our society, for every argument against women in combat relies upon stereotypes of women being the inferior sex.[19]

Women want equality, and even though not all women will choose to join a ground-combat unit, just as not all men do, they want the choice to be theirs, not the government's. "War doesn't give a damn what your job is, we're getting killed anyway," as Sgt. Miriam Barton said. "We're getting blown up right alongside the guys. We're manning whatever weapons we can get our little hands on. We're in combat! So there's no reason to keep us segregated anymore."

- Reform the military handling of sexual abuse. The way the Defense Department currently approaches this problem is riddled with contradictions. Some examples: The DoD has been creating a database to track sexual assault and other criminal incidents for fifteen years without completing it. Although Congress ordered the DoD to form a task force to investigate military sexual assault in 2005, the task force never met until August 2008.[20] Of the sexual assaults reported and recorded by the DoD in the fiscal year 2007, 47 percent were dismissed as unworthy of investigation and only 8 percent of the cases investigated that year were referred to court martial—the majority of assailants were given what the DoD calls "nonjudicial punishments, administrative actions and discharges." (By contrast, in civilian life, 40 percent of those arrested for sex crimes are prosecuted.)[21] And then for a long time the Sexual Assault Prevention and Response (SAPR) Web site (www.sapr.mil) displayed on its main page the headline, SEXUAL ASSAULT PREVENTION BEGINS WITH YOU. Under it was a picture of a woman.

The fact is that too many members of the military remain more interested in protecting male soldiers from scandal than female soldiers from assault. Here are the reforms necessary to correct this problem:

- Include female doctors and gynecologists among the medics currently deployed.
- Include sexual assault counselors in the combat stress expert teams already in place. These counselors should be trained in civilian rape crisis centers, not by the military alone. Ideally, they should be independent of the military, like the Red Cross.
- Train these counselors to help male and female soldiers not only with war trauma and sexual assault but also with childhood abuse.
- Provide a toll-free telephone number of a civilian organization where female soldiers can report rape and sexual assault. The organization would offer advice on steps to take within the military, monitor its response, and step in to help the victim if the command attempts to silence her.

- Make the act of intimidating women out of reporting sexual abuse a violation of the Uniform Code of Military Justice, punishable by court-martial.
- Enforce the rule that no victim should ever have to confront the accused or his lawyer without an advocate at her side.
- Train victim advocates to expose anyone who tries to intimidate the victim out of reporting an assault, even if this means conflicting with superiors. A victim advocate is supposed to put the needs of the victim first.
- Protect the victim from the assailant. If she is assaulted by someone she has to keep working with, offer these options: 1) Have him removed from contact with her until the trial and all following procedures are over. 2) Transfer her in such a way that is neither punitive nor suspicious, regardless of whether she presses charges or the accused is found guilty. 3) Allow her to take an immediate medical leave. *These options must never be forced on a victim but must be her choice.*
- Revise the definition of rape on the SAPR Web site to prominently display the fact that anyone who uses his rank to coerce someone into sexual relations is guilty of rape.[22]
- Strike the following rule under the Restricted Reporting (i.e., anonymous) option on the SAPR Web site, which is essentially a gag order that prevents women from seeking help or advice from friends: "You will not be able to discuss the assault with anyone, to include your friends, without imposing an obligation on them to report the crime. The only exceptions would be chaplains, designated healthcare providers, your assigned victim advocate, and the sexual assault response coordinator." Telling friends is the most common first step in seeking help and should be encouraged.
- Strike the following suggestions on the Web site listed under "Safety" for women, which foster the view of women as too weak and vulnerable to be soldiers, lead to blaming the victim, and happen to be laughable in the face of war: "Do not allow yourself to be isolated with a person you do not know or trust. Travel with a friend or in a group. Plan your outings and avoid getting into a bad situation. Walk only in lighted areas after dark. Keep the doors to homes, barracks, and cars locked. Know where the phone is located." Everyone, women and men, should be streetwise, of course, but the military's emphasis should be on stating clearly and visibly that sexual violence

is a man's problem, not a woman's, and that it violates all ideas of military honor.

- Pass the bipartisan bill to halt rape and sexual assault in the military that was introduced to Congress by Rep. Jane Harman (D-CA) and Rep. Michael Turner (R-OH) on July 31, 2008.[23]

AS WOMEN RETURN FROM WAR

As explained, many thousands of women soldiers are returning from Iraq and Afghanistan with health and psychological problems that the military and VA are failing to address. These are some of the reforms that are urgently needed:

- Open more health clinics for women nationwide, including inpatient clinics for those traumatized by sexual violence, combat, or both.
- Train and hire more therapists to treat women who have suffered multiple traumas.
- Train therapists to understand how women react differently than men to combat-related PTSD and to treat them accordingly.
- Train soldiers, officers, doctors, and counselors to regard PTSD as equal to physical war wounds, not something of which to be ashamed.
- Train therapists to treat trauma without making soldiers permanently dependent on drugs. Too many veterans are addicted to painkillers, such as morphine and OxyContin, and to antidepressants and sleeping pills, which are causing their own cycle of trauma and tragedy.[24]
- Test and treat soldiers for pathogens and diseases caused by depleted uranium, contaminated water, radiation, and anthrax and other vaccines.
- Train military doctors to recognize and treat diseases specific to the Middle East.
- Create more support networks for women outside the VA and military.
- Make it easier for soldiers with trauma or medical problems to separate from the military if they choose.
- Transfer soldiers to the VA benefits system automatically the instant they are discharged.
- Change the VA so that it automatically pays for veterans' medical

needs, rather than putting the burden on veterans to prove that their mental and physical injuries were acquired at war. The VA could periodically audit soldiers' claims to correct for fraud, but the bulk of veterans would be presumed honest and deserving of benefits. This is how it is done in other countries, including Britain and Australia.[25]

At least 160,500 women have served in Iraq by now, risking their lives, limbs, and well-being, as they will again in future wars. It is wrong for us as a nation to ask women to do this and then treat them as inferior to men. We must end this war that is misusing them so tragically. We must demand that our politicians, soldiers, and commander-in-chief stop the violence against them. And we must insist that our government provide women with the services, recognition, and honors they are so overdue. It is time to renew women's hopes that they can serve their country with dignity and noble purpose, the way every American soldier should.

Military Ranks and Organization

ENLISTED RANKS

An enlisted soldier joins the army without going to ROTC (Reserve Officers' Training Corps) or officer school. *E* stands for "enlisted"; the number denotes pay scale. The ranks are: Private E-1, Private E-2, Private First Class E-3, Specialist or Corporal E-4.

Promotions through these four ranks are automatic, unless a soldier gets into trouble. To be promoted to a noncommissioned officer (NCO), one must pass a review board and an interview. The NCO ranks are: Sergeant E-5, Staff Sergeant E-6, Sergeant First Class E-7, First Sergeant or Master Sergeant E-8, Sergeant Major or Command Sergeant Major E-9 +.

OFFICER RANKS

Officers must graduate from ROTC or officer school. The ranks are: Second Lieutenant, First Lieutenant, Captain, Major, Lieutenant Colonel, Colonel, Brigadier General, Major General, Lieutenant General, General.

ORGANIZATION

Each level contains groups of the level below, so a squad, for example, will contain two or three teams; a platoon, several squads; and a unit, several platoons.

Team: 2–5 soldiers

Squad: 6–10 soldiers
Platoon: 30–60 soldiers
Company or Unit: 60–300 soldiers
Battalion: 300–1,000 soldiers
Brigade: 3,000–5,000 soldiers
Division: 10,000–15,000 soldiers
Corps: 25,000–45,000 soldiers

Where to Find Help

TO FIND COUNSELORS AND APPLY FOR BENEFITS:

W.O.W., Women Organizing Women: www.vetwow.com

S.W.A.N., Service Women Action Network: www.servicewomen.org

(These two organizations are independent of the VA or military and will put women veterans in touch with one another and provide advice and services, from help with sexual assault to getting benefits.)

National Sexual Assault Hotline: 800-656-HOPE

Voices and Faces Project: www.voicesandfaces.org. A national non-profit network of rape survivors willing to speak out about sexual violence.

National Center for Posttraumatic Stress Disorder (a VA site): www.ncptsd.va.gov

National Coalition for Homeless Veterans—Women Veterans: www.nchv.org/women.cfm

Women's Mental Health Center (a VA site): www.womenvetsptsd .va.gov. Offers information about where to go for help and how to find residential centers for women.

TO FIND VETERANS, FIGHT FOR VETERANS' RIGHTS,

OR PROTEST THE WAR OR THE WAY SOLDIERS ARE TREATED:

Veterans for Peace: 314-725-6005, www.veteransforpeace.org

Iraq Veterans Against the War (IVAW): 215-241-7123, www.ivaw.net

Iraq and Afghanistan Veterans of America (IAVA): www.iava.org
Military Families Speak Out: 617-983-0710, www.mfso.org
Gold Star Families for Peace: 562-500-9079, www.gsfp.org

FOR HELP LEAVING THE MILITARY:

The G.I. Rights Hotline 24-hour telephone: 800-394-9544,
   www.objector.org/girights/
Military Counseling Network, Germany: 06223-47506, www.getting
   .out.de
Central Committee for Conscientious Objectors: (Philadelphia)
   215-563-8787; (Oakland) 510-465-1617; www.objector.org

ACKNOWLEDGMENTS

First, my deepest thanks to all the forty or so veterans who have talked to me for this book, especially Terris Dewalt-Johnson, Mickiela Montoya, Eli PaintedCrow, Abbie Pickett, and Jennifer Spranger. I wish there were room to name you all, for it is because of your honesty, generosity, and courage that this book exists.

Thank you also to the veterans who helped me from the start: Rolanda Freedman-Ard, Laura Taylor, Jennifer Hogg, Ellen Barfield, Leah Bolger, Christina Taber, April Fitzsimmons, Lily Jean Adams, Jimmy Castellanos, Ann Wright, and Dan McSweeney.

Much gratitude to my friends Karen Malpede and Ynestra King, who inspired me to begin this book; to Amalia Coro, Sarah Solon, and Pablo Calvi for their invaluable help with research; to Beth Hillman for her expert feedback; and to the ever-generous Mary Marshall Clark, who offered me the resources of the Oral History Department at Columbia University, without which I would have been transcribing for years to come. Thank you all.

Thank you also to Gayatri Patnaik, Kim Witherspoon, and Alexis Hurley for their support and enthusiasm, which has meant so much, and to the Corporation of Yaddo for time and peace in which to write.

And of course gratitude and love to Stephen O'Connor, whose faith in this book and willingness to read its many drafts has never flagged, and to Simon and Emma, whose ebullience always warms me, even in thoughts of war.

ONE: THE LONELY SOLDIER

1. Le Moyne College/Zogby Poll, "U.S. Troops in Iraq: 72% Say End War in 2006," Zogby International, February 28, 2006, www.zogby.com/news/readnews .dbm?id=1075. The rates among women were sent to the author by e-mail on March 18, 2007.

2. DoD databases, "Profile Ever Deployed Personnel," March 31, 2008, and "Females in GWOT as of September 6, 2008," sent to the author by the DoD on request, September 11, 2008. GWOT, the Global War on Terror, refers to Afghanistan, Iraq, supporting countries such as Kuwait and Bahrain, and nearby seas. The DoD counts also include these areas. When Afghanistan is added, the total counts in September 2008 for women are 608 wounded and 114 dead.

3. Madeline Morris, "By Force of Arms: Rape, War, and Military Culture," Duke Law Journal 45, no. 4 (1996): 708, 716–20.

4. DoD databases, "Profile Currently Deployed," March 31, 2008, and "Reserve Guard Population," September 2007, sent to the author by the DoD on request, May 5 and 6, 2008; "Information on Women Veterans," Department of Veterans Affairs Center for Women Veterans, ww1.va.gov/womenvet/; "History of Women in War," Women's Research & Education Institute, www.wrei.org/Publications_ WomeninMilitary.htm.

5. Morris, "By Force of Arms," 653; Anne G. Sadler et al., "Factors Associated With Women's Risk of Rape in the Military Environment," American Journal of Industrial Medicine 44, no.1 (2003).

6. Maureen Murdoch et al., "The Association between In-service Sexual Harassment and Post-traumatic Stress Disorder among Department of Veterans Affairs Disability Applicants," Military Medicine 171, no. 2 (2006): 166–73.

7. Terri Spahr Nelson, *For Love of Country: Confronting Rape and Sexual Harassment in the U.S. Military* (Binghamton, NY: Haworth Maltreatment and Trauma Press, 2002); Ann Scott Tyson, "Sexual Abuse is Called Rife in Guard and Reserves," *Washington Post,* September 30, 2005.

8. *Uniform Code of Military Justice,* U.S. Code 10, art. 120, § 920, www.sapr .mil/contents/news/newlaw.pdf; "Department of Defense FY07 Report on Sexual Assault in the Military," DoD Sexual Assault Prevention and Response, www.sapr .mil/contents/references/2007%20Annual%20Report.pdf.

9. Helen Benedict, *Virgin or Vamp: How the Press Covers Sex Crimes* (New York: Oxford University Press, 1992), 13–19; A. Nicholas Groth and H. Jean Birnbaum, *Men Who Rape: The Psychology of the Offender* (New York: Plenum Press, 1979).

10. Helen Benedict, *Recovery: How to Survive Sexual Assault* (New York: Columbia University Press, 1994); Paula Schnurr (deputy executive director of the Veterans Affairs' National Center for PTSD), interview by the author, December 2006; Amy Street and Jane Stafford, "Military Sexual Trauma: Issues in Caring for Veterans," National Center for PTSD, www.ncptsd.va.gov; Edna B. Foa and Barbara Olasov Rothbaum, *Treating the Trauma of Rape: Cognitive-Behavioral Therapy for PTSD* (New York: Guilford, 1998).

11. Author interviews; Amy Herdy and Miles Moffeit, "Betrayal in the Ranks," *Denver Post,* November 16, 17, 18, 2003.

12. Traci Carl, "Marine Killing Suspect Caught in Mexico," Associated Press, April 11, 2008.

13. Josh White, "Military Deaths in Iraq Reach 2,000," *Washington Post,* October 25, 2005; Ann Wright, "Is There an Army Cover Up of Rape and Murder of Women Soldiers?" Common Dreams NewsCenter, April 28, 2008, www.commondreams.org/archive/2008/04/28/8564; Ann Wright, interview by the author, April 28, 2008; Donna St. George, "A Drunken Night in Iraq, a Soldier Is Left Behind," *Washington Post,* January 4, 2008.

14. Pfc. LaVena Johnson, http://lavenajohnson.com.

15. Erica Sharkansky, "How Common Is Sexual Trauma among Women?" National Center for PTSD, www.ncptsd.va.gov/ncmain/ncdocs/fact_shts/fs_female_primary.html?opm=1&rr=rr99&srt=d&echorr=true; M.P. Koss, P.G. Koss, and M.S. Woodruff, "Deleterious Effects of Criminal Victimization on Women's Health and Medical Utilization," *Archives of Internal Medicine* 151 (1991): 342–47; R. Kimerling and K.S. Calhoun, "Somatic Symptoms, Social Support, and Treatment Seeking among Sexual Assault Victims," *Journal of Consulting and Clinical Psychology* 62 (1994): 333–40; R.C. Kessler et al., "Posttraumatic Stress Disorder in the National Comorbidity Survey," *Archives of General Psychiatry* 52 (1995): 1048–60; J.S. Robohm, and M. Buttenheim, "The Gynecological Care Experience of Adult Survivors of Childhood Sexual Abuse: A Preliminary Investigation," *Women and Health* 24 (1996): 59–75.

16. Erik Eckholm, "Surge in Number of Homeless Veterans Is Anticipated," *New York Times,* November 8, 2007.

17. Deborah J. Bostok and James G. Daley, "Lifetime and Current Sexual Assault and Harassment Victimization Rates of Active-Duty United States Air Force Women," *Violence Against Women* 13 (2007): 927, 940; Colleen Dalton, "The Sexual Assault Crisis in the United States Air Force Academy," *Cardozo Women's L.J.* 177 (2004); Nelson, *For Love of Country*.

18. Sadler et al., "Women's Risk of Rape." See erratum, *American Journal of Industrial Medicine* 44 (2003): 110, which corrects rape rate from 28 to 30 percent. Anne G. Sadler et al., "Gang and Multiple Rapes During Military Service: Health Consequences and Health Care," *Journal of American Medical Women's Association* 60, no. 1 (2005); Maureen Murdoch, "Prevalence of In-service and Post-service Sexual Assault among Combat and Noncombat Veterans Applying for Department of Veterans Affairs Posttraumatic Stress Disorder Disability Benefits," *Military Medicine* 169, no. 5 (2004); M. Murdoch and K. L. Nichol, "Women Veterans' Experiences with Domestic Violence and With Sexual Harassment While in the Military," *Archives of Family Medicine* 4, no. 5 (1995): 411–18.

19. "Who Are the Victims?: Breakdown by Gender and Age," Rape, Abuse & Incest National Network, www.rainn.org/get-information/statistics/sexual-assault-victims.

20. "Reporting Options," DoD Sexual Assault Prevention and Response, www .sapr.mil/HomePage.aspx?Topic=Sexual%20Assault&PageName=reporting.htm.

21. One in six civilian women is raped in her lifetime. "Who Are the Victims?: Breakdown by Gender and Age," Rape, Abuse & Incest National Network, www .rainn.org/get-information/statistics/sexual-assault-victims.

TWO: FROM GIRL TO SOLDIER

1. *No Child Left Behind Act of 2001*, Public Law 107–110, U.S. *Statutes at Large* 115 (2002): 1983; www.rethinkingschools.org/archive/19_03/military_enlistment .pdf

2. Associated Press, "Military Recruiting Slips among Foreign Nationals," *USA Today*, April 14, 2005, www.usatoday.com/news/nation/2005-04-14-foreign-recruits_ x.htm; Joseph Williams and Kevin Baron, "Military Sees Big Decline in Black Enlistees," *Boston Globe*, October 7, 2007.

3. Tom Bearden, "Army Recruiting," *NewsHour*, PBS, May 12, 2005, www.pbs .org/newshour/bb/military/jan-june05/recruiting_5-12.html.

4. "Cameras Show Army Recruiters Misleading Students," ABC News, November 3, 2006; "Military Recruiters Lie About Dangers in Iraq," WLWT, May 18, 2005, www.wlwt.com/news/4508233/detail.html.

5. Bianca Solorzano, "Sexual Abuse by Military Recruiters," CBS News, August 20, 2006.

6. L. N. Rosen and L. Martin, "The Measurement of Childhood Trauma among Male and Female Soldiers in the U.S. Army," *Military Medicine* 161 (1996): 6, 342–45; Jessica Wolfe et al., "Gender and Trauma as Predictors of Military Attrition: A Study of Marine Corps Recruits," *Military Medicine* 170 (2005): 12, 1037.

7. U.S. Census Bureau Fact Sheet, http://factfinder.census.gov/home/saff/main
.html?_lang=en; DoD databases, "Annual Report on Military Services Sexual Assault,"
March 14, 2007, www.sapr.mil/contents/references/2006%20Annual%20Report.pdf,
and March 13, 2008, www.sapr.mil/contents/references/2007%20Annual%20Report
.pdf; DoD database, "Profile Ever Deployed Personnel," July 31, 2007, sent to the
author by the DoD on request, September 18, 2007.

8. Tim Kane, "The Demographics of Military Enlistment After 9/11," The Heri-
tage Foundation, November 3, 2005, www.heritage.org/research/nationalsecurity/
em987.cfm; Katherine S. Newman, *The Missing Class: Portraits of the Near Poor in
America* (Boston: Beacon Press, 2007).

9. Charles Moskos, "Overcoming Race: Army Lessons for America," *Military
Officer,* February 2003, www.moaa.org/magazine/February2003/f_race.asp; DoD,
Defense Manpower Data Center, "Women in the U.S. Military: Selected Data,"
Feminism and Women's Studies, http://feminism.eserver.org/workplace/professions/
women-in-the-military-data.txt/document_view.

10. Williams and Baron, "Decline in Black Enlistees"; DoD database, "Profile
Ever Deployed Personnel," March 31, 2008, sent to the author by the DoD on request, May 6, 2008.

THREE: THEY BREAK YOU DOWN, THEN BUILD YOU BACK UP

1. *Kevlar* is a trademark for a synthetic fiber used to reinforce bulletproof vests
and helmets, but soldiers often use the word to mean *helmet*.

2. Rick Rogers, "Drill Instructor Charged in Abuse of Marine Recruits," *San
Diego Union-Tribune,* August 23, 2007.

3. Brian Mockenhaupt, "The Army We Have," *Atlantic,* June 2007, 87–99; Mark
Thompson, "Boot Camp Goes Soft," *Time,* June 24, 2001.

4. Lizette Alvarez, "Army Giving More Waivers in Recruiting," *New York Times,*
February 14, 2007; Mockenhaupt, "Army We Have," 90.

5. James Der Derian, *Virtuous War: Mapping the Military-Industrial-Media Entertainment Network* (Boulder, CO: Westview Press, 2001).

6. This basic training rhyme was also cited by Iraq War army veteran Sholom
Keller in Lovella Calica, ed., *Warrior Writers: Re-making Sense: A Collection of
Artwork* (Philadelphia: Iraq Veterans Against the War, 2008), 34.

7. CS stands for o-*chlorobenzalmalononitrile.*

8. Alicia Borlik, "Physical Training Differences Explored," American Forces Press
Service, May 13, 1998, www.defenselink.mil/news/newsarticle.aspx?id=41344.

9. Anne S. Mavor and Paul R. Sackett, eds., *Assessing Fitness for Military Enlistment: Physical, Medical, and Mental Health Standards* (Washington, D.C.: National Academies Press, 2006).

10. Dave Grossman, *On Killing: The Psychological Cost of Learning to Kill in
War and Society* (New York: Little, Brown, 1996), 3–4, 29–30, 35.

11. Madeline Morris, "Force of Arms: Rape, War, and Military Culture," *Duke
Law Journal* 45, no. 4 (1996): 691; Carol Burke, *Camp All-American, Hanoi Jane,*

and the High-and-Tight: Gender, Folklore, and Changing Military Culture (Boston: Beacon Press, 2004), 44.

12. Burke, *Camp All-American*, xi.

13. Les Roberts et al., "Mortality before and after the 2003 Invasion of Iraq: Cluster Sample Survey," *Lancet* 364, no. 9448 (2004).

14. Professor James Der Derian of Brown University described the marine's use of Iraqi immigrants, female soldiers, and soldiers of color at a Harvard University panel, "Human Rights and the Media," in April 2007; Wells Tower, "Under the God Gun," *Harper's*, January 2006, 57–66.

15. Grossman, *On Killing*, 169–70.

16. Theodore Nadelson, *Trained to Kill: Soldiers at War* (Baltimore: Johns Hopkins University Press, 2005), 45; Chris Hedges and Laila Al-Arian, "The Other War: Iraq Vets Bear Witness," *Nation*, July 30, 2007, 23; Evan Wright, *Generation Kill: Devil Dogs, Icemen, Captain America, and the New Face of the American War* (New York: Berkeley Caliber, 2004).

17. The Compassionate Care for Servicewomen Act of 2007 attempted to reintroduce Plan B. As of September 2008 it had not been passed.

FOUR: THEY TOLD US WE WERE GOING TO BE PEACEKEEPERS

1. "Influenza (pandemic): Influenza Virus," Milvax, www.vaccines.mil/default .aspx?cnt=disease/minidv&dID=57.

2. Richard Currey, "The Needle and the Damage Done: Vaccinating America's Soldiers," *VVA Veteran: The Official Voice of Vietnam Veterans of America* 25 (2005). In early 2008 the DoD changed its smallpox vaccine from Wyeth's Dryvax brand to Acambis' supposedly safer ACAM2000.

3. Meryl Nass, "DoD Anthrax Safety Claims Debunked," Anthrax Vaccine, March 22, 2007, www.anthraxvaccine.org/NassDOD.htm; Greg Guma, ed., "Effects of Anthrax Vaccine Downplayed," *Vermont Guardian*, December 20, 2005.

4. "Vaccines/Diseases," Milvax, www.vaccines.mil/default.aspx?cnt=disease/ diseaseHome.

5. "Anthrax," CDC, www.cdc.gov/nczved/dfbmd/disease_listing/anthrax_gi.html; David Ruppe, "DoD Switches Policy on Voluntary Vaccinations," Global Security Newswire, May 6, 2005.

6. "Possible Side-Effects from Vaccines," CDC, June 12, 2007, www.cdc.gov/ vaccines/vac-gen/side-effects.htm; "The Vaccine Is Effective: Anthrax Vaccine Protects People from Anthrax Infection," Anthrax Vaccine Immunization Program, www.anthrax.osd.mil/vaccine/protect.asp.

7. Meryl Nass, "No Weapons of Mass Destruction Found in Iraq, but Forced Anthrax Vaccinations Are Back Anyway," Anthrax Vaccine, January 20, 2007, www .anthraxvaccine.org/wmd.shtml.

8. "The Vaccine Is Safe: Consistent With U.S. National Vaccine Guidelines, by DoD Policy, Pregnant Women Are Not Vaccinated With Anthrax Vaccine or Any Vaccine Routinely," Anthrax Vaccine Immunization Program, www.anthrax.osd

.mil/vaccine/safe5.asp, which includes the statement, "Preliminary findings suggest vaccination during pregnancy might lead to increased odds of birth defects"; Meryl Nass, interviews by and e-mail messages to the author, October 26, 2007, and June 5, 2007. Dr. Nass attributed the rise in miscarriages to aluminum hydroxide in the vaccine, which binds to proteins and creates a nonspecific immune reaction. A British study said all vaccines can cause fevers that can trigger miscarriages. "Anthrax Vaccine," Health Protection Agency, January 25, 2008, www.hpa.org.uk/webw/HPA web&Page&HPAwebAutoListName/Page/1158945065499?p=1158945065499.

9. Meryl Nass, "Anthrax Vaccine Related to Multiple Cancers and Other Illnesses: Army Statistics Provided to Institute of Medicine in 2001 but Never Published," The Anthrax Vaccine Blog, comment posted June 4, 2007, http://anthraxvac cine.blogspot.com.

10. Meryl Nass, "Back to Basics: What's the Evidence that Anthrax Vaccine Will Protect People After a Bioterrorist Attack?" The MBVP News Blog, comment posted June 5, 2007, http://mbvic.blogspot.com.

11. Julie Weisberg, "Pentagon Conducting Research into Adverse Effects of Anthrax Vaccine While Maintaining It Is Safe," The Raw Story, March 27, 2007, http://rawstory.com/news/2007/Pentagon_conducting_research_into_adverse_effects_0327.html.

12. "Birth Control Shot (Depo-Provera)," Planned Parenthood, February 8, 2008, www.plannedparenthood.org/health-topics/birth-control/birth-control-shot-depo-provera-4242.htm.

FIVE: THE ASSAULT WAS JUST ONE BAD PERSON, BUT IT WAS A TURNING POINT FOR ME

1. DoD database, "Profile Ever Deployed Personnel," March 31, 2008, sent to the author by the DoD on request, May 6, 2008.

2. The soldier who wrote this wishes to remain anonymous to protect her identity.

3. Thomas Ricks, Fiasco: The American Military Adventure in Iraq (New York: Penguin Books, 2007), 8–13.

4. "Military Translators—Iraq," Kwikpoint, www.kwikpoint.com/military_translators/iraq.html.

SIX: THESE MORONS ARE GOING TO GET US KILLED

1. Les Roberts et al., "Mortality before and after the 2003 Invasion of Iraq: Cluster Sample Survey," Lancet 364, no. 9448 (2004). The more conservative Iraq Body Count estimated war-caused civilian deaths at 20,000 and "spiraling upwards" by the war's second anniversary.

2. Paul Fussell, Wartime: Understanding and Behavior in the Second World War (New York: Oxford University Press, 1989), 80.

3. Brian Mockenhaupt, "The Army We Have," Atlantic, June 2007, 91.

SEVEN: THIS WAR IS FULL OF CRAZY PEOPLE

1. Terri Spahr Nelson, "Assessing the Problem," in *For Love of Country: Confronting Rape and Sexual Harassment in the U.S. Military* (Binghamton, NY: Haworth Maltreatment and Trauma Press, 2002), 77–94.

2. "Army Rape Accuser Speaks Out," CBS News, February 20, 2005, www.cbsnews.com/stories/2005/02/17/60minutes/main674791.shtml.

3. Sara Rich (Suzanne Swift's mother), interviews by the author, 2006–2007; "Stop 'Command Rape': You Are Not Alone," Suzanne Swift, www.suzanneswift.org; "Suzanne Swift," Courage to Resist, www.couragetoresist.org/x/content/blog category/23/37/.

4. Erik Holmes, "Woman Who Claimed Gang Rape Faces Trial," *AirForce Times,* August 19, 2007.

5. Lizette Alvarez, "Army Giving More Waivers in Recruiting," *New York Times,* February 14, 2007; Alvarez, "Moral Waivers and the Military," *New York Times,* February 20, 2007; Mark Benjamin, "Out of Jail, Into the Army," *Salon,* February 2, 2006, www.salon.com/news/feature/2006/02/02/waivers/.

6. Lolita C. Balder, "More Convicted Felons Allowed to Enlist in Army, Marines," Associated Press, April 22, 2008.

7. Jim Dwyer and Robert F. Worth, "Accused G.I. Was Troubled Long before Iraq," *New York Times,* July 14, 2006, www.nytimes.com/2006/07/14/us/14private.html?_r=1&n=Top/Reference/Times%20Topics/People/W/Worth,%20Robert%20F.&oref=slogin.

8. Lisa Chedekel and Matthew Kauffman, "Mentally Unfit, Forced to Fight," *Hartford Courant,* May 14, 2006.

9. DoD databases, "Annual Report on Military Services Sexual Assault," March 14, 2007, www.sapr.mil/contents/references/2006%20Annual%20Report.pdf, and March 13, 2008, www.sapr.mil/contents/references/2007%20Annual%20Report.pdf; Congresswoman Jane Harman, House Oversight Committee testimony, July 31, 2008, http://nationalsecurity.oversight.house.gov/documents/20080731133916.pdf.

EIGHT: IT'S PRETTY MUCH JUST YOU AND YOUR RIFLE

1. Patrick Cockburn, *The Occupation: War and Resistance in Iraq* (London: Verso, 2006); Riverbend, *Baghdad Burning: Girl Blog from Iraq,* (New York: Feminist Press, 2005), xiv–xv, 9.

2. Thomas Ricks, *Fiasco: The American Military Adventure in Iraq* (New York: Penguin Books, 2007), 36–39.

3. Paul Rieckhoff, *Chasing Ghosts: A Soldier's Fight for America from Baghdad to Washington* (New York: Penguin Books, 2006), 35.

4. Dina Rasor and Robert Bauman, *Betraying Our Troops: The Destructive Results of Privatizing War* (New York: Palgrave MacMillan, 2007), 6–7, 16–17.

5. Michael Massing, "Iraq: The Hidden Human Costs," *New York Review of Books,* December 20, 2007, 87.

6. Rasor and Bauman, *Betraying Our Troops,* 22.

7. John Kampfner, "Saving Private Lynch Story 'Flawed,'" BBC News, May 15, 2003; Rick Bragg, *I Am a Soldier, Too: The Jessica Lynch Story* (New York: Knopf, 2003), 95–96.

8. Ricks, *Fiasco,* 36, 68, 70, 75.

9. About 20 percent of the bomblets in cluster bombs don't explode immediately and are particularly deadly to children because they look like brightly colored tin balls. In 2006 the U.S. Senate voted down a bill to comply with the Geneva prohibition.

10. Evan Wright, *Generation Kill: Devil Dogs, Icemen, Captain America, and the New Face of the American War* (New York: Berkeley Caliber, 2004), 78–80, 89–10, 112–113.

11. Cockburn, *Occupation,* 53–54.

12. Y. K. J. Yeung Sik Yuen, "Human Rights and Weapons of Mass Destruction, or With Indiscriminate Effect, or of a Nature to Cause Superfluous Injury or Unnecessary Suffering" (working paper, Economic and Social Council, United Nations Commission on Human Rights, June 27, 2002), 33.

13. "US/British Forces Continue Use of Depleted Uranium Weapons Despite Massive Evidence of Negative Health Effects," Project Censored, www .projectcensored.org/top-stories/articles/8-us-british-forces-continue-use-of-depleted-uranium-weapons-despite-negati/; Neil Mackay, "US Forces 'Use of Depleted Uranium Weapons Is Illegal,'" *Sunday Herald,* March 30, 2003; Dan Kaplevitz, "Toxic Troops: What Our Soldiers Can Expect in Gulf War II," *Hustler,* June 2003; Reese Erlich, "The Hidden Killer," Children of War, March 2003, www.warchildren. org/hidden_killer.html.

14. Asaf Durakovic, "On Depleted Uranium: Gulf War and Balkan Syndrome," *Croatian Medical Journal* 42 (2001): 130–34; Mike Barber, "First Gulf War Still Claims Lives," *Seattle Post-Intelligencer,* January 16, 2006, http://seattlepi .nwsource.com/local/255812_gulfvets16.html; Byron Harris, "Studies Link Birth Defects, Gulf War. Pentagon Says There Is No Proven Correlation," WFAA-TV, February 24, 2004, www.iacenter.org/depleted/du-birthdefects-wfaa.htm; Maria Rosario G. Araneta et al., "Prevalence of Birth Defects Among Infants of Gulf War Veterans in Arkansas, Arizona, California, Georgia, Hawaii, and Iowa, 1980–1993," *Birth Defects Research. Part A, Clinical and Molecular Teratology* 67 (2003): 246–60; H. Kang et al., "Pregnancy Outcomes among U.S. Gulf War Veterans: A Population-Based Survey of 30,000 Veterans," *Annals of Epidemiology* 11 (2001): 504–11; Martin Williams, "First Awarded for Depleted Uranium Claim," *Herald* (Glasgow), February 9, 2004.

15. Richard Garfield (professor of nursing and coordinator of the WHO/PAHO Nursing Collaborating Center at Columbia University), e-mail interview by the author, October 29, 2007.

16. Yuen, "Human Rights and Weapons of Mass Destruction."

17. Kristen Lombardi, "Stirring Up the Toxic Dust," *Village Voice*, June 21, 2005, www.villagevoice.com/news/0525,lombardi,65154,5.html.

18. G. C. Jiang and M. Aschner, "Neurotoxicity of Depleted Uranium: Reasons for Increased Concern," *Biological Trace Element Research* 110 (2003): 1–17.

19. Rory McCarthy, *Nobody Told Us We Are Defeated: Stories from the New Iraq* (London: Chatto & Windus, 2006), 142; A. Ascherio et al., "Effect of the Gulf War on Infant and Child Mortality in Iraq," *New England Journal of Medicine* 327 (1992): 931–36.

20. Mark Danner, "Abu Ghraib: The Hidden Story," *New York Review of Books,* October 7, 2004; Janis Karpinski, *One Woman's Army: The Commanding General of Abu Ghraib Tells Her Story* (New York: Hyperion, 2005), 153.

21. "Lie by Lie: How Our Leaders Used Fear and Falsehood to Dupe Us into a Mideast Quagmire," *Mother Jones,* www.motherjones.com/bush_war_timeline/archives/quagmire/.

22. Jen's statements were corroborated by other Camp Bucca soldiers in a CBS *60 Minutes* program in May 2004. "A G.I.'s Iraq Prison Video Diary: Exclusive Video Shows U.S. Soldier's Disdain for Iraqi Prisoners," CBS News, May 12, 2004, www.cbsnews.com/stories/2004/05/11/60II/main616849.shtml.

23. "The Taguba Report," FindLaw, http://news.findlaw.com/hdocs/docs/iraq/tagubarpt.html.

24. Karpinski, *One Woman's Army.*

25. Ibid., 207–37; David Cole, "The Grand Inquisitors," *New York Times,* July 19, 2007; Scott Shane et al., "Secret U.S. Endorsement of Severe Interrogations," *New York Times,* October 4, 2007; Seymour Hersh, *Chain of Command: The Road from 9/11 to Abu Ghraib* (New York: Harper Collins, 2004); Danner, "Abu Ghraib: The Hidden Story."

26. *CONEX* stands for *Container Express.*

27. Heater Meals, www.heatermeals.com/eestotherm.html.

28. Cyril Connolly, *The Unquiet Grave: A Word Cycle by Palinurus* (New York: Persea Books, 2005).

29. Army veteran Nathan Lewis, in Lovella Calica, ed., *Warrior Writers: Remaking Sense: A Collection of Artwork* (Philadelphia: Iraq Veterans Against the War, 2008), 82.

30. "Mefloquine (Lariam): Information for Military Service Members and Their Families," DoD Deployment Health Clinical Center, www.pdhealth.mil/downloads/Mefloquine_SM_fs_4104.pdf.

31. *Iraq for Sale: The War Profiteers,* DVD, directed and produced by Robert Greenwald (Culver City, CA: Brave New Films, 2006).

32. Rasor and Bauman, *Betraying Our Troops,* 7, 155, 205.

33. DoD Inspector General, "Audit of Potable and Nonpotable Water in Iraq," Democratic Policy Committee, March 7, 2008, http://dpc.senate.gov/docs/03-10-08igreport.pdf.

34. Patrick Crosby, "Former Army Official, His Wife, and a Businessman Indicted on Bribery Charges," Department of Justice, February 12, 2008, www.usdoj.gov/usao/gan/press/2008/02-12-08c.pdf.

NINE: YOU'RE JUST LYING THERE WAITING
TO SEE WHO'S GOING TO DIE

1. Thomas Ricks, *Fiasco: The American Military Adventure in Iraq* (New York: Penguin Books, 2007), 161–65; Rory McCarthy, *Nobody Told Us We Are Defeated: Stories from the New Iraq* (London: Chatto & Windus, 2006), 59–60.

2. Patrick Cockburn, *The Occupation: War and Resistance in Iraq* (London: Verso, 2006), 75.

3. George W. Bush, interview by TVP, Poland, May 29, 2003, White House press release, www.whitehouse.gov/g8/print/interview5.html.

4. Paul Rieckhoff, *Chasing Ghosts: A Soldier's Fight for America from Baghdad to Washington* (New York: Penguin Books, 2006), 157–58.

5. Antoine B. Hannoun et al., "Effect of War on the Menstrual Cycle," *Obstetrics & Gynecology* 109 (2007): 929–32.

6. "Suicide Bomber Suspected in Mess Hall Attack," CNN, December 25, 2004, www.cnn.com/2004/WORLD/meast/12/22/iraq.main/.

7. *Iraq for Sale: The War Profiteers,* DVD, directed and produced by Robert Greenwald (Culver City, CA: Brave New Films, 2006).

8. "Halliburton's Abusive Practices in Iraq Are in the Spotlight," Agence France Presse, June 28, 2005; Griff Witte, "Ex-Workers Testify about Halliburton," *Washington Post,* September 19, 2006.

9. James Risen, "Limbo for US Women Reporting Iraq Assaults," *New York Times,* February 13, 2008; Matt Kelly, "GOA challenges $150B Contract Awarded by Army," *USA Today,* October 31, 2007; Democratic Policy Committee, "Contracting Abuses in Iraq: Is the Bush Administration Safeguarding American Taxpayer Dollars?" Halliburton Watch, April 28, 2008, www.halliburtonwatch.org/news/DPChearing042808.pdf.

10. Riverbend, *Baghdad Burning: Girl Blog from Iraq* (New York: Feminist Press, 2005), xv, xix; McCarthy, *Nobody Told Us We Are Defeated,* 130–133.

11. Cockburn, *The Occupation,* 107

12. McCarthy, *Nobody Told Us We Are Defeated,* 143.

13. Corey Flintoff, "Baghdad Officials Fear Outbreaks from Dirty Water," NPR, July 13, 2008, www.npr.org/templates/story/story.php?storyId=91874191.

14. Cockburn, *The Occupation,* 83, 173; Riverbend, *Baghdad Burning,* 228, 276–78; Janis Karpinski, *One Woman's Army: The Commanding General of Abu Ghraib Tells Her Story* (New York: Hyperion, 2005), 175–82.

15. Dina Rasor and Robert Bauman, *Betraying Our Troops: The Destructive Results of Privatizing War* (New York: Palgrave MacMillan, 2007), 217; Rieckhoff, *Chasing Ghosts,* 28.

16. Chris Hedges and Laila Al-Arian, "The Other War: Iraq Vets Bear Witness,"

Nation, July 30, 2007, 24. *The Ground Truth* documentary (2006) records several soldiers talking about running over children in Iraq.

17. Cockburn, *The Occupation,* 4

18. See *Lioness,* a documentary about women in combat in Iraq, directed and produced by Meg McLagan and Daria Sommers (New York: Room 11 Productions, 2008).

19. Tinnitus is constant buzzing or ringing in the ears.

20. Cockburn, *The Occupation,* 86, 95, 123; Riverbend, Baghdad Burning Blog, comments posted October 2003, http://riverbendblog.blogspot.com/2003_10_01_riverbendblog_archive.html.

21. Pamela Constable, "Women in Iraq Decry Decision to Curb Rights," *Washington Post,* January 16, 2004; Nancy Trejos, "Women Lose Ground in the New Iraq," *Washington Post,* December 16, 2006; Daniel Smith, "Women in a Hostile Nation," *New Haven Advocate,* July 19, 2007.

22. Cockburn, *The Occupation,* 197.

23. "Stronger Women, Stronger Nations: 2008 Iraq Report," Women for Women International, www.womenforwomen.org/documents/IraqReport.03.03.08.pdf.

TEN: YOU BECOME HOLLOW, LIKE A ROBOT

1. *Occupation Dreamland,* directed and produced by Garrett Scott, directed and edited by Ian Olds (Wilmington, NC: Working Films, 2004); Rory McCarthy, *Nobody Told Us We Are Defeated: Stories from the New Iraq* (London: Chatto & Windus, 2006), 271–72; Thomas Ricks, *Fiasco: The American Military Adventure in Iraq* (New York: Penguin Books, 2007), 332–33.

2. Dan Baum, "The Price of Valor," *New Yorker,* July 12 and 19, 2004.

3. Patrick Cockburn, *The Occupation: War and Resistance in Iraq* (London: Verso, 2006), 158–59.

4. Paul Rieckhoff, *Chasing Ghosts: A Soldier's Fight for America from Baghdad to Washington* (New York: Penguin Books, 2006), 329.

5. "Transcript: Senate Intelligence Committee Report Released," *Washington Post,* July 9, 2004, www.washingtonpost.com/wp-dyn/articles/A38650-2004Jul9.html.

6. Rieckhoff, *Chasing Ghosts,* 321.

7. "U.N. Secretary General Kofi Annan Declares Iraq War Illegal," BBC, September 16, 2004.

8. Dana Priest and Anne Hull, "Soldiers Face Neglect, Frustration at Army's Top Medical Facility," *Washington Post,* February 18, 2007.

9. Mark Benjamin, "Behind the Walls of Ward 54," *Salon,* February 18, 2005, http://dir.salon.com/story/news/feature/2005/02/18/walter_reed/. Knight Ridder newspapers ran a long series of the failures of Veterans Affairs in 2004 and 2005, which were published in many of its newspapers, including the *News Tribune,* December 31, 2005; the *Lexington Herald-Leader,* March 6, 2005; and the *Pioneer Press,* March 28, 2005.

10. Hope Yen, "Months After 'Wash Post' Walter Reed Revelations and Official

Promises GOA Finds Not Enough Done," Associated Press, September 26, 2007; Matt Renner, "Ongoing Problems at Walter Reed," Truthout, January 15, 2008, www .truthout.org/article/ongoing-problems-walter-reed.

11. Joseph Shapiro, "Army Improves Care for Injured, Study Says," NPR, February 28, 2008, www.npr.org/templates/story/story.php?storyId=87775239; Shapiro, "Injured GI's Care Reflects Army's Uneven Progress," NPR, May 2, 2008, www.npr.org/tem plates/story/story.php?storyId=90109327.

ELEVEN: I WASN'T CARRYING THE KNIFE FOR THE ENEMY,
I WAS CARRYING IT FOR THE GUYS ON MY OWN SIDE

1. Iraq Body Count, March 3, 2005, www.iraqbodycount.org/database/.

2. "Filipino Workers in Iraq Deceived, Abused," *Migrant News Monitor,* July 31, 2007; Guy Raz, "U.S. Contractors in Iraq Rely on Third-World Labor," NPR, October 10, 2007; Carlos H. Conde, "Despite Risk and a Government Ban, Filipinos Line Up for Iraq Jobs," *International Herald Tribune,* September 2, 2004; Debra McNutt, "Is the Iraq Occupation Enabling Prostitution?" Common Dreams NewsCenter, July 11, 2007.

3. Christin M. Damiano, "Lesbian Baiting in the Military: Institutionalized Sexual Harassment Under 'Don't Ask, Don't Tell, Don't Pursue,'" *Journal of Gender, Social Policy & the Law* 7, no. 499 (1998–1999): 500–22.

4. Thom Shanker, "'Don't Ask, Don't Tell' Hits Women Much More," *New York Times,* June 23, 2008.

5. Paul Rieckhoff, *Chasing Ghosts: A Soldier's Fight for America from Baghdad to Washington* (New York: Penguin Books, 2006), 33; Janis Karpinski, *One Woman's Army: The Commanding General of Abu Ghraib Tells Her Story* (New York: Hyperion, 2005), 148–49.

6. Dina Rasor and Robert Bauman, *Betraying Our Troops: The Destructive Results of Privatizing War* (New York: Palgrave MacMillan, 2007), 63, 141, 143–44.

7. "Iraq: Violence against Women Increases Sharply," Amnesty International, March 31, 2004, www.amnesty.org/en/library/info/MDE14/009/2004.

8. Patrick Cockburn, *The Occupation: War and Resistance in Iraq* (London: Verso, 2006), 170, 200.

9. Rieckhoff, *Chasing Ghosts,* 322.

10. Karpinski, *One Woman's Army,* 100–101.

11. "Army Misses Recruiting Target for Previous Fiscal Year by Widest Margin Since 1979," Associated Press, September 30, 2005.

12. Tom Regan, "Stop-Loss Used to Retain 50,000 US Troops," *Christian Science Monitor,* January 31, 2006.

13. John Murtha, "Iraq Must Be Freed from the US Occupation," *CounterPunch,* November 17, 2005, www.counterpunch.org/murtha11172005.html.

TWELVE: MOMMY, LOVE YOU. HOPE YOU DON'T GET KILLED
IN IRAQ

1. Ed Vulliamy, "Troops 'Vandalise' Ancient City of Ur," *Observer,* May 18, 2003.

2. Dina Rasor and Robert Bauman, *Betraying Our Troops: The Destructive Results of Privatizing War* (New York: Palgrave MacMillan, 2007), 67.

3. Dave Grossman, *On Killing: The Psychological Cost of Learning to Kill in War and Society* (New York: Little, Brown, 1996), 243–45.

4. Rasor and Bauman, *Betraying Our Troops,* 44, 61, 159, 235.

5. DoD database, "Number of Service Members by Service, Child Status and Gender," November 2007, sent to the author by the DoD on request, September 18, 2007.

6. Ewen MacAskill, "Pressure on Bush to Help Military Families Fighting on Two Fronts," *Guardian* (Manchester), May 8, 2007; Alison Williams, "Toll on Deployed Soldiers' Children Is Studied: Neglect—Mostly by Female Spouses—Rises When One Parent Goes to War, Researchers Say," August 1, 2007, *Los Angeles Times,* http://articles.latimes.com/2007/aug/01/science/sci-abuse1.

7. Le Moyne College/Zogby Poll, "U.S. Troops in Iraq: 72% Say End War in 2006," Zogby International, February 28, 2006, www.zogby.com/news/readnews .dbm?id=1075.

THIRTEEN: COMING HOME

1. Hart/McInturff, "Study #6056," NBC News/*Wall Street Journal*, September 9–12, 2005, http://online.wsj.com/public/resources/documents/poll20050914.pdf.

2. Marine Matt Howard in Lovella Calica, ed., *Warrior Writers: Re-making Sense: A Collection of Artwork* (Philadelphia: Iraq Veterans Against the War, 2008), 163.

3. C. W. Hoge et al., "Combat Duty in Iraq and Afghanistan, Mental Health Problems, and Barriers to Care," *New England Journal of Medicine* 351, no. 1 (2004): 13–22 (see table 2).

4. "Mental Health Injuries Scar 300,000 Troops," Associated Press, April 17, 2008, www.msnbc.msn.com/id/24183188/; Brett T. Litz, "A Brief Primer on the Mental Health Impact of the Wars in Afghanistan and Iraq," National Center for PTSD, www.ncptsd.va.gov/ncmain/ncdocs/fact_shts/fs_iraq_afghanistan_lay_audien.html; Patricia Resnick, "Military Sexual Assault," *NOW,* PBS, May 23, 2008, www.pbs .org/now/shows/336/fact-check-military-sexual-trauma.html.

5. C. W. Hoge et al., "U.S. Iraq War Veterans with PTSD Suffer Significant Physical Health Problems," *American Journal of Psychiatry* 164 (2007): 150–53; Dave Grossman, "The Weight of Exhaustion," in *On Killing: The Psychological Cost of Learning to Kill in War and Society* (New York: Little, Brown, 1996), 67–73; Dan Baum, "The Price of Valor," *New Yorker,* July 12 and 19, 2004; "Hearing on Mental

Health Problems Confronting Soldiers Returning from Iraq, Afghanistan," Committee on Oversight and Government Reform, May 24, 2007, http://oversight.house.gov/story.asp?ID=1330.

6. Terri Tanielian and Lisa. J. Jaycox, eds., "Invisible Wounds of War: Psychological and Cognitive Injuries, Their Consequences, and Services to Assist Recovery," RAND, 2008, xxi.

7. Hoge, "Combat Duty"; Daniel Zwerdling, "Soldiers Say Army Ignores, Punishes Mental Anguish," NPR, December 4, 2006, www.npr.org/templates/story/story.php?storyId=6576505; Litz, "Mental Health Impact of the Wars."

8. Janet W. Wohlberg, in e-mail discussion with the author, March 18, 2007; Dana Priest and Anne Hull, "The War Inside," *Washington Post,* June 17, 2007.

9. Dana Priest, "Soldier Suicides Reach Record Level," *Washington Post,* January 31, 2008; Deborah Sontag and Lizette Alvarez, "Across America, Deadly Echoes of Foreign Battles," *New York Times,* January 13, 2008; Phyllis Bennis and Erik Leaver, "The Iraq Quagmire: The Mounting Costs of War and the Case for Bringing Home the Troops: A Study by the Institute for Policy Studies and Foreign Policy in Focus," IPS Iraq Task Force, August 31, 2005; DoD, "Directive No. 1010.4: Drug and Alcohol Abuse by DoD Personnel," Defense Technical Information Center, September 3, 1997, www.dtic.mil/whs/directives/corres/pdf/101004p.pdf; DoD, "Defense Task Force on Domestic Violence, No. 102–01," Defense Technical Information Center, March 9, 2001, www.defenselink.mil/releases/release.aspx?releaseid=2851.

10. Dana Priest and Anne Hull, "Soldiers Face Neglect, Frustration at Army's Top Medical Facility," *Washington Post,* February 18, 2007; Editorial, "Veterans Without Health Care," *New York Times,* November 9, 2007; Editorial, "The Plight of American Veterans," *New York Times,* November 12, 2007.

11. Linda J. Bilmes (coauthor of *The Three Trillion Dollar War: The True Cost of the Iraq Conflict* [New York: Norton, 2008]), interview, *Fresh Air,* NPR, March 3, 2008, www.npr.org/templates/story/story.php?storyId=87855957.

12. Maj. Gen. Irene Trowell-Harris (director of Veterans Affairs Center for Women Veterans), interview by the author, May 22, 2008; Meri H. Mallard (deputy field director of Women Veterans Health Strategic Healthcare Group), interview by the author, May 22, 2008; "Women Veterans: Past, Present and Future, Revised and Updated," Department of Veterans Affairs, September 2007, www1.va.gov/womenvet/docs/WomenVet_History.pdf.

13. Dawne Vogt, "Women, Trauma and PTSD," National Center for PTSD, www.ncptsd.va.gov/ncmain/ncdocs/fact_shts/fs_women_lay.html.

14. D. U. Himmelstein et al., "Lack of Health Insurance Coverage among U.S. Veterans from 1987 to 2004," *American Journal of Public Health* (December 2007), www.pnhp.org/PDF_files/uninsured_veterans_study.pdf.

15. Kimberly Hefling, "Study Sees Discrepancies in VA Care for Men, Women," Associated Press, June 8, 2008.

16. "Tuition Support," Today's Military, www.todaysmilitary.com/benefits/

tuition-support; Central Committee for Conscientious Objectors, "Joining the Military Is Hazardous to Your Education," *Objector,* www.objector.org/before-you-enlist/gi-bill.html.

17. Joseph Shapiro, "A Woman Guard Member's Struggle with PTSD," *Morning Edition,* NPR, June 2, 2005; Marti Brant, "Women Soldiers More at Risk for Stress Disorder," *Newsweek,* July 5, 2005.

18. Catherine A. Simmons and Donald K. Granvold, "A Cognitive Model to Explain Gender Differences in Rate of PTSD Diagnosis," *Brief Treatment and Crisis Intervention* 5, no. 3 (2005): 291–95; E. B. Foa, T. M. Keane, and M. J. Friedman, *Effective Treatments for PTSD: Practice Guidelines from the International Society for Traumatic Stress Studies* (New York: Guilford Press, 2000); R. C. Kessler et al., "Posttraumatic Stress Disorder in the National Comorbidity Survey," *Archives of General Psychiatry* 52 (1995): 1048–60; Amy Street and Jane Stafford, "Military Sexual Trauma: Issues in Caring for Veterans," National Center for PTSD, www.ncptsd.va.gov/ncmain/ncdocs/fact_shts/military_sexual_trauma.html?opm=1&rr=rr145&srt=d&echorr=true.

19. Simmons, "Gender Differences in Rate of PTSD Diagnosis."

20. Editorial, "Plight of American Veterans."

21. Erik Eckholm, "Surge in Number of Homeless Veterans Is Anticipated," *New York Times,* November 8, 2007.

22. Ibid.

23. In the 2008 Research and Development (RAND) Corporation study of PTSD among Iraq and Afghanistan war veterans, the largest such study to date, veterans were asked if they'd been responsible for deaths of citizens or witnessed brutality toward prisoners, but this is not the same as asking if they feel shame or remorse. Tanielian and Jaycox, eds., "Invisible Wounds of War," RAND, 2008, 97.

24. Chris Hedges and Laila Al-Arian, "The Other War: Iraq Vets Bear Witness," *Nation,* July 30, 2007"; Dan Baum, "The Price of Valor," *New Yorker,* July 12 and 19, 2004.

FOURTEEN: FIXING THE FUTURE

1. "Operation Iraqi Freedom (OIF) U.S. Casualty Status," September 22, 2008, DoD, www.defenselink.mil/news/casualty.pdf. The counts include casualties in Iraq and other countries and seas of support.

2. "Women in the Army: AR600-13 Army Policy for the Assignment of Female Soldiers," DoD, www.army.mil/usapa/epubs/pdf/r600_13.pdf; DoD database, "Profile Ever Deployed Personnel," March 31, 2008, sent to the author by the DoD on request, May 6, 2008; Steve Fainaru, "Silver Stars Affirm One Unit's Mettle," *Washington Post,* June 26, 2005.

3. Susan Brownmiller, *Against Our Will: Men, Women, and Rape* (New York: Simon & Schuster, 1975.)

4. Sara L. Ziegler and Gregory G. Gunderson, *Moving Beyond G.I. Jane: Women and the U.S. Military* (Lanham, MD: University Press of America, 2005), 88; Joanna

Bourke, "From Surrey to Basra, Abuse Is a Fact of British Army Life," *Guardian* (Manchester), February 26, 2005; John Phillips, "Women Chased from Italian Army; 'Molesters in Uniform' Blamed," *Washington Times,* August, 2004.

5. Madeline Morris, "By Force of Arms: Rape, War, and Military Culture," *Duke Law Journal* 45, no. 4 (1996): 680, 721; Elizabeth L. Hillman (professor of law at Rutgers University School of Law at Camden), in e-mail discussion with the author, March 14, 2008; Hillman, "Front and Center: Sexual Violence in U.S. Military Law" (working paper, Rutgers University School of Law at Camden, 2008).

6. L. N. Rosen and L. Martin, "The Measurement of Childhood Trauma among Male and Female Soldiers in the U.S. Army," *Military Medicine* 161 (1996); Jessica Wolfe et al., "Gender and Trauma as Predictors of Military Attrition: A Study of Marine Corps Recruits," *Military Medicine* 170 (2005); A. Nicholas Groth and H. Jean Birnbaum, *Men Who Rape: The Psychology of the Offender* (New York: Plenum Press, 1979).

7. Robert Jay Lifton, "Conditions of Atrocity," *Nation,* May 31, 2004.

8. Marine Martin Smith in Lovella Calica, ed., *Warrior Writers: A Collection of Artwork* (Philadelphia: Iraq Veterans Against the War, 2008), 34.

9. Morris, "By Force of Arms," 715; Anne G. Sadler et al., "Factors Associated With Women's Risk of Rape in the Military Environment," *American Journal of Industrial Medicine* 44, no.1 (2003).

10. "Divide to Conquer: Gender and Sexuality in the Media" (Winter Soldier panel testimony, Silver Spring, MD, March 13–16, 2008).

11. Donna St. George, "A Drunken Night in Iraq, a Soldier Is Left Behind," *Washington Post,* January 4, 2008.

12. Sadler et al., "Women's Risk of Rape."

13. Clara Bingham, "Code of Dishonor," *Vanity Fair,* December 2003; Carol Burke, *Camp All-American, Hanoi Jane, and the High-and-Tight: Gender, Folklore, and Changing Military Culture* (Boston: Beacon Press, 2004), 20–21.

14. "Women in the Army: AR600-13 Army Policy for the Assignment of Female Soldiers," DoD, www.army.mil/usapa/epubs/pdf/r600_13.pdf.

15. Morris, "By Force of Arms," 738.

16. Canada, Italy, and Chile allow women in ground combat. Belgium, Canada, and Holland have opened certain limited combat jobs to women, mostly in the navy. Linda D. Kozaryn, "NATO Military Women Share Views," American Forces Press Service, February 15, 2009, www.defenselink.mil/news/newsarticle.aspx?id=41587.

17. "Women in the Army: AR600-13 Army Policy for the Assignment of Female Soldiers," DoD, www.army.mil/usapa/epubs/pdf/r600_13.pdf.

18. For more on women in combat, see Ziegler, *Moving Beyond G.I. Jane.*

19. Margaret C. Harrell et al., "Assessing the Assignment Policy for Army Women," RAND, 2007.

20. Oversight Hearing on Sexual Assault in the Military, Part 2, http://oversight.house.gov/story.asp?ID=2154; Ann Wright, "Sexual Assault in the Military: A DoD

Cover-Up?" August 1, 2008, www.truthdig.com/report/item/20080801_sexual assault_in_the_military_a_dod_cover_up/.

21. Rep. Jane Harman (D-CA), July 29, 2008, press release, www.house.gov/apps/list/press/ca36_harman/July29_mst.shtml.

22. Uniform Code of Military Justice, U.S. Code 10, art. 120, § 920, www.sapr.mil/contents/news/newlaw.pdf.

23. Rep. Jane Harman (D-CA), July 29, 2008, press release.

24. U.S. General Accounting Office, *Oxycontin Abuse and Diversion and Efforts to Address the Problem,* report prepared for congressional requesters, December 2003, Committee Print GAO-04-110.

25. Joseph E. Stiglitz and Linda J. Bilmes, *The Three Trillion Dollar War: The True Cost of the Iraq Conflict,* New York: Norton, 2008.

Najaf, 156

Nasiriyah, Iraq, 102–3

Nass, Meryl, 61, 62

National Center for Posttraumatic
Stress Disorder, 235

National Coalition for Homeless
Veterans—Women Veterans, 235

National Sexual Assault Hotline, 235

Native Americans: alcoholism in,
20–24; loss of ceremony, women's
issues, 160; similarity of culture to
Iraqis, 158–59; tradition of enlistment, 24; warrior ethos of, 24, 84,
85. *See also* PaintedCrow, Eli

Naylor, Laura: on deformed children,
109; on Sunni bombing of police
station, 142–43; on women in combat roles, 135–36

near-death experience, 139

Night Vision goggles (NVG), 53

9/11, 15–16, 65–66, 73–74

"Nintendo warfare," 53

No Child Left Behind Act, 16

Nuclear Biological Chemical (NBC)
mask, 46

O'Herrin, Liz, 94

Operation Pencil, 130–33

PaintedCrow, Eli: background of, 19–
25; at Camp Cedar II, 149–52; at
Camp Scania, 155–59; counseling
career of, 84; on cultural role playing, 52; disillusionment of, 155–59;
health of, 159–62; injury of son,
85–87; Iraq War training phase of,
85, 87–89; issues with ineffective
leadership, 152–54; Kuwait deployment of, 149; postwar adjustment
of, 218–22; on sexual assault,
80–81; on sexual promiscuity, 169;
training phase of, 79–80

Palestine Hotel, bombing of, 142

pastimes/diversions, 101, 117–18, 126,
137

Phillabaum, Jerry L., 114

Pickett, Abbie: background of, 33–36;
at Camp Speicher, 125–29, 145–47;
at Camp Warhorse, 136–40; convoy
missions of, 134–36; "fronting" by,
140–42; on group ethos, 58; Kuwait
deployment of, 123–25; medical
training of, 143–44; and Operation
Pencil, 130–33; postwar adjustment
issues of, 207–11; prewar staging
phase of, 69–72; on sexual assault
classes, 90; on sexual assault,
67–69; training phase of, 65–67

pornography, 50–51, 129, 225–26, 227

Post-9/11 Veterans Educational Assistance Act of 2007, 209

post-traumatic stress disorder (PTSD):
due to sexual violence, 5, 7, 200,
209–10; lack of VA programs for,
203–4; in returning veterans,
199–200, 207, 209, 216, 218

Posttraumatic Stress Disorder,
National Center for, 235

postwar adjustment issues: Abbie
Pickett, 207–11; Eli PaintedCrow,
218–22; family support, 214–15;
Jennifer Spranger, 211–18, 213–18;
Mickiela Montoya, 197–99, 204;
overview, 198–201, 202–4; Terris
Dewalt-Johnson, 205–6

poverty: enlistment as escape from, 27,
35, 224; in family background, 14,
20–25; in Iraq, 111, 124, 177–78; in
veterans, 205, 213–14, 218

pregnancy: active-duty, 39, 54–55,
163–64; and anthrax vaccine, 62,
110, 204; and depleted uranium,
109-10, 204; postwar, 201–2, 204;
preenlistment, 22, 23

pride of service: Abbie Pickett, 36, 66;
Claudia Tacson, 2–3; Eli Painted-
Crow, 83–84; Jennifer Spranger,
28, 217; Meredith Brown, 3; Mickiela Montoya, 18

prisoners: at Abu Ghraib, 114, 117, 149;